{ Crazy Book }

Advanced praise for **Crazy Book:**

"We often miss the humor and iconoclasm that pulses through the Bible. These guys don't. This book is hilarious, refreshingly irreverent and delightfully alive."

Debbie Blue,
Author of *Sensual Orthodoxy* and *From Stone to Living Word*

{Crazy Book}

A Not-So-Stuffy Dictionary of Biblical Terms

Rolf A. Jacobson
Karl N. Jacobson
Hans H. Wiersma

For our parents,
Delmar and Katherine Jacobson
and Hylke Wiersma.
And in memory of Anna Wiersma.

CRAZY BOOK
A Not-So-Stuffy Dictionary of Biblical Terms

Cover design: Laurie Ingram
Book design: Christa Rubsam
Interior art: Profile images courtesy of the Digital Image Archive, Pitts Theology Library, Candler School of Theology, Emory University.

Library of Congress Cataloging-in-Publication Data
Jacobson, Rolf A.
Crazy book : a not-so-stuffy dictionary of Biblical terms / Rolf A. Jacobson, Karl N. Jacobson, Hans H. Wiersma.
p. cm.
Includes index.
ISBN 978-0-8066-5765-3 (alk. paper)
1. Bible—Dictionaries. I. Jacobson, Karl N., 1969- II. Wiersma, Hans H., 1964- III. Title.
BS440.J28 2009
220.3—dc22
2008051062

The paper used in this publication meets the minimum requirements of American National Standard for Information Sciences — Permanence of Paper for Printed Library Materials, ANSI Z329.48-1984.

Printed in Canada

13 12 11 10 2 3 4 5 6 7 8 9 10

Contents CRAZY BOOK

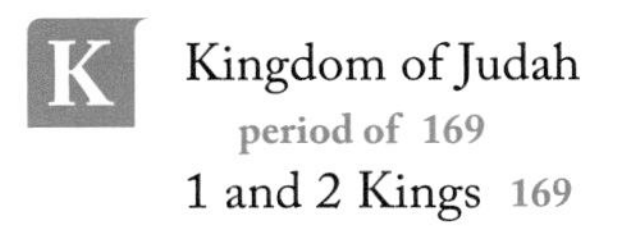

Introduction

Back when a few of us put together *Crazy Talk: A Not-So-Stuffy Dictionary of Theological Terms*, the very first entry that we drafted was the one that defined the Bible as "a book that Christians believe is so holy and inspired that they almost never read it for fear that it might draw them closer to God and neighbor or change their lives in some other inconvenient way."

And, as many of us learned to say when we were teenagers, "This is most certainly true!"

But there are also other reasons why many of us don't read the Bible as much as we would like to. For starters, the Bible can be hard to understand. The customs and metaphors of the Bible are often so foreign to us that we don't know what to make of them. Don't believe us? Consider the custom of Levirate marriage, which held that if a man died without an heir, his brother was required to sleep with the man's widow in order to give the man an heir (and to give the woman a child who could grow up and take care of her in old age—for more on this, see TAMAR).

We know what you are thinking: "That's crazy!" And there are a lot more foreign customs and metaphors where that one came from . . . in the Bible.

To many of us, the Bible often does seem like a crazy book. But the truth is, the Bible is the most sane thing around. The Bible brings God's sanity to us. In the process, it exposes the insane,

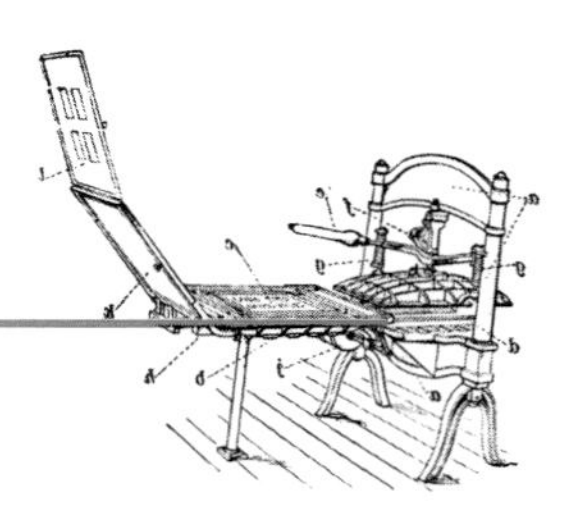

crazy illusions that we have built our lives around. Insane beliefs such as, "Yes, you can have it all." Crazy notions such as, "I have it all under control and I don't need any help."

We know what you are thinking: "That's crazy!" And there are a lot more insane illusions where we got those . . . in our lives.

It turns out that the crazy book we call the Bible actually teaches us the sanity that we need. The sanity that lets us know who God is, who we are in light of God's love, and where God's love can be found and experienced. This little book introduces the reader to the places, books, and most importantly to the people of the Bible. The entries here are short. That is on purpose. They don't contain everything that the Bible has to say—just a taste. Just an appetizer. But believe us, the Bible serves up a whole feast that is worth sitting down to. We hope that, having had a taste, you'll know where you can find the whole meal.

Aaron \EHR-uhn\

Status:
Aaron hates it when Moses disappears for months at a time.

Profile

Vocations:	Levite/Priest, Prophet—mouthpiece for God and for my baby brother
Family:	Moses (brother), Miriam (sister)
Interests:	Fine craftsmanship of gold-plated bobble-head cows; eating, drinking, and reveling on the festival day of the Lord
Guilty Pleasure:	Speech impediments
Favorite Song:	"He Ain't Heavy, He's My Brother" by the Hollies

So here's the deal, when it comes to old school Old Testament prophets—the who's who of who they are, what they had to say, and to whom they said it—Aaron gets the short end. He was right there with his little brother Moses (or "camel-breath" as he was known to Aaron), talking to Pharaoh on behalf of God, turning sticks into snakes and water into blood. He was Moses' right hand man (*literally* at the battle of Rephidim—check it out in Exodus 17:8-12; it's awesome). And yet we're guessing that if you, dear reader, were asked to list ten prophets and told that you couldn't use any of the four major prophets (FYI that's Isaiah, Jeremiah, Ezekiel and James Brown) you'd still probably come up short, and if you didn't you'd still be more likely to come up with the unnamed prophet in Judges 6 before you thought of Aaron. When it comes to the prophets, Aaron can't get no love.

Why? Because Aaron made a mistake, and we're not talking about misplacing your keys or eating that extra hot dog or forgetting to zip that fly. No, this was a big mistake. And like politicians, CEOs, sculptors, and hair-stylists, there are some mistakes that a prophet has a hard time recovering from. Aaron made exactly that kind of mistake.

When Moses (and Aaron don't forget) had led the people of Israel out of Egypt, they beat feet to Mount Sinai to make the 8:30 worship service of the Lord. While Moses was up on the mountain consulting with the Great I AM, the people got a little anxious. It's hard to blame them—hanging out in the desert without the leeks and onions upon which they loved to snack (not to mention the melons and the garlic...mmm *garlic*), without a land to call their own. And so they asked Aaron to get the service started. And Aaron? He did what priests (and pastors) do best; he took up an offering, melted down the proceeds, and formed an image of a golden calf.

You can read the whole story in Exodus 32, but before the calf-god-stand-in finished cooling, Aaron led a liturgical conga-line, dancing and praying and whooping it up in front of this statue, and he declared, "Tomorrow there will be a festival to the Lord!" Notice something—most people think that Aaron made an image of a false god. But actually, Aaron made a false image of the true God ("the Lord")—which was not allowed.

Needless to say, Moses and the Lord were a little miffed. If Aaron could have waited just a little longer (or he could have just read the travelogue that Moses was keeping during Exodus 20—it's right there in verses 4-5) he would have known that what he was doing was wrong (dudes, it's called "idolatry"; perhaps you've heard of it), silly (c'mon, dancing *while* praying?), and frankly just a little tacky (gold against a desert palette?! Please).

Kind of like a politician, Aaron survived his mistake. He is never really seen as Moses' equal or as one of the great prophets of Israel, but he is represented as one of the big time priests and religious leaders for the people of Israel.

Key Verse: "The Lord has been mindful of us; he will bless us; he will bless the house of Israel; he will bless the house of Aaron… " (Ps 115:12; see also Exod 4 and 32)

See also: Moses, Prophets.

A

Abel \Ā-buhl\

Status:
Abel's blood is crying from the ground.

Profile

Vocation:	Keeper of the Sheep (are you the Gate Master?)
Interests:	Making offerings to the Lord of the firstlings from my flock; animal-husbandry; darning
Pet Peeves:	Older brothers; jealous brothers; getting killed by older, jealous brothers
Favorite Song:	"I'm Ready [Willing, and Abel to Rock 'n Roll All Night]" by Fats Domino

The name Abel means "breath" or "puff of smoke." He was called that either because his parents weren't very nice (c'mon, why not go with something nice like Hans or Karl or Rolf? Okay, maybe not Rolf) or because his name summarizes the length of his stay in the biblical story—just ten verses. We don't learn much about Abel in those ten verses, but we do learn something crucial about God: God cares for each and every one of us. And when one of us suffers—even though in the sight of eternal God our lives flit by like the shadow of a speeding car—God notices; God cares; and God responds.

Key Verse: "By faith Abel offered to God a more acceptable sacrifice than Cain's. Through this he received approval as righteous, God himself giving approval to his gifts; he died, but through his faith he still speaks" (Heb 11:4; see also Gen 4:1-10).

See also: Cain, Genesis.

Abraham \ Ā-bruh-ham\

Status:
Abraham is the father of many nations.

Profile

Vocation:	Life-long temp with experience in itinerant wandering and flock-tending
Family:	Wife: Sarah; Sons: Ishmael and Isaac
Pet Peeve:	Having my name changed. Don't get me wrong I get the symbolism of "Abraham," but re-printing business cards on papyrus is expensive and messy; besides, there's something short and sweet about Abram (and something confident with a hint of the darkly handsome, as well).
Favorite Song:	"Baby-hair with a woman's eyes; I can feel you watching in the night"— opening line of "Sarah Smile" by Hall and Oates; greatest slow-jam *ever*!

Being in relationship with God is all about trust. This is true of pretty much every relationship, but it is extremely true of the Abraham-God relationship. There are a bunch of things we could say about Abraham, for example that he was originally called Abram. Abram means "exalted father" (ironic in that he was childless at the time), but his name was changed to Abraham when God promised to make him the father of many nations (thereby putting the "Ha!" in Abram—Sarah laughs and so does her beau). What's more, he gave up everything to relocate (and relocate and relocate) because God told him to. And he was willing to use his son as a burnt offering to the Lord, again because God seemed to think this screwy math (1Son + 1Sacrifice = many, many sons) was a good way to keep a promise. All interesting parts of Abraham's story. But the main recurring theme in Abraham's story is faith. The most important thing about Abraham is that he believed, he trusted. God spoke, and Abraham listened.

Granted, Abraham's faith wasn't perfect. There was that time (okay, okay... those *times*) when he thought he'd pass Sarah off as his sister (Gen 12:10-20; 20). And he and Sarah tried to jump-start their promised family with a little help from Hagar (see Gen 16). But still Abraham's faith is held up all over the place in the Bible as pretty flippin' sweet. His faith isn't perfect, it isn't always steady or exactly right, but the Bible tells us that Abraham's faith was good, that it was right, and that it was in fact righteous. And so we can take both hope and inspiration from this imperfect faith, which we would say looks a lot like ours. And probably yours too.

Key Verse: "And he believed the Lord; and the Lord reckoned it to him as righteousness" (Gen 15:6; see also Gen 12–22).

See also: Hagar, Isaac, Ishmael, Sarah.

Absalom \AB-suh-lahm\

Status:
Absalom is swinging in the tree.

Profile

What's in a Name?	My name means "father of peace," which is ironic.
Family:	Father: David; Sister: Tamar; Brothers: one too many
Likes:	Long-range planning
Dislikes:	Unpruned trees
Favorite Quotation:	"The best laid schemes o' Mice an' Men, Gang aft agley"—"To a Mouse" by Robert Burns

Say this for Absalom: he was a unique combination of passion and cool reasoning. After his half-brother Amnon raped their sister Tamar, Absalom took his time—two years' worth of it—to plan his revenge for Tamar's rape. And he got his man. Of course that didn't sit well with David, who pretty much gave Absalom the silent treatment for five or ten years.

But Absalom used that time well, too. He used at least four of those years to plan his rebellion against David. Which went pretty well. Absalom seized Jerusalem and the king's wives, but his father got away. Which gave Absalom an adult reason to dread those child-fearing words, "Just you wait until your father gets home!"

Absalom still might have gotten away with it all, too, if he hadn't tried to ride his get-away mule under an oak tree with a low-hanging branch. You could say that he didn't have much of a head for leadership.

Key Verse: "Thus Absalom did to every Israelite who came to the king for judgment; so Absalom stole the hearts of the people of Israel" (2 Sam 15:6; see also 2 Sam 16–19).

See also: David.

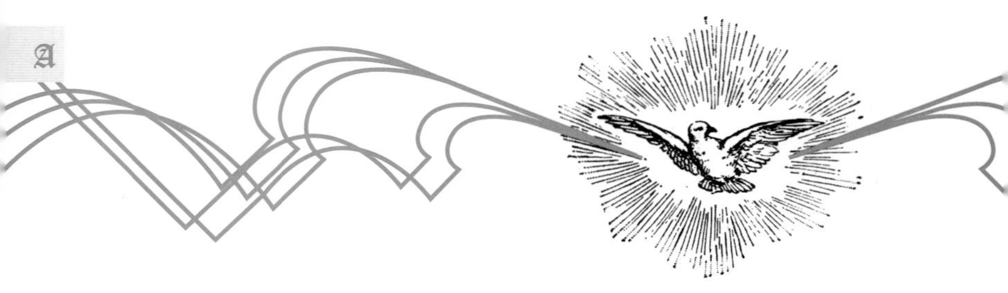

Acts of the Apostles, The

\thee-AX-uhv-thee-uh-PAH-suhlz\

by Luke* (New Testament, History, twenty-eight chapters)

Acts is a romp. You may not think that "romp" is the best word to use when describing a book of the Bible. But "romp"—here defined as "boisterous, lively play or frolic"—fits. The one doing most of the romping in Acts is the Holy Spirit, the Spirit of the Risen Christ, promised by Jesus (in John 14:26). This is not to say that the spread of the gospel is not serious business. Nor is it to minimize the persecution and suffering those earliest Christians experienced. But come on. A Spirit that gets things going with the sound of a rushing wind, tongues of fire, and the neat trick of getting people to preach in languages they do not otherwise speak, is romping. And speaking of preaching, the preaching in Acts is often preaching that is powered by the Holy Spirit—like Peter when he's on trial (Acts 4:8), and Stephen when he's on trial (7:55), and Paul when he's speaking out against the magician Elymas (13:9). The point in Acts is that things really *go* when the Spirit is working—things like preaching and teaching, things like disciples and apostles, things like the church. So romp-on Acts, romp-on church, and romp-on, you *Crazy Book* reading child of God!

* The Acts of the Apostles—also addressed to a guy named Theophilus (lover of God)—was written by the writer of Luke's gospel.

See also: Luke (The Gospel according to), Stephen.

Adam \AD-uhm\

Status:
Adam is homesick.

Profile

Vocation:	Father of all humankind, what's on top of your résumé?
Family:	Everybody . . . ever
Likes:	The Name Game; getting to know Eve; long-range planning
Dislikes:	Fig leaves (they chafe and they aren't particularly slimming), and snakes
Favorite Quotation:	"I don't know you from Adam." Which is kind of confusing.

Adam was the original man. He was also the original dupe and buck-passer, and one of the original liars. Lest you think he was just the first disappointment we should point out that he had some good firsts too—first father and husband, first date (both "eating of" and "going on"), and first kiss. That's a lot of firsts for Adam, but then he was bound to be the first to do, try, or be most everything considering that he was the first person.

The name "Adam" is a play on words in Hebrew (the main language of the Old Testament). When you read the creation story in Genesis 2 it goes something like, "God formed man (Hebrew: *adam*) from the dust of the ground (Hebrew: *adamah*)." The pun emphasizes that we all have a basic connection with the earth, from which we spring. Maybe it should be translated, "God formed the earthling from the dust of the earth." Adam was given the responsibility of watching over God's garden—tilling and keeping it and naming all the animals. "Ground-boy" was given the job of "groundskeeper" (okay, he was *assistant* groundskeeper, but he had a six-year schedule to become head groundskeeper).

Adam was allowed free reign of the garden, meaning he could do and eat just about whatever he wanted. *Just* about. God gave Adam and his wife Eve one rule: don't eat from one—just one—of the trees in the garden, the tree of the knowledge of good and evil. Which probably just gave him the idea and made him want to break the rule. Like when parents say to a kid: House-sit, no loud parties, cut the grass, and you'll get free room and board. And the kid says, "Loud party? What a great idea."

You know the rest of the story—a talking snake, temptation, sin, nakedness, and deceit. After all this, Adam's name was mud (get it?), and he and Eve got a one-way ticket out of Eden (if you *don't* know the story you can read up on it in Genesis 3).

The story of Adam is the story of the first sin (another of Adam's firsts) and the results of making mistakes. The key to understanding what's at stake in Adam's story is recognizing that it is really *our* story. "Adam" isn't actually a proper name, as we said, it's a play on words that is probably best understood not just as a specific person but as a representation of human beings in general. We are just like Adam and Eve: quick to sin, bad at covering it up, and slow to owning it. That's a human being for you. So come to think of it, maybe you don't know Adam from you.

Key Verse: "Then the LORD God formed man from the dust of the ground, and breathed into his nostrils the breath of life; and the man became a living being" (Gen 2:7; see also Gen 2–3).

See also: Eve, Genesis.

Ahab \Ā-hab\

Status:
Ahab can't understand why leaders aren't more respected.

A

Profile

Vocation:	King—are you *down* with the King?
Family:	Omri was my father; he was king before me and the Moabites call Israel the "House of Omri"; so I bet my dad could beat up your dad.
Interests:	Jezebel (my queen—she's a hottie); ruling, which is what other kings wish they did and which I define
Disinterests:	Prophets, who need to lighten up on the whole "worshipping Baal is not cool" thing
Favorite Quotation:	"And Ahab piled upon the whale's white hump the sum of all the rage and hate, if his chest had been a canon he would have shot his heart upon it." Okay, that's a different Ahab, but Melville rocked.

Ahab was a milk-toast. Oh don't get us wrong, he was super kingly in that he brought the battle to Israel's enemies and cut such a dashing figure at the battle of Qarqar that the Assyrians were impressed enough to include *his* name on one of *their* monuments. But rocking on the battle-field doesn't make you a strong man—that is, a man of strong character or a man who takes strong stands. He may have been king, but his wife Jezebel wore the pants in that family. She was the bizz-oss.

Ahab did just about everything she thought best (either he did what she told him to do or he could sleep in the summer palace). He let Jezebel bring Baal worship into Israel; he let her get away with killing Naboth and stealing his vineyard; he even let her kill the prophets of Yahweh when those prophets spoke out against The Man (since he was The Man, he didn't care for this). All in all, Ahab was every bit of a king, but he was even more of a milk-toast.

In the end, Ahab was so impressed with himself, he thought that he could outsmart God. God sent him a warning: If the king goes into battle, the king will die. So Ahab forced Jehoshaphat of Judah to dress up as himself, while he dressed up as a common soldier. To God, this probably looked like the typical four-year-old kid hiding under a blanket and shouting out to mom and dad, "Bet you don't know where I am!" If he had only taken God seriously, he might have lived. But then, we suppose, if he had taken God seriously, he would not have been Ahab.

Key Verse: "Ahab son of Omri did evil in the sight of the LORD more than all who were before him" (1Kgs 16:30; see also 1 Kgs 17–22).

See also: Baal, Jezebel.

Ahaz \ā-haz\

Status:
Ahaz is weary of prophets.

Profile

Vocation:	King (of Judah)
Likes:	Child sacrifice, preferably at some high place
Dislikes:	Prophets—no matter what they say, I hate 'em all

When it comes to being a lousy king, not many were lousier than Ahaz. He did just about all the bad stuff a king of Judah can do—he stripped the Temple sanctuary to make the Assyrians happy, and he *actually sacrificed his own son* as a burnt offering. Ahaz was so bad... (now you go: "How bad was he?")...Ahaz was so bad that the author of 2 Kings says he "walked in the way of the kings of Israel." Which is like saying of a Vikings fan that she cheered in the way of the Cheeseheads of Green Bay (or vice versa). And that's just yuck.

Ahaz's signature moment of un-faith came when the prophet Isaiah came to deliver *good news* to him! Isaiah brought the message that the Lord would protect Ahaz from attack. But Ahaz had already made plans to protect himself from attack by selling off the kingdom to the Assyrians in exchange for Assyrian protection. From there, he was only a step away from taking his own son's life.

Key Verse: "[Ahaz] did not do what was right in the sight of the LORD his God, as his ancestor David had done . . ." (2 Kgs 16:2b; see also 2 Kgs 16 and Isa 7).

See also: Assyrians.

Amos \Ā-muhs\ (book)

by Amos Ha-Noqer (Old Testament, Minor Prophets, nine chapters)

The plot of this deliciously sarcastic book can be summed up by the first words out of the prophet's mouth: "The Lord roars from Zion" (Amos 1:2). At whom does the Lord roar? Why at the rulers and residents of the Northern Kingdom, sometime around the year 760 BCE. But also at you and me, dear reader, for we are prone to the same sins as they were. Why does the Lord roar? Because they—we!—"have rejected the law of the Lord, and have not kept his statutes" (Amos 2:4).

To unpack Mr. Ha-Noqer's sarcastic condemnations, at times it will be helpful to know something about daily life in his times. Mr. Ha-Noqer uses many metaphors and illustrations from daily life to get his points across. For example, the prophet said, "The LORD was standing beside a wall built with a plumb line, with a plumb line in his hand. And the LORD said to me, 'Amos, what do you see?' And I said, "A plumb line." Then the LORD said, 'See, I am setting a plumb line in the midst of my people Israel; I will never again pass them by'" (Amos 7:7-8). A plumb line is a carpenter's tool used to assure that walls and the like are, well, plumb (meaning straight up and down). The prophet's point was that the people were not "upright." God had measured them and found them less than righteous.

It will help if the reader has an ear for sarcasm, because the prophet's words drip with it, like a leaky faucet. For that reason, this book might find a potential audience among teenagers, who have been known to enjoy sarcasm.

See also: Amos, Prophets.

A

Amos \Ā-muhs\

Status:
Amos is not impressed by your fancy theology degree or your ordination.

Profile

Vocation:	Herdsman/Dresser of Sycamore Trees
Home:	Tekoa (Home of the Tekoa High *Fighting Pruners*)
Likes:	Obscure metaphors for God's plans like "plumb-line" or "basket of summer fruit"
Dislikes:	Priests who think they're all that and get too big for their britches (no names, but his initials are . . . Amaziah)
Favorite Quotation:	"To them I will give as leaders Abraham, Isaac, and Jacob, and Hosea and *Amos* and Micah and Joel and Obadiah and Jonah." Some dude named Esdras whose books (unlike mine) didn't make it into the Bible. But check out the company I'm keeping!

Amos wasn't always a prophet. In fact, you might say he was never a prophet in the full-time sense. God called Amos from his home and life to preach a particular message to a particular people. Amos was sent by God to get Israel to straighten up and fly right.

The name Amos means "burden." Amos's arch rival's name, Amaziah, means "Yahweh is wickedly-kicking strong" (or pretty close to that anyway). If you're considering becoming a prophet you might keep that in mind—it's a dirty business, just ask Amos's boys Isaiah or Hosea.

Amos' message was that Israel was out of whack—they didn't know God and they weren't treating each other right. Amos used metaphors and plays on words to make his point. The plumb line, used in construction to build straight, solid walls, would show that the "wall" that is the kingdom of Israel is crooked and flawed—which at least hinted that it had to be torn down and rebuilt. He also talked about a basket of "summer fruit" (in Hebrew: *qayitz*) as a play on the word "end" (*qetz*), meaning, "You all see a bowl of ripe fruit, but I see that you are ripe for the end that you so justly deserve: The Punishment of the Lord!!!" You can imagine how the king of Israel and the priest of Bethel took that.

But Amos wasn't interested in being a pain in the priest's posterior just for the sake of being a pain. He wanted God's people to pay attention to their relationship with God and each other. Amos wanted them to get right theologically (that is, to have a right understanding of and relationship to God)—walking humbly with their God, and to get right socially—doing justice, loving mercy, and generally avoiding the abuse of widows and cruelty to the poor. He said, "You've got blood on your hands, but you think God will take an offering from those very same hands! Stop it. God wants you to live and love right."

One last lesson from "the Burden." Amos was not one of the insiders: he was no priest, no prophet, no senator's son, he was an everyday guy called by God to do his best. If God can use the Burden, he can use you too.

Key Verse: "Then Amos answered Amaziah, "I am no prophet, nor a prophet's son; but I am a herdsman, and a dresser of sycamore trees, and the LORD took me from following the flock, and the LORD said to me, 'Go, prophesy to my people Israel'" (Amos 7:14-15; see the entire book of Amos).

See also: Amos (book), Prophets.

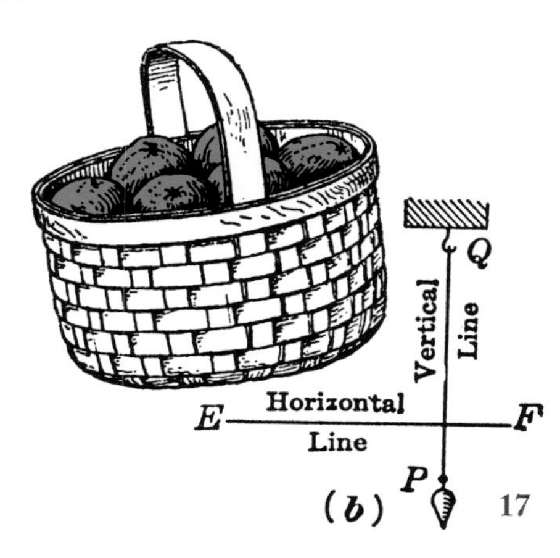

A

Ananias

\an-uh-NI-uhs\ or \an-un-NEE-uhs\

Status:
Ananias thinks that maybe someone has overreacted, just a little.

Profile

Vocation:	Huge Tract of Land Owner
Interests:	Along with my wife Sapphira I enjoy real-estate speculation.
Dislikes:	Communism
Favorite Quotation:	"What's yours is mine and what's mine is mine."

The story of Ananias is a little unsettling, especially in capitalistic cultures that prize freedom, individualism, and the piling up of wealth. Ananias sold a piece of property and he was supposed to share all of the profits with the community of believers, because in those days the church "held all things in common." But Ananias, he kept some of the money for himself. And that just wasn't how the Church rolled in the book of Acts. Ananias was accused of lying and having Satan running all through him; on top of that, he was struck dead.

Makes a measly ten percent offering look pretty good, doesn't it?

Key Verse: "How is it that you have contrived this deed in your heart? You did not lie to us but to God" (Acts 5:4b; see also Acts 5).

See also: Acts of the Apostles.

Ancestral Period \an-SEHS-truhl-PEER-ee-uhd\

Yesteryear; the Good Old Days; the Olden Days; back in the day; that stuff great-grandpa is always talking about.

In the Old Testament there is a lot of talk about the time of the Ancestors. This period includes a long stretch of Israel's history, from Abraham and Sarah, through Isaac and Rebekah, down to

Jacob, Leah and Rachel, and should include Joseph, his cool coat, and his uncool brothers, as well. This time, this collection of the "oldies but goodies" tells how God moves from the "scattering of the nations" that happened in the tower of Babel to the Exodus. It is difficult to put a date on this era and is perhaps best not to worry about that too much. What *is* important is that this era was the time of God's jump-starting of the nation of Israel—of choosing one nation (Israel) to be the "priestly nation" through which God would work to bless all of the other nations. References to the days of Abraham, Isaac, and Jacob are almost always meant to point to what God was doing in that time—which was working so that through one nation all the world would be blessed.

See also: Abraham, Isaac, Jacob.

Andrew \AN-droo\

Status:
Andrew says, "You shoulda seen the one that got away."

Profile

Vocation:	Fisherman, Apostle
Hometown:	Bethsaida (of Galilee)
Family:	Simon Peter is my older brother; yes, *that* Simon Peter.
Nickname:	In an old tradition, I'm known as "Protocletos"—First to be Called.
Interests:	Fishing for trout, bass, tilapia, people

Andrew is your typical story: A fisherman from Galilee becomes a follower of Jesus becomes a martyred apostle becomes a beloved saint becomes a city in Scotland with a world-famous golf course. Okay, Andrew is not your typical story. Traditions about what happened to Andrew abound: he spread the gospel in Asia Minor; he was the first bishop of Constantinople; he was crucified on an X-shaped cross; his skull and bones—first enshrined in Patras, Greece—have been scattered about, with pieces buried in places as far flung as Italy, Poland, Turkey, and Scotland (the X on the Scottish flag is in honor of St. Andrew). As you might have guessed, Andrew is the patron saint of Scotland. But did you know he's also the patron saint of Russia, Romania, Ukraine, and Greece? Yeah, Andrew really got around.

So what should we make of Andrew when so much has been made of him already? Truth be told, Andrew gets scant mention in the Gospels. After Pentecost, the New Testament doesn't mention him at all. Nevertheless, Andrew is remembered as one of the very first to be called. And so we have that one vivid, lasting image of Andrew: there he is, standing on the lakeshore, tending his nets, when along comes Jesus, who says to Andrew, "Follow me." In other words, there's Andrew, minding his own business, doing his own thing, not bothering anybody, when along comes Jesus . . . and Andrew's life is never the same. We can relate.

Key Verse: "As Jesus passed along the Sea of Galilee, he saw Simon and his brother Andrew casting a net into the sea—for they were fishermen. And Jesus said to them, 'Follow me and I will make you fish for people'" (Mark 1:16, 17).

See also: Mark (The Gospel according to).

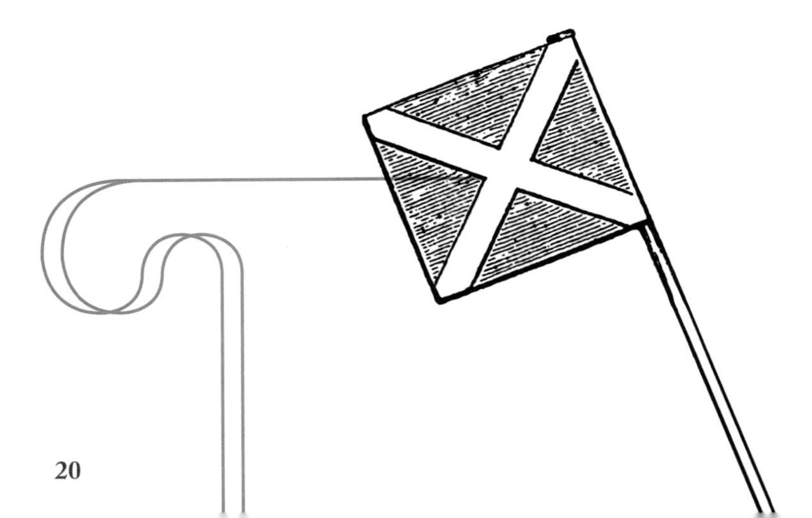

Anna \AN-nuh\

Status:

Anna has a good vibe about Mary and Joseph's kid.

Profile

Vocation:	Prophetess
Hometown:	Jerusalem
What's in a Name?	My name means "grace" or "favor" (same as Hannah).
Hobbies:	Hanging out in the Temple, fasting, praying—you know, the usual

Anna makes the most of her brief appearance at the end of Luke's Christmas story. Anna is a person of "great age" who likes to spend her days (and nights, apparently) in Jerusalem's Temple. She's part of the Simeon-Anna Elderly Person Tag-Team that gave the little Lord Jesus their wizened blessing (see also SIMEON). As Luke tells it, when the infant Jesus is brought to the Temple to be circumcised, Anna arrives—not to do the circumcision, mind you, but to preach. We're told that Anna sang the child's praises and told about how the tot would have something to do with the redemption of Jerusalem. Since Anna was 84 years old at the time, we can hardly blame her for only seeing as far as Jerusalem's city limits. But she was on the right track. That babe born in Bethlehem came not only to redeem Jerusalem and its inhabitants, but all cities and all people everywhere.

Key Verse: "At that moment Anna began to praise God and to speak about the child to all who were looking for the redemption of Jerusalem" (Luke 2:38; see also Luke 2:36-38).

See also: Luke (The Gospel according to), Simeon.

A

Apocalyptic Literature

\uh-PAH-kuh-lihp-tihk-LIH-duhr-uh-chuhr\

If you don't know how to read apocalyptic literature, it's the end of the world; if you do know how, it isn't.

Apocalyptic literature is a kind of story that God's people found particularly helpful during times of oppression. These stories have recurring features. *Ancient heroes of the faith*: perhaps because the people were being persecuted, they felt safer telling stories about people who had lived long ago. *Dreams*: these ancient heroes have visions, often featuring strange imagery. *Angels*: an angel appears who interprets the meaning of the visions. *Predictions*: the meaning of these visions is often a prediction by the long-gone hero of the faith concerning the situation in which God's people were suffering.

Daniel was written in a time when God's people were oppressed by the Seleucid empire (c. 167 BCE). Revelation was written when the church was oppressed by the Roman empire (c. 90 CE). If you know how to read this literature, you'll know these books are about the Seleucid and Roman empires, respectfully. If you don't know how to read this literature, you might get tempted to pull a "Chicken Little" and run around yelling, "The sky is falling! The sky is falling!" Which would be entertaining. Misguided, yes. But certainly entertaining.

See also: Daniel, Revelation.

Apocrypha \uh-PAH-krih-phah\

Those things that didn't make it into the "approved and authoritative" version of the Bible and which are therefore great subjects for people to make both hay and money with.

Marginalized! Suppressed! Treated unfairly! You might think any one of these is what the Greek word *apocrypha* means, but they aren't. Apocrypha means something that is hidden, something that is removed from sight and sound. In biblical terms the Apocrypha is a collection of books that never gained the same level of authority or influence as did the canonical books of the Bible. Books that make up the Apocrypha include Maccabees (vols 1–4), Esdras (vols 1–2), the Letter of Jeremiah, the Wisdom of Solomon, and additions to a couple of the books that *do* make it into the Bible (like "Bel and the Dragon" in Daniel or Psalm 151). There are various reasons why these books were hidden away—because there is little of "God" in them, because they are obviously not a part of the books they've been added to and so on. The important thing to remember is that for a lot of folks for a lot of years these other apocryphal books were not so much hidden as they were put out of sight and mind because they just aren't that important to the everyday believer.

What's kind of funny about all of this is that not everyone thinks of the same set of material as apocryphal in the same way. Roman Catholics, for example, have a bigger Old Testament than Protestants do. So do the Orthodox. Why? Because no Hebrew copy of these other books survived (only Greek copies)—so Judaism didn't accept these books in the canon (and Protestants followed the Jews on this issue).

To confuse matters more, there are books that some people call the New Testament Apocrypha, such as the Gospel of Thomas. But no Christian church accepts any of these books in the New Testament. All Christian groups have the same twenty-seven books in the New Testament. And no, Emperor Constantine did not decide which twenty-seven books were in. Sorry, Dan.

See also: Old Testament, New Testament.

𝔄

Apostolic Mission (period of)

\ap-uh-STAH-lihk-MIH-shuhn\

A loosely organized effort to spread the word that, after a period of about seventy years, pretty much succeeded.

The story of the "Apostolic Mission" begins with Pentecost. *Pentecost* refers, literally, to the fiftieth day of the season of Easter—that is, the Sunday that follows forty-nine days after Easter Sunday. On the first Pentecost, Jerusalem was crowded with foreign-born Jews who were in town for the Jewish festival of weeks.* The followers of Jesus had been told to stay in Jerusalem and "wait for the gift my Father promised" (Acts 1:4). There they sat. Until that fateful fiftieth day when—woosh! The Holy Spirit came upon those followers and, spilling into the streets, they began to tell about Jesus. And here's the neat trick: they told about Jesus by speaking in the native language of those foreigners that were in the city that day. A crowd gathered, and Peter had to explain that everyone was perfectly sober, since it was only nine o'clock in the morning. (We're not sure why the time of day makes a difference, but maybe that says more about us than anything else.) Then Peter, filled with the Holy Spirit, preached. It was the first Christian sermon and it must have been a pretty good one since "about three thousand were added to their number that day."

The miracle of Pentecost is, in fact, a perfect metaphor of the Apostolic Mission. The mission of those early apostles was, put simply, to get the word out—to translate the gospel into other tongues, cultures, and world-views. The members of Jesus' inner circle of followers were called "Apostles," and it was these twelve Apostles who were originally charged with leading the mission to spread the word. (When you think "apostle," think "emissary," or "ambassador," or "messenger.") Generally speaking, these apostles were eye- and ear-witness to the life, death, and resurrection of Jesus. In addition, "signs, wonders, and miracles" were "the things that mark an apostle" (2 Cor 12:12).

The Apostle Paul, because of his own encounter with the Risen Christ, was, after some hazing, welcomed into the Apostles' Club. Some have called this Apostles' Club a "boys club," but there were female apostles as well (see JUNIA and MARY MAGDALENE). In the end, the apostolic age came to an end when the last of the eyewitnesses to Jesus died out during the first century. On the other hand, with about two billion people around the world who name Jesus as Lord, it's clear that despite the deaths of those long-ago apostles, their apostolic mission did not die with them. Mission accomplished.

*The Jewish Festival of weeks is a "week of weeks" (7 x 7) after Passover. It is a harvest festival at which the gift of the Law at Mount Sinai is celebrated.

See also: Acts of the Apostles, Paul, Pentecost.

Assyria \uh-SEER-ee-a\

Other than in the assonance of its name, nothing whatsoever is funny about Assyria.

Assyria was one of the great super powers of the ancient world. In fact it could be considered the first great super-power, spanning most of the ancient near eastern world and lasting from 934–609 BCE. It was the Assyrian empire that conquered the Northern Kingdom of Israel in 722 BCE. Assyria, and its capital city of Nineveh, are the object of a lot of anger, hatred and thirst for revenge in Old Testament because of its cruel dominance of its neighbors. Nahum promises its destruction—"I will throw filth at you and treat you with contempt, and make you a spectacle." Then Nahum asks the $64,000 question (or in these days of inflation, the $1 million dollar question)—"Then all who see you will shrink from you and say, 'Nineveh is devastated; who will bemoan her?'" No one, we guess.

See also: Assyrians, Monarchy.

Assyrians \uh-SEER-ee-uhns\

The people responsible for the Neo-Assyrian empire and other scary concepts.

The Neo-Assyrian Empire is generally assigned the dates of 934–609 BCE. When one sets these dates alongside those of the Kingdom of Judah, 922–587 BCE, one can imagine the obvious beginnings of a great drama—or at least a decent made-for-TV mini-series. The Assyrian Empire was based in what is now Iraq, with its capital in Nineveh. The Assyrian emperors included Tiglath-Pileser III, Sargon the Great, Sennacherib, Esarhaddon, and Ashurbanipal—a line up to make the '27 Yankees quiver. At its largest, the empire dominated the entire Middle East—from Egypt in the west to the Persian Gulf in the East. And when we say dominated, we mean dominated. Here is what one biblical author had to say about them: "Devastation, desolation, and destruction! Hearts faint and knees tremble, all loins quake, all faces grow pale!... City of Bloodshed, utterly deceitful, full of booty—no end to plunder" (Nahum 2:10, 3:1).

The Empire (cue up Darth Vader music) was responsible for the destruction of Samaria in 722 BCE, the end of the Northern Kingdom, and the exile of that kingdom's people. The Kingdom of Judah became a vassal of Assyria at about the same time. Part of Assyrian policy was the imposition of Assyrian religion on the nations that came under her sway. The biblical prophets, as a rule, didn't approve.

See also: Assyria, Monarchy.

Baal

Status:
Baal is . . . maybe meditating, or has wandered off, or is conducting some personal business, or is sleeping.*

Profile

What's in a Name?	Baal means "lord" or "prince," but I would prefer it if you didn't think of it in a "wooden" sense.
Family:	I've always felt a close kinship to the Easter Island heads.
Fun Fact:	In the Old Testament my name is both *my name* (Baal, 2 Kgs 3:2), and a general term for other gods or deities (the baals, cf. Judg 8:33).
Favorite Quotation:	Baal ♥s Asherah—carved into trees all around Canaan

Baal was a god from the Canaanite pantheon of gods and was worshipped by a lot of the folks who lived in the Promised Land before (and for a good while after) it was promised to Abraham and his descendents.

In the Old Testament Baal is the primary challenger to Yahweh's championship belt in the heavyweight divinity division. But as Elijah's contest with that whole bunch of Baal's prophets (450 BCE, to be exact) shows, Baal isn't much of a contender. In fact, you might say that Baal is the "straw-man" to Yahweh's all-consuming fire. Ultimately the Old Testament tells us that Yahweh is God, and no-body, and no-thing else is. And that includes Baal.

So maybe Baal's status line should just be: **Baal** is . . . n't.

***Key Verse:** "At noon Elijah mocked them [the prophets of Baal], saying, 'Cry aloud! Surely he is a god; either he is meditating, or he has wandered away, or he is on a journey, or perhaps he is asleep and must be awakened.'" (1 Kgs 18:27).

See also: **Elijah.**

Babylon \BAB-ih-lahn\

"Mother of whores and of earth's abominations."*

"Babylon" refers both to an empire and to that empire's capital. In Israel's history, only the city of Nineveh, capital of the Assyrian empire, is more hated. Babylon conquered Israel in 587 BCE, devastated Jerusalem, destroyed the Temple, and took the best and brightest of its citizens away into captivity. The Israelites held a bit of a grudge, which you can probably imagine. If you want a taste of just how passionately Babylon was hated, check out Psalm 137. Yikes.

In the New Testament, in Revelation in particular, Babylon is used as a figurative name both for Rome, which was the capital of the new empire that was oppressing the fledgling Christian church, and for what is wrong with all the kingdoms of the earth—hunger for power and disregard for God's sovereignty.

*We didn't come up with that one. This definition is straight from the Bible: Rev 17:5.

See also: **Babylonians, Nebuchadnezzar, Temple.**

Babylonians \bab-ih-LOH-nee-uhns\

If the Kingdom of Judah was the fish and the Assyrian Empire was the frying pan, then the Babylonian Empire was the fire.

At first, the people of Judah may have celebrated the news that arrived in 609 BCE that the dreaded Assyrian Empire had finally been defeated. But to borrow from something Jesus later said, it was like when one evil spirit is cast out of a house, only to have seven worse ones move in (see Luke 11:24-26). Because the Assyrians were just replaced by the Babylonians, who were no better, and were probably a little "badder."

The Babylonians, whose capital was conveniently located in Babylon, worshiped many gods, but their chief god was the idol Marduk. The kings included the famed Nebuchadnezzar, under whose leadership Babylon destroyed Jerusalem and its Temple in 587 BCE, and who deported Judah's leaders to live in Babylon. The Neo-Babylonian Empire was short-lived. It ended in 539 BCE, when Cyrus of Persia gained ascendancy in the region.

See also: Babylon, Nebuchadnezzar, Temple.

B

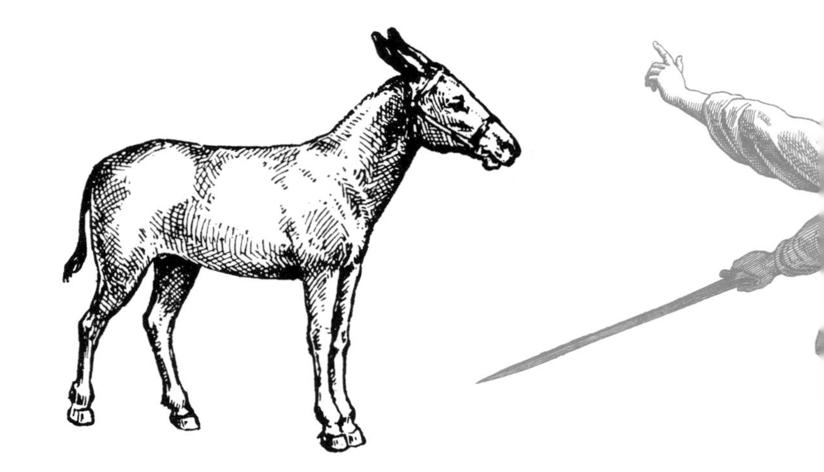

Balaam \BĀ-luhm\

Status:
Balaam wishes that he had stayed in bed.

Profile

Vocation:	Prophet
Fun Fact:	I may not be an Israelite, but I'm still a prophet of the LORD.
Favorite Celebrity:	Johnny Carson—he talked to animals all the time and check out *his* career (Jack Hanna is a close second).
Political Views:	I'm a democrat—not for any policy reason, but I have this thing for donkeys.

Ever talk to yourself? Ever answer? If so you might want to seek counseling, or at least do it quietly and with as little lip movement as possible. Don't worry, though; lots of people talk to themselves, but even the chronic self-talker ain't got nothin' on our guy Balaam.

Balaam was a prophet of the Most High (one of Yahweh's many titles), living during the time when the people of Israel were on their way up from Egypt. You've got to feel sorry for Balaam. He was caught between the rock of a changing political world and the hard place of a divine calling. A king (Balak of Moab) summoned him to curse the oncoming Israelites. The LORD told him not to go (Duh! God *of the Israelites*, what would you expect?). So Balaam didn't go. But the king, being a king, didn't take no for and answer, and summoned him again. This time God told Balaam "Okay, changed my mind, go. Just make sure you say what I tell you to say and only what I tell you to say." As Balaam rode his mule (the original low-emissions hybrid) to go prophesy to/for/against/near Israel, the Good LORD got good and mad (even though God had just told him to go, which is a little confusing) and sent an angel to stop them. And here's where the story gets a little nuts; the mule, she sees the angel of the LORD, but Balaam, prophet of the LORD, doesn't (ironic, no?). The long and the short of it is that the mule ends up lying down on the job instead of taking on a sword-wielding angel. Low-emissions and smart! What a combo.

You can imagine Balaam's frustration. Mixed messages and a mule that won't go; we'd wager denarii to donuts that he was talking to himself. So Balaam dropped smack on his mule's behind to try to get her rear in gear. That's when Balaam talked to his mule. Well, to be fair the mule started it and Balaam answered. "What's up with beating me like a rented mule when you've ridden me all your life?!" To which Balaam answered, "I have sinned." Confessing your sins to a mule, tell us that's not crazy talk!

When Balaam finally made it to Balak, God ordered him to bless Israel. "Let's try again," said Balak, "but this time if you can't curse Israel, at least don't bless it." And you got it. Again, Balaam blessed Israel. After four tries, Balak threw his hands in the air and gave up.

The story of Balaam is a strange one. There seem to be at least two important things happening. The first is delivered with this incredible irony. The Lord uses a mule to talk to a prophet to get him to deliver the right message. If we wanted to push we might even say that the mule is the true prophet here. There's a message there for all of us who want to know and share God's word. Second, the story drives home the point that God's word is God's word. Rulers can't make God deliver a particular message for their nation or against their enemies; prophets can't choose to shape the message according to their own desires (ask Jonah); God's word is God's word. Period.

Key Verse: "They did not meet the Israelites with bread and water, but hired Balaam against them to curse them—yet our God turned the curse into a blessing" (Neh 13:2; see also Balaam's story in Num 21–24).

See also: Prophets.

Barabbas \buh-RAB-uhs\

Status:
Barabbas is enjoying his fifteen minutes.

Profile

Vocation:	Notorious Prisoner
Favorite Movie:	*Barabbas* (1961); what? It does me way more justice than the Gospels.
Favorite Quotation:	"He chose poorly." —The knight guarding the grail in *Indiana Jones and the Last Crusade*
What's in a Name?	My name means "Son of the Father"—in fact, my whole name is Jesus Barabbas—which is pretty ironic, because in order to set me free, the crowd had to condemn the other Jesus, who was the real "Son of the Father."

Barabbas was a criminal, probably an insurgent or guerilla warrior type. Along with Jesus of Nazareth, he was offered to the crowd as a choice. They could have one released—the itinerant teacher who, it turned out, was the Messiah. Or the bad-news Barabbas who was an outlaw. They chose Barabbas. Barabbas was set free, and we know nothing more about him. Jesus was crucified and saved everybody from their sins. For a poor choice, it worked out pretty well, don't you think?

Key Verse: "Now the chief priests and the elders persuaded the crowds to ask for Barabbas and to have Jesus killed. The governor again said to them, 'Which of the two do you want me to release for you?' And they said, 'Barabbas.'" (Matt 27:20-21)

See also: Matthew (The Gospel according to).

Bathsheba \bath-SHEE-buh\

Status:
Bathsheba is considering a sunbath. Does anyone have any SPF 30?

Profile

Biggest Accomplishment:	Hmmmm, I think perhaps it was helping my son Solomon become the next king of Israel.
Favorite Song:	"Up on the Housetop"
Favorite Movie Star:	Susan Hayward (Her best role was when she played me opposite Gregory Peck, who was passable in his role as David.)
Hobby:	Playing chess—surely you noticed that the king isn't the most powerful piece!
Favorite Quotation:	"Think like a queen. A queen is not afraid to fail. Failure is another stepping-stone to greatness."—Oprah Winfrey

See David.

Key Verse: "It happened, late one afternoon, when David rose from his couch and was walking about on the roof of the king's house, that he saw from the roof a woman bathing; the woman was very beautiful" (2 Sam 11:2; see also 2 Sam 11–12; 1 Kgs 1–2).

Bethel \BEH-thuhl\

B

"House of God": simply divine; 3 bedroom, 2 bath, rambler; all appliances, including altar, will stay; near Jerusalem; will throw in ladder.

Bethel is not a house or a church even though the Hebrew *Beth-El* means "house of God." Bethel, just north of Jerusalem, is a favored stomping ground for all kinds of Old Testament characters. It starts with Abraham (in Genesis 13) who sets up an altar near the site that would come to be called Bethel. Eventually, Jacob builds an altar at Bethel proper—an altar that would become an important place for all sorts of kings and prophets. Genesis 28 records how Bethel got its name. In Jacob's famous dream—the one featuring the very, very long extension ladder—the Lord promised Jacob that the whole world would be blessed through Jacob's family line. When he awoke, Jacob exclaimed: "Surely, God is in this place." (To which God said, "True. Now stop calling me Shirley.") Impressed with the experience Jacob exclaimed, "This is none other than the house of God!" Fortunately, Jacob knew the source of his dream and of the blessing bestowed in it. Otherwise he might have ended up naming the place Beth-a-bit-of-undercooked-potato-which-is-fouling-up-my-digestion.

See also: Genesis, Jacob.

Bethlehem \BETH-luh-hehm\

A little town, which may be seen lying still just south of Jerusalem, in whose dark streets shineth an everlasting light; there the hopes and fears of all the years are met.

You probably think you know all that there is to know about Bethlehem. Sure, you know it's the place where there was no room at the inn, and where Jesus was born in a manger, and where shepherds and wise men dropped by for a visit. You may even know that Bethlehem was known as the city of David and that there was an expectation among some that the Messiah was to be born in David's hometown (Mic 5:2; Matt 2:5-6). But did you know that *Beth-Lehem* is Hebrew for "house of bread"? And did you know that Bethlehem is the site of Rachel's tomb, the site of Ruth's "hook-up" with Boaz, the site of David's anointing by Samuel? And did you know that all of these Bethlehem fun facts pale in comparison to what's most important about Bethlehem—namely, that Bethlehem is the place where the Word became flesh and dwelt among us (John 1:14), where when the fullness of time had come, God sent his Son, born of a woman (Gal 4:4)? What's that? You knew that last bit? Well, okay then! Excellent!

See also: Jesus, Matthew (The Gospel according to).

Birth of Jesus (Christmas)

\BUHRTH-uhv-JEE-zuhs\

The reason for the season and Santa's biggest competition.

Since the modern calendar had not yet been invented, we have to rely on the clues given by Matthew and Luke to figure out the exact year of the birth of Jesus. Luke tells us that Mary gave birth to a son "while Quirinius was the governor of Syria," and Matthew explains that Jesus was born "in the time of King Herod." Wait a minute! Quirinius ruled Syria from 6 CE to 12 CE and Herod the Great ruled Judea from 37 BCE to 4 BCE. Something does not compute! Today, most scholars agree that Jesus was born around 4 BCE, when Herod was still alive and Quirinius was governor of Pamphylia and Galatia (Central Turkey). You can blame some of the calendar confusion on a sixth-century monk named Dionysius Exiguus. He's the one who put the birth of Jesus (1 CE) on the wrong year. (There is no zero CE—blame Dionysius again.) So it's not Jesus' fault that he was born four years "Before Christ." Perhaps we can agree that the point is not to know *when* Jesus was born but to know *that* Jesus was born? Because you have to admit: the Common Era (CE) wouldn't be the same without him.

See also: Jesus, Luke (The Gospel according to), Matthew (The Gospel according to).

B

Boaz \BOH-az\

Status:
Boaz is listening to the Eric Clapton song, "After Midnight."

Profile

Profession:	I am a land-owner, with a penchant for barley-winnowing.
Interests:	Moabitesses; camping out on the threshing room floor
Favorite Fashion Accessory:	Long, feather-entwined scarves

Boaz is described in the book of Ruth as a good and righteous man (and also a smooth ladies man, cf. Ruth 2:8, 14-15), who lives according to the Torah (see Deut 24:19). Perhaps it was just Boaz's concern for Torah that made him deal so kindly with Ruth—a homeless, impoverished, widow from Moab. Boaz saw her gleaning—which is a fancy word that means she was walking behind the harvesters, picking up the pieces of grain that they dropped, so that she and her mother-in-law would have something to eat. This wasn't always a safe thing for women to do, but what choice did she have? So Boaz made sure none of the young men bugged her. And on top of what she could gather, Boaz threw in six measures of grain for good measure. And then he thought, "Heck, in for a penny, in for a pound. Let's get married." And long story short, Boaz became the great grandfather of King David. And the über-über-über-Grandfather of Jesus.

Key Verse: "Boaz instructed his young men, "Let her glean even among the standing sheaves, and do not reproach her" (Ruth 2:15).

See also: Ruth.

Caesar \SEE-zuhr\

Status:
Caesar can't understand why the fiddle is considered the devil's instrument.

Profile

Vocation:	Caesar *is* a vocation—it means emperor, dictator, all around swell guy.
Family:	Well, lots of neat folks have shared my name/title, such as Julius, Augustus, Nero, and Romero—okay, he was the original Joker in the old Batman TV show, but we still count him.
Likes:	Having things rendered unto me
Dislikes:	Barbarian hordes from the north—they're murder on the real estate values
Favorite Food:	Salad—obviously, but hold the anchovies. They taste like eyebrows.

Caesar was ruler of the Roman Empire. During the New Testament period there were several Caesars: Augustus, real name Octavian (27 BCE–14 CE); Tiberius (14–37 CE); Caligula (37–41 CE); Claudius (41–54 CE); and Nero (54–68 CE), just to name a few. In the Roman Empire, the Caesar was considered a god. Not a god in the sense of being really good looking or popular, but as in being a god. And Caesar thought he really was all that. He could shout at a map, and people in far away countries would jump. But according to the

C

Bible, someone else is actually in charge of history: God. So when "a decree went out from Caesar Augustus that all the world should be registered" (Luke 2:1), Caesar thought he was doing his usual trick of moving world affairs from the comfort of his Lazy Boy. But the one who was actually at work behind Caesar's little registration fixation was the Lord God—who was moving Mary and Joseph to Bethlehem in order that the Savior of the world would be born.

Key Verse: [Jesus] said to them, "Then give to the emperor [that is, Caesar] the things that are the emperor's, and to God the things that are God's" (Acts 20:25).

See also: Luke (The Gospel according to), Acts of the Apostles.

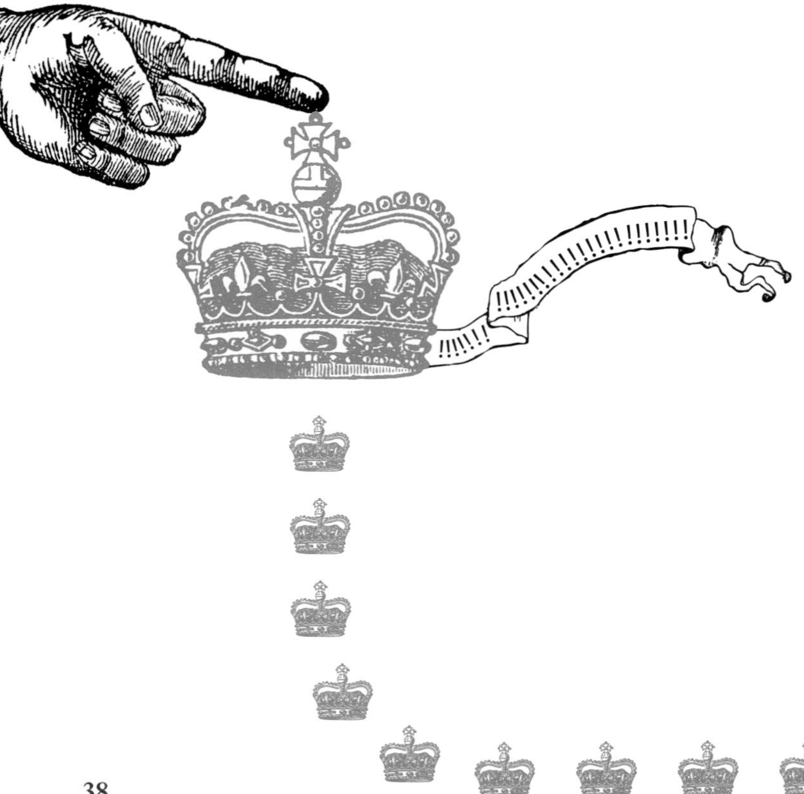

Caiaphas \KI-uh-fuhs\

Status:
Caiaphas is glad that his name didn't make it into the Apostles' Creed.

Profile

Vocation:	High Priest
Likes:	Simple, straightforward solutions to complex, thorny problems
Dislikes:	The idea of the Romans destroying my holy place and my nation; also sign-performing, dead-guy-raising rabbis with a messiah complex

Caiaphas was the high priest who came up with the big idea of having Jesus die for a whole bunch of folks, in order to avoid a whole bunch of folks dying for Jesus. Pretty ironic, huh? He and the other priests in power (the chief ones who weren't quite so high as he was) were worried that the people would believe in Jesus, get uppity about having a messiah, and would start a revolt against Roman rule. Who would then reciprocate by dropping Roman smack down on Jerusalem and Israel like a ton of matzos. So Caiaphas, for at least some of the right reasons, did the wrong thing. Which turned out to be the right thing in a totally different way. Funny old world, isn't it?

For the record, about forty years after Jesus, the Judean populace did revolt against Rome. And the results were every bit as bloody as Caiaphas feared.

Key Verse: "He did not say this on his own, but being high priest that year he prophesied that Jesus was about to die for the nation . . ." (John 11:51).

See also: John (The Gospel according to).

Cain \kān\

Status:
Cain is wondering if this mark washes off.

C

Profile

Vocation:	I am a tiller of the ground and a fugitive wanderer.
Favorite Celebrity:	David Carradine—loved his work in *Kung Fu*
Pet Peeves:	Little brothers; mysterious marks
Favorite Quotation:	"Am I my brother's keeper?" I said that; pretty clever if I do say so myself—my brother's "keeper," get it? Just like he was a sheep keeper? In this scenario that makes *him* the sheep.

Cain was not Abel, and that's what did him in. In the original story of sibling rivalry—a story of jealousy, murder, deceit and cold, hard justice—Cain takes his brother's life, apparently because he feels that Abel has gotten the better of him. Both brothers offer a sacrifice to God, but God prefers Abel's. Why? Well, maybe because Cain's offering came from the ground, which was cursed. And that was more than Cain could handle. Poor Abel followed when Cain lured him out into the field, and that was the end of it. One of the striking parts of this story is the way God handles Cain's punishment. God doesn't go all eye-for-an-eye, tooth-for-a-tooth, life-for-a-life Old Testament Law on Cain. Instead, God shows Cain mercy and lets him live. And even more, God puts the mysterious "Mark of Cain" on Cain, so that everyone would know that Cain was under God's protection and that nobody had the right to kill him. Maybe the punishment was that God let him live with the pain of what he has done and who he is. Ouch.

If you're like us you've probably had it in for a sibling or a friend or just some random Joe or Jane Schmoe on the street. You've been mad, jealous, put out, looking for an excuse to let them have it—maybe not to kill, but to abuse verbally or payback with one of the little nastinesses that sometimes seem to make life so interesting. But beware, as someone once said. "Sin is lurking at the door; and its desire is for you." And whatever we do to our brother or sister, we get to live with it.

Key Verse: "And the LORD had regard for Abel and his offering, but for Cain and his offering he had no regard. So Cain was very angry, and his countenance fell" (Gen 4:4-5; see also Gen 4).

See also: **Abel, Genesis.**

1 and 2 Chronicles

\FUHRST-and-SEH-kihnd-KRAH-nih-kuhlz\

by Anonymous (Old Testament/History, sixty-five chapters)

1–2 Chronicles is Mr. Anonymous' editing and revising of Mr. Anonymous' (no relation) earlier work in 1–2 Samuel and 1–2 Kings. This second helping of history is remarkable in large part for two things. First, it evidences an outrageous and unsubtle concentration on the Southern Kingdom (Judah), all but ignoring the Northern Kingdom (Israel) and its history. Second, it celebrates the building of Solomon's Temple in much greater detail, to the point where specific groups of Levitical singers are identified according to their role in Solomon's praise ensemble. These among other changes mark Mr. Anonymous' work in Chronicles as something almost completely different.

While one hesitates to suggest that 1–2 Chronicles is not worth reading it certainly is important to have read Samuel and Kings in order to appreciate the subtle nuances and differences in emphasis that one finds in Chronicles. Mr. Anonymous' work is also commendable because he has preserved some pieces of Judah's story that the earlier mentioned Mr. Anonymous did not include in the epic 1–2 Kings.

See also: **Monarchy, Temple.**

C

Cleopas \KLEE-uh-puhs\

Status:
Cleopas really, really, really thought that This One might have been The One.

Profile

Likes:	Long walks in the evening, a good loaf of bread and cup of wine
Dislikes:	Gossip, silly tales
Motto:	"Wait 'til next year" (the unofficial slogan of the old Brooklyn Dodgers' fans)

Cleopas and his buddy picked up their signs, banners, and pennants, and started walking. When your hopes are crushed, yet again, there's nothing like a long walk to work off some of the frustration.

Cleopas said, "When he came in on the donkey and all of the crowds were cheering and throwing down clothes for the donkey to walk on, I thought *for sure* he was the one who was going to restore glory and honor to Israel. And then he gets himself crucified without even putting up a fight. What a letdown! Well, maybe next year. There's always a candidate for messiah springing up somewhere."

Presently, a third traveler joined them, "What's this about the Messiah?"

"Are you the only one who hasn't heard? We had hoped Jesus of Nazareth would lead us to victory. But, turns out he was just a prophet. True, some women who followed him were spreading around a silly tale about him being raised from the dead. But we are men of action, we don't cotton much to foolish women's prattle."

"How foolish are you?" Jesus replied. "For years I have been telling you that I am not that kind of messiah. I am not about war and restoring David's kingdom but about God's mission to love, save, forgive, and bless the world. Suffering and dying did not mean I wasn't the Messiah, but that I am—I had to suffer, because the world would not accept a humble, forgiving, loving Messiah. It isn't what the world wants. But it's what they get, and that is a little something that I like to call The Good News."

Jesus taught them the Scriptures. He took bread, broke it, gave it to them. And they recognized him.

Key Verse: "They got up and returned to Jerusalem; and they found the eleven and their companions gathered together. They were saying, 'The Lord has risen indeed, and he has appeared to Simon!'"
(Luke 24:33-34; see also Luke 24:13-35).

See also: Luke (The Gospel according to).

Colossians \kuh-LAH-shunz\

by Paul (New Testament, Letters, four chapters)

Jesus is Lord. That's what Colossians wants to make abundantly clear, especially chapter one. But Colossians wants to make other things abundantly clear as well. For instance: Watch out for those false teachers whose words captivate (2:8). Beware of those legalists who tell you "you can't touch this" and "you can't taste that" (Col 2:21). But on the other hand, put to death fornication and impurity and passion and evil desire and greed (Col 3.5—please note: that whole "put to death" language is metaphorical; please don't actually put anyone to death for these transgressions). Oh, and while you're at it, clothe yourselves with Col 3:12-17, a passage that's also nice to read at weddings (please note: again this "clothing" language is purely metaphorical, if you show up at a wedding in just Colossians 3 you probably won't get in). For more about the writing of Colossians, see the end of the Ephesians entry.

See also: Paul (Saul of Tarsus).

1 and 2 Corinthians

\FUHRST-and-SEH-kihnd-kuhr-IHN-thee-uhnz\

by Saul of Tarsus, a.k.a. the Apostle Paul
(New Testament, Letters, twenty-nine chapters)

Readers familiar with Paul's other works will certainly welcome Corinthians to the collection. This work is divided into two volumes and represents a compilation of letters that Paul wrote to the Christians living in Corinth, Greece. As many folks know, Paul is the one who planted the seed of the gospel in Corinth—no easy feat in that polytheistic metropolis. Anyway, thanks to others who watered that seed, the church in Corinth was a growing concern with growing concerns. Paul's letters address these concerns.

Part of the fun of reading Corinthians is reading between the lines. Like listening to one side of a phone conversation, we can only guess as to the exact nature of the questions and concerns arising out of the Christian community in Corinth. It's clear that there were conflicting opinions—and conflicting opinion-leaders—and that such conflict inspired some in Corinth to seek the counsel of their founder, Paul. Paul readily offers such counsel, covering a variety of subjects, including how to handle differences of opinion, how to "know nothing except Christ crucified," how to think about food sacrificed to idols, how to deal with issues of marriage and the single life, how to honor the Lord's Supper, how to share the wealth, and, in general, how to be the "Body of Christ" with all its parts working together. Not to be missed is Paul's hilariously "foolish" boasting jag (in 2 Corinthians 11) by which he exposes the "super-apostles" who were stirring things up in there Corinth. Wait... foolish boasting? What's next? Army intelligence? Jumbo shrimp?

Not intended to be the theological tour de force represented by Paul's Romans, 1 and 2 Corinthians nevertheless offer a profound "inside look" at the struggles of an early Christian community, not to mention sound guidance for Christian communities everywhere.

See also: Paul (Saul of Tarsus).

Creation \kree-Ā-shuhn\

That which God alone is capable of doing—often through other creatures.

Here's the thing about Creation, there really isn't any detailed time frame for when it started and how long it lasted. Sure, Genesis talks about seven days, but that's probably more of an attempt to explain the seven day week than anything else. So when is Creation? What time period are we talking about here?

In the simplest sense Creation is the time before "history" begins. This is pre-anything that we know of, pre-stone age, pre-Paleolithic era, pre-primordial goo, pre-everything. In other words, we're talking a long time ago, and just how long ago is hard to say. But that's OK 'cause here's the cool thing: Creation is still going on right now! This is true of our world around us—things grow and are made and are discovered every day; it's true of our bodies—we may not "grow" anything but fatter and bigger of ear and nose, but our bodies are constantly regenerating dead cell tissue; and if the stellar and galactic physicists are correct (and let's face—it they probably are; after all, they're rocket scientists) the universe is continuing to grow and expand. So creation is now. It is still. It is the way God continues to work on/in/around the world.

See also: Adam, Genesis, Jesus.

Daniel \DAN-yuhl\ (book)

by Anonymous (Old Testament/Major Prophets, twelve chapters)

Mr. Anonymous has once again posed a puzzle for readers. The first question is, exactly what kind of literature is this? In the Christian tradition, the book has been considered one of the major prophets. But it is unlike other prophetic books in many ways. In the Jewish tradition, the book is not considered a prophetic book, but one of the *writings* (along with books such as Psalms, 1 and 2 Chronicles, and Job). The present reviewer is of the opinion that the Jewish tradition is closer to the mark. This isn't a book by Daniel or containing his prophetic speeches (at least not in the same way that Hosea or Amos contain the speeches of those prophets). Rather, it is a narrative that was written many years after Daniel lived, using stories about him to talk about the challenges of living a faithful life in the midst of a hostile world and culture. Daniel lived during the Babylonian exile, when the people of God struggled beneath the yoke of Babylonian tyranny. The author of the book of Daniel lived around the year 165 BCE, during a time when the people of God suffered greatly under the tyranny of a kingdom known as the Seleucids. The stories told about Daniel gave the people who lived under the Seleucids courage and hope as they struggled to remain faithful.

Daniel is probably the latest book in the Old Testament—it was not completed until perhaps 164 BCE. The first part, chapters 1–6, is composed of six stories set in the court of the kings of Babylon. If you aren't much for fiery furnace, lions, or wall graffiti, you might not like them. The second part, chapters 7–12, is made up of four visions. Don't read them to the kids before bed, unless you like wet sheets.

See also: Apocalyptic Literature, Daniel.

Daniel \DAN-yuhl\

Status:
Daniel is slightly claustrophobic.

Profile

Vocation:	Dream Therapist
What's in a name:	Daniel means "God is my judge." Sometimes I think I'd prefer something less serious, like Dannyboy or Skip or Belteshazzar, but Daniel has stuck.
Dislikes:	Dens; circuses; zoos
Least Favorite Celebrity:	Freud—or should I say Fraud, he's such a wanna-be
Favorite Quotation:	"I want you to hold on to God's unchanging hand. 'Cause he helped Joshua fight the battle of Jericho. Yes! He helped Daniel get outta the lions den. He helped Gilligan get off the Island. Lord!"—Arsenio Hall as Rev. Brown in *Coming to America*.

It all started with a dream (as these things so often seem to). The king of Babylon, we'll call him Buck, had bad dreams. Daniel, to whom God had given the ability to interpret dreams, did just that for the Buckster. Now able to sleep more soundly, the king promoted Daniel to be one of the chief governors of the whole kingdom. That might have been the end of it. But along with Daniel's promotion there came an unfortunate side effect (as there often does with these things). Certain members of Buck's court, other leaders and governors, became jealous of Daniel and began to plot to discredit him so that they could get ahead. Their plot came to a head during the reign of Darius (the king of Persia, who had conquered Babylon after Buck had passed on). These court members, we'll call them "satraps"—'cause that's what they're called—arranged for a law to be written that made praying to anyone other than King Darius a capital crime (that's if you broke it you bought it—figuratively). Daniel, being a devout and faithful Jew, couldn't do that. So he went right ahead and kept praying to the Lord alone. And naturally the satraps had him arrested.

To be fair, Darius wanted to spare Daniel; he probably thought the law was pretty silly anyway, but the law is the law and he was forced to uphold it (which just goes to show you that while the law can be good it really isn't "all that"). So Daniel was sent into a cave full of lions, and a stone was rolled in front of the entrance (which seems like a strangely specific sentence for a crime, don't you think?). He was in there all night. And when morning came? Out strolls Daniel, without a scratch or a scrape, without so much as a cat hair on his clothes.

When we read Daniel's story we might be tempted to stress his faithfulness, the fact that even facing death he would pray only to his God. Or we might stress God's power, the fact that the LORD can save a person from anything—even a den full of lions. But the real punch of the story comes in the impact that Daniel's faithfulness and God's power have on people—even kings. Check it out:

Key Verse: "'I [Darius] make a decree, that in all my royal dominion people should tremble and fear before the God of Daniel: For he is the living God, enduring forever. His kingdom shall never be destroyed, and his dominion has no end. He delivers and rescues, he works signs and wonders in heaven and on earth; for he has saved Daniel from the power of the lions'" (Dan 6:26-27).

See also: Babylonians, Daniel (book).

David \DĀ-vihd\

Status:
David does not believe in term limits.

Profile

Vocation:	Shepherd, King, Paradigm
What's in a name:	My name means "beloved one," and I am too—both of God and my parents. We youngest usually are.
Family:	Jesse is my father (Dad, that's what I call him); my seven older brothers are Eliab (not king), Abinadab (not king), Shimmea (not king), Nathanel (not king), Raddai (not king), Ozem (not king), Elihu (not king), and then me —king, go figure
Dislikes:	Uncircumcised Philistines
Favorite Psalm:	Since it would be prideful to pick one of my own, I'd say Psalm 78 is my fav. I love the way it ends.
Favorite Quotation:	"What then is this bleating of sheep in my ears?" Nathan said that to Saul. You should have seen the look on his face.
Least Favorite Quotation:	"Alas for those . . . who sing idle songs to the sound of the harp, and like David improvise on instruments of music." Amos. What was his deal anyway? Improvisation is trickier than it seems, especially on a lyre.

David was the Captain Kirk of Israel's kings. If that's too 1966 for you, think of him as the Brad Pitt or the Ashton Kutcher (without the pranks) of Israel's kings. When he got his mack on, he was virtually irresistible. He was charming, handsome, and knew how to get his way. While this isn't all the Bible has to say about David, it does play a prominent role in his story.

We encounter one of the not so subtle biblical ironies when the prophet Nathan is sent out to find a replacement for Saul. He meets Jesse's boys, and one after another as they came up to him. Nathan would think: *Hey, he's tall . . . strong . . . good looking, I bet he's the one.*

And of course Nathan would be wrong. Then the Lord would say to Nathan, "This ain't no GQ model hunt; don't look at them from the human point of view, but from my point of view which I think we can all agree is the superior point of view. It's a perspective thing." The seven older boys all passed by and none of them was chosen to be king. Finally, up comes David, Jesse's youngest son, who had been out watching the sheep. If you don't already know the story you've probably guessed what happens next—David is the one. He's the one God chooses to take over for Saul. And strangely enough here's how the Bible then describes him: "Now he [David] was ruddy, and had beautiful eyes, and was handsome. The Lord said, 'Rise and anoint him; for this is the one.'" It's not about appearance... except when it is. Double standard much?

David's story is really long. *Really* long—it is in fact the longest story about an individual in the Old Testament, and David is mentioned more in the OT than any other human. But the highlights of his story are familiar enough that even folks who don't read the Bible too much or too closely have probably seen a reference to them out there somewhere. And how about when little school beats big school in the throws of March Madness and next day's headline reads: *David upsets Goliath*. And of course David did. Sort of. Outsized and out-armed he faced a bigger, stronger, more experienced, and better armed warrior. Now if you know the story you're probably thinking—here comes the sling and stone bit. And you're not wrong. Instead of a sword or a spear or even a bow and arrow, David used sling and stone. He knocked Goliath down by hitting him between the eyes with the stone, then took Goliath's own sword and finished the job. But according to both the Bible and David himself it wasn't a stone or a sword that killed Goliath. "This very day," David said to Goliath, "the Lord will deliver you into my hand, and I will strike you down and cut off your head."

David was the champion, but he was God's champion—all that he was and all he accomplished were God's doing. When David remembered this, that's when he was at his best. But David was by no means perfect. In fact, he was *perfectly sinful*. For just one example, take the Bathsheba incident. He not only got a married woman pregnant but tried to get out of it by getting her husband (Uriah) drunk. When that didn't work, he went for the gusto and had him killed so that he could have Bathsheba as his own wife. Then along comes Nathan with another story with another sheep—maybe Nathan was in a rut—showing David where he had gone wrong (for the uncondensed version see 2 Samuel 11). Maybe David was a champion, but he was also a bit of a goat, too.

And maybe that is, finally, the most important thing to take away from his story. David was not so much a role model for how people of faith ought to live as he was typical of the kind of person God chooses and loves—a sinner, with all the good and despite the bad that we bring to the table. We may not be royalty like David, and we may not even sin as spectacularly as he did. But we are sinners, and still we are beloved of God. And God can still use us as part of God's plan for the world. Crazy talk? Maybe, but crazy good news too.

Key Verse: "When God had removed Saul, he made David their king. In his testimony about him he said, 'I have found David, son of Jesse, to be a man after my heart, who will carry out all my wishes'" (Acts 13:22).

See also: **Absalom, Goliath, Saul, Uriah the Hittite.**

Deborah \DEHB-ruh\

Status:
Deborah is judging Israel.

D

Profile

Vocation:	Prophet, Judge, Military Mastermind
Fun Fact:	Judges 5 "The Song of Deborah"—that's my jam—is considered to be among the oldest passages in the Old Testament
Favorite Song:	I should think that's obvious.
Favorite Quotation:	"No matter how many times you save the world it always manages to get back in jeopardy again. Sometimes I just want it to stay saved, you know? For a little bit? I feel like the maid: I just cleaned up this mess—can we keep it clean, please, for ten minutes?!" Mr. Incredible in *The Incredibles*—substitute "Israel" for "world" and I couldn't say it any better.

Deborah is introduced in Judges 4:4: "At that time Deborah, a prophetess . . . was judging Israel," but she wasn't judging Israel like an Internet opinionator (ripping the Israelites for some fashion faux pas or their dating habits), or a disapproving uncle ("Can't you get a real job? Your cousin Marty is so much more talented and successful than you. Don't you wish you could be more like him?"). No, Deborah didn't judge like that, she settled disputes among the people; she was the star of The Chosen People's Court. But there was more to Deborah's judging. She was also a prophet, delivering judgments/messages from God, and she was a military leader—which is part of what the judges did in Israel. Talk about your multi-tasking. Under Deborah's direction—direction she first received from God—Barak (a military leader from the tribe of Naphtali) defeated the Canaanite King Jabin, his general Sisera, nine hundred "chariots of iron" (the premier war machine back in the day), and an unspecified number of foot soldiers.

Deborah is an important figure from Israel's early days. She was a vital spiritual and political leader during the fledgling days of the people. The simple fact that Deborah is a woman is also important. While the book of Judges doesn't make a huge deal out it, it is clear that strong leadership, wisdom, and vision can come from women. And in the person of Deborah, with all the different hats she wore—prophet, judge, military strategist, all around queen bee for Israel—we meet an extraordinary woman called by God to save God's people.

Key Verse: "The peasantry prospered in Israel, they grew fat on plunder, because you arose, Deborah, arose as a mother in Israel" (Judg 5:7).

See also: **Judges (book), Judges (period of).**

Delilah \duh-LI-luh\

Status:
Delilah has fallen just slightly short of "faithful 'til death."

D

Profile

Vocation:	Nagger-unto-death
Homeland:	I come from the valley of Sorek (pronounced sow-rake), which is on the Philistine/Judah border.
Interests:	I like shiny things, like scissors, razors, and Philistine silver.
Fun Fact:	The name of the valley where I live is a play on words in Hebrew; according to Jewish tradition *sorek* means "fruitless tree" and *req* means "empty," which is what Samson's head was when he fell in love with me.
Favorite Book:	*Tempting Strong Men for Dummies* (it's an old franchise)
Favorite Song:	"Fire" by Bruce Springsteen ("Romeo and Juliet, Samson and Delilah . . .")

Delilah was the beginning of the end for Samson. The Philistines wanted to get to Samson, who had defeated them several times in battle, and offered Delilah a couple camel loads of silver to learn the secret of his incredible strength. So Delilah, all smooth and subtle like, goes, "Please tell me what makes your strength so great, and how you could be bound, so that one could subdue you." Now Samson may not have been the brightest judge on the bench, you know, one gavel short of a ruling, but he didn't fall for it; he lied. So Delilah asked him again. And again. And again. And finally, apparently just to get Delilah to shut her yapper, he told her the truth: it was all in the hair. Okay, that's not the *whole* secret, but it's all that mattered to Delilah and the Philistines. Delilah gave him what is believed to be the original buzz cut, and the Philistines captured him and took him away.

Far as we know Delilah lived happily ever after. Rumor has it she opened a successful chain of hair salons. You might find her listed in the Yellow Papyrus under "Sorek: Stylists/Seductions."

Key Verse: "Finally, after she had nagged him with her words day after day, and pestered him, he was tired to death" (Judg 16:16).

See also: Judges (book), Philistines.

Deuteronomy \doo-duhr-AH-nuh-mee\

by the Deuteronomist (Old Testament, Pentateuch, thirty-four chapters)

In this thirty-four-chapter dissertation, Mr. Deuteronomist has produced what might well be described as Exodus version 2.0. Mr. D. begins by reviewing, revisiting and retelling the story of Israel's recent past (starting with the covenant at Mt. Sinai—called Horeb in Deuteronomy), using that history as a launching pad for reviewing, revisiting, and revising the law and the terms of covenant relationship between God and Israel. Mr. D. takes the English title for his work from this characterization, namely that it is a "second" presentation of "the Law" (*deutero* = second; *nomos* = Law).

Deuteronomy is written as though it is an address or perhaps sermon delivered by Moses to the people of Israel just prior to their occupation of the Promised Land. Here Mr. D. repeats the giving of the Ten Commandments, and reiterates a series of laws meant to guide life with God and with one another. While some readers might feel, and at times this reviewer felt, that Deuteronomy as a revision of the law is somewhat redundant, there are important additions and shifts in emphasis to this second volume.

In Deuteronomy, which was written close in both time and theology to the reforming work of Judah's King Josiah, Mr. D. addresses issues of *covenant loyalty*. His contention is that Israel's trials and tribulations can be directly traced to its faithlessness, to its worship of gods other than Yahweh. Only through reestablishing a right relationship with God, according to D., will Israel have hope for the future. There are symptoms which show up when Israel is out of step with the covenant. Primary among these for Deuteronomy, as for several of the prophetic authors such as Amos, Micah, and Hosea, is neglect of the poor. For Deuteronomy, right relationship with God and right relationship with one's neighbor go hand-in-hand.

D

See also: Pentateuch.

Deuteronomy \doo-duhr-AH-nuh-mee\

by the Deuteronomist (Old Testament, Pentateuch, thirty-four chapters)

In this thirty-four-chapter dissertation, Mr. Deuteronomist has produced what might well be described as Exodus version 2.0. Mr. D. begins by reviewing, revisiting and retelling the story of Israel's recent past (starting with the covenant at Mt. Sinai—called Horeb in Deuteronomy), using that history as a launching pad for reviewing, revisiting, and revising the law and the terms of covenant relationship between God and Israel. *Are you really reading this entry too? What, so hungry for information on Deuteronomy that you'll read anything that smacks of this second law that you'll dive right in?*

Deuteronomy is written as though it is an address or perhaps sermon delivered by Moses to the people of Israel just prior to their occupation of the Promised Land. *Here the authors of* Crazy Book *are repeating some of the information that you've already read and reiterating the joke about the "secondness" of Deuteronomy.* While some readers might feel, and at times this reviewer felt, that Deuteronomy as a revision of the law is somewhat redundant, *even more redundant is the fact that you're still reading this entry. Move on!* Anyway, in Deuteronomy, which is tied closely to the reforming work of Judah's King Josiah, Mr. D. addresses issues of covenant loyalty. His contention is that Israel's trials and tribulations can be directly traced to its faithlessness, to its worship of gods other than Yahweh. Only through reestablishing a right relationship with God, according to D., will Israel have hope for the future. Primary among these for Deuteronomy, as for several of the Prophetic authors such as Amos, Micah and Hosea, is neglect of the poor. *For those of you still reading, maybe looking for another insight or, let's hope, another joke here it is: the joke's on you for reading this Deuteroentry.*

See also: Pentateuch.

Dinah \DI-nuh\ or \DEE-nuh\

Status:
Dinah is in the kitchen.

Profile

What's In a Name:	My name means "skillfully shaped"—not too shabby, eh?
Fun Fact:	I have always suffered from a serious existential quandary: will I or will I not blow my horn?
Favorite Celebrity:	It's a tie between Dinah Shore and Judy Strangis (she played Dyna Girl in *Electra Woman and Dyna Girl*)

Dinah's story is not a pleasant one. A guy named Shechem, who was a Hivite (guess he was into bees), took a shine to Dinah and, being a "prince among men," and thinking he could get away with anything, he raped her. After the fact, he *did* want to marry her and so he "spoke tenderly to her," but as far as we're concerned, that does absolutely nothing to redeem him or make up for the awful violence he did to Dinah. He is a criminal, plain and simple.

Apparently, Dinah's brothers agreed with us, because they put into play one of the nastiest tricks in the Bible (or anywhere for that matter). Dinah's brothers agreed that Shechem could marry Dinah, and his boys could marry other members of Jacob's family, under one condition—that they all get circumcised. The Hivites agreed, and while they were recovering and "still in pain" from their conversion experience, Dinah's brothers dropped in and made a rather large iron deposit. With swords. That means they killed them all. Not that we are endorsing revenge.

Dinah's story is not a pleasant one, but the Bible is about real life. And her story is skillfully shaped.

Key Verse: "And they said, 'Should our sister be treated like a whore?'" (Gen 34:31; see also Gen 34).

See also: Genesis.

Ecclesiastes \eh-KLEE-zee-AS-teez\

by Mr. Qoheleth (Old Testament, Poetry, twelve chapters)

"Of making many books there is no end, and much study is a weariness of the flesh." So writes Mr. Qoheleth toward the end of his little book, and one does not doubt that the irony is entirely intentional. The wearisome making of books by *preachers* in particular seems endless and wearisome, but Mr. Qoheleth—a pseudonym for the author of Ecclesiastes which traditionally was translated as "preacher"—offers a fresh, if somewhat melancholic, entry upon the field.

Ecclesiastes stands in stark contrast to the current best-selling, prosperity-driven and prosperity-promising literature in the area of religious writing. Mr. Qoheleth charges that all pursuits—and one suspects in particular the pursuits of success-oriented spirituality—are "vanity." In other words, the press toward happiness, fullness, richness, righteousness and blessedness is empty, like a puff of smoke on the wind, amounting to nothing and leading nowhere. What does Mr. Qoheleth preach in the place of the prosperity gospel? Realism. Contentment in the moment. Happiness where one can find it in the blessings one has at hand. "Take joy in your life," Mr. Qoheleth might preach, "for this is your time—a time for the present time, the moment." Or in the Preacher's own words: "There is nothing better for mortals than to eat and drink, and find enjoyment in their toil. This also, I saw, is from the hand of God." You can see why we like this particular preacher.

See also: Poetry.

Eglon \EHG-lahn\

Status:
Eglon is . . . relieving himself in the cool chamber.

Profile

E

Vocation:	King of Moab
What's in a name?	In Hebrew my name means "little bull," which I guess is supposed to be ironic since I'm a little big boned. Ha, ha, ha, ha, ha, that's not funny.
Favorite Celebrity:	Fat Elvis
Favorite Quotation:	"My doctor says I've been swallowing a lot of aggression, along with a lot of pizzas." —Dewey "Ox" Oxberger (John Candy), *Stripes*

Key Verse: "The Israelites again did what was evil in the sight of the LORD; and the LORD strengthened King Eglon of Moab against Israel, because they had done what was evil in the sight of the LORD" (Judg 3:12).

See also: Ehud, Judges (book).

Egyptians \ee-JIHP-shuhnz\

The wondrous pyramid-building people, with one-sided faces and L-shaped arms, whose civilization was centered around the Nile River.

When you see the pictures that the Egyptians painted of themselves, you wonder whether they weren't a people completely obsessed with making sure the artist captured their better side. And speaking of capture, the Egyptians' main moment in the biblical drama is one in which they play the villains in the Exodus story. But don't get the idea that Egypt and Israel were always at odds with one other (they often were, but at times they were allies), or the idea that the Israelites and Egyptians had nothing in common (they shared many things, including technology and many ideas about government and law).

The Egyptians were a polytheistic people, worshiping gods such as Horus and Isis. They believed that their king (pharaoh) was divine. They were also a seriously commercial and intellectual people with an open and cosmopolitan society. After the fall of Jerusalem in 587 BCE, a group of Judeans, including the prophet Jeremiah and his scribe Baruch, took up residence in Egypt, helping to preserve God's people. So in a rather fitting what-comes-around-also-goes-around kind of way, the Egyptians, who had played the villains earlier in the Old Testament story, came to play the merciful harborers of refuge toward its end.

See also: Israelites, Moses, Pharaoh.

Ehud \Ā-ood\

Status:
Ehud is sharpening Q-bit.

Profile

Vocation:	Judge
Who I am:	I am a left-handed Benjaminite which, if you know your Hebrew, is pretty funny because "benjamin" means "son of the right hand."
Favorite Celebrities:	John McEnroe, Rocky Balboa, Jimmie Hendrix. All southpaws.
Favorite Movie Dialogue:	*Vizzini*: We'll head straight for the Gilder frontier. You catch up with us there. If he falls, fine. If not, the sword. *Inigo Montoya*: I'm going to duel him left-handed. *Vizzini*: You know what a hurry we're in! *Inigo Montoya*: Well, is only way I can be satisfied. If I use my right . . . over too quickly. *Vizzini*: [exasperated] Oh, have it your way. —*The Princess Bride*

Most of us, when we think about the biblical judges, think of Samson, Gideon, and maybe Deborah. But one of the most interesting, crazy and, for our money, hee-haw hi-larious stories in the book of Judges is about Ehud and Eglon; Ehud is the Israelite judge and Eglon the Moabite king. As the book of Judges tells us over and over again (and over and over and over again which is what in English circles they call the "concentric circle method"), Israel blows its relationship with God and needs to be rescued from the wages of its sin. There are three things you need to keep in mind as you read this story recorded in Judges 3:12-30:

1. It's gross; nasty stuff happens, the kind of stuff that the average 13-year-old boy can't get enough of and the average 13-year-old girl will "Ew!" at.
2. It is written using the original Bible code; when we say this we don't mean things hidden in numbers or mysterious re-sequencing of words and letters that reveal some prophecy of the future, but euphemism that avoids using naughty or unpleasant words in holy writ.
3. Ehud is clever, his craftiness is the tool that God uses to save Israel.

Eglon and the Moabites had been in control of Israel for eighteen years, demanding regular tribute. So Israel sends Ehud to render unto Eglon what is Eglon's.

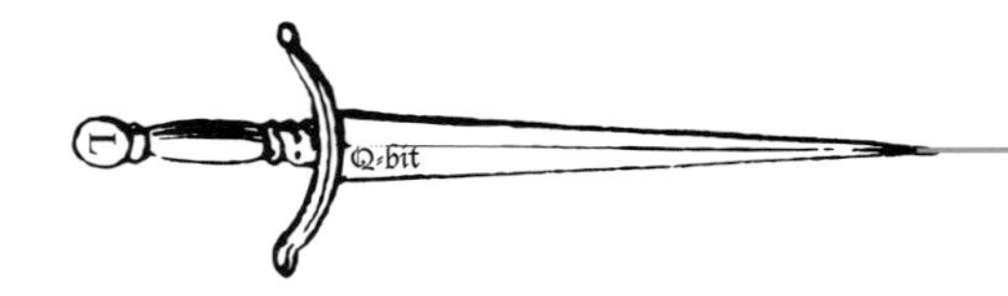

Hint: Remember that Ehud is clever; this "tribute" is going to be something other than shekels and sheep.

In preparation for his visit to king Eglon, Ehud made a special sword—sharpened on both edges and short, just a cubit in length (and that's what he called it, Q-bit; X-calibur was taken).

Note: Remember that Ehud is clever; a cubit is about the length from your elbow to the tip of your middle finger—that's a little different for everybody but pretty short for a sword no matter who you are, go ahead and measure your cubit (feel free to make a note of it here:_____, being careful not to insult yourself) and you'll see what we mean: short. The point of all this detail is that such a small sword would be easier to hide. On top of all this, Ehud is left handed which apparently nobody expected back in the day so the guards probably didn't search his right side too thoroughly.

Now, your average vigilante judge would probably have taken the tribute in to old Eglon, pulled out his sword, and gotten right down to business. Not Ehud—remember, he's clever. He delivers the tribute and then makes like he's going back to Israel like a good little vassal. But all of the sudden he stops and goes back and says to Eglon, "I've got a secret message just for you. From God." So Eglon sends all of his retainers out so that he can hear this secret message in secret. Of course we all know what "message" Ehud is talking

See answer on pg. 113

about, don't we? 45.72 centimeters of a message sharper than any two edged sword (FYI, 45.72 centimeters is Da Vinci's Antediluvian Man's cubit). And here's where the story gets a little gross—so if you're squeamish we suggest you turn the page now. Ehud stabs Eglon in the belly and stabs him so hard (now you go "How hard was it?"), so hard that the whole sword goes into him, all the way up to and over the handle, and the fat flops over the hilt. Just so you don't think we're being intentionally over-the-top-gross just to sell this book let us quote directly from Judges here:

"Ehud reached with his left hand, took the sword from his right thigh, and thrust it into Eglon's belly; and the fat closed over the blade, for he did not draw the sword out of his belly; and the dirt came out."

Decoder: So we know what you're thinking (among other things we guess you're thinking): what is this business about "dirt"? Here we have an example of Judge's bible code. "Dirt" is a polite way of saying "guts," "innards," "intestines," "entrails," "viscera,"—sorry, you get the point. Yuck, right? Or, as a confirmation-aged boy might say, "Cool!"

What happens next is one of the crazy details that the Bible sometimes includes for who knows what reason, but it's in there. Ehud, having slipped his tribute between Eglon's ribs, locks the door to the king's chambers to make time for his getaway. The servants of the Moabite court are waiting for their king and they say to themselves, "He'll be out in a minute he's just relieving himself in the cool chamber." *Decoding*: Actually this is a case of double-decoding; "relieving himself" (can we agree that we know what that means?) is the newer translation for what the servants think Eglon is doing, the older translation is "covering his feet," the ancient Israelite euphemism for "going potty." We're not making this stuff up.

Needless to say the king was on the throne for a long time. So long, in fact, that the king's servants became embarrassed. In the war that ensued the Israelites prevailed, winning a decisive victory. With their number one out of the way, the Moabites finished number two, and the LORD redeemed Israel and brought them back to a right relationship with their God.

We make up all kinds of children's songs about Ezekiel and the dry bones, Noah and the animals two-by-two...why not a little ditty about Ehud, Eglon the fat king, and going potty? O.K. maybe not. But in this interesting, crazy, hee-haw hi-larious (and did we mention gross?) story, which you might not believe is actually *in* the Bible, the problem of human sin separating humanity from God—probably the main subject of the book of Judges—is dealt with head on. And in this wild story the pattern for the way that God deals with us sinful people, a pattern that ultimately leads to the life, death and resurrection of God's only Son, is laid out in plain and even vulgar language. And that's not yuck. That's cool.

Key Verse: "Ehud came to [Eglon], while he was sitting alone in his cool roof chamber, and said, 'I have a message from God for you'" (Judg 3:20).

See also: Eglon, Judges (book).

Elijah/Elisha

So Elijah and Elisha—which one is which? Who came first? Who rode the chariot of fire? Who told the prophets of Baal to go suck eggs? Not sure? Have a hard time keeping them straight? Well, you're not the only one. So allow us to let you in on a little secret: Elijah and Elisha are actually the same guy. Heard of Bruce Wayne and Batman? Peter Parker and Spiderman? Clark Kent and Superman? Same guys right? Same here. The whole "passing of the mantle" bit was just a cover up.

O.K., that's not actually true, but their stories are so similar that you could understand why someone would make the mistake. What we offer here is a little look at each prophet and a comparison of the similarities (and differences) between them.

Elijah \ee-LI-zhuh, -juh\

Status:
Elijah is trash-talking.

Profile

E

Vocation	Prophet
What's in a Name?	My name means "Yah is God."
Pet Peeves:	I'm so over the "still small voice" thing—in fact sometimes I wish God would raise the divine voice a little. I also hate being mistaken for John the Baptist. I do have some professional pride.
Favorite Holiday:	The Passover; it's nice to know that so many people are saving me a seat.
Favorite Pastime:	Trash talking
Favorite Quotation:	"So, because you are lukewarm, and neither cold nor hot, I am about to spit you out of my mouth" (John in Rev 3:16). Sounds like something I'd say (1 Kgs 18:21).

Time: High noon. Place: Mount Carmel. The Contest: 450 prophets versus Elijah—to see who can end the drought and bring rain to Israel. So Elijah says, "Here's the deal, gang: we'll take two bulls and set them up to sacrifice. Then you pray to Baal and I'll pray to Yahweh. Whoever sends down fire to burn up the offering—there's your God." So Baal's prophets get all set up and they call out for Baal to do his thing. Surprise, surprise, nothing happens. Now faced 450 to 1, we might have just gone about our business and said our prayer and made our sacrifice. Not Elijah. He talks trash to Baal and his prophets: "What? No answer? Go, Baal, go! Some 'god.' He must be on a Zen meditation retreat. Or at the salon. Or catching forty winks." Elijah talked a little smack, which we've got to respect. Then he added a little more umpf to the insult. Elijah prepared his bull for sacrifice, and doused it with water—not once but twice—enough water to form a big moat around the altar. And when he called out

to Yahweh, what do you know, fire fell from the sky and burned up the offering and burned so hot that all the water was toasted too. And then, just to add a little injury to the insult, Elijah had all of Baal's prophets killed. Talk about rubbing in your victory. . . .

In the end the Bible says that Elijah did not die. He was taken away into heaven in a chariot of fire and the prophet Malachi promised that he would come again to usher in the day of the Lord (Mal 4:5). For this reason many devout Jews still set an extra place for Elijah when they celebrate the Passover—just in case he decides to start the day of the Lord at their house. In the New Testament John the Baptist is taken for Elijah, and in the Gospel of Matthew Jesus actually says that John the Baptist played the part of Elijah and prepared the way for the Messiah (mostly by suffering as the Messiah also suffered and preparing his way).

Key Verse: "Elijah has already come, and they did not recognize him, but they did to him whatever they pleased. So also the Son of Man is about to suffer at their hands" (Matt 17:12-13; see also 1 Kgs 17—2 Kgs 2).

See also: Baal, 1 and 2 Kings, Prophets.

Elisha \ee-LI-shuh\

Status:
Elisha is wearing a fancy, hand-me-down mantle.

Profile

€

Vocation:	Prophet; Successor to Elijah
Likes:	Shares of the Spirit. Make mine a double.
Dislikes:	Snot nosed brats; teasing; street magicians (if you want to see something float, come with me to the Jordan River)
Favorite Joke:	The balding middle-aged man asked his barber, "Why charge me the full price for cutting my hair? There's so little of it." "Well," said the barber, "actually, I make little charge for cutting it. What you're paying for is my searching for it!" My barber told me that joke. He laughed real hard until he got home and found a couple of she-bears in his front yard.

Elisha did some great things, no doubt. He very much followed in Elijah's footsteps. But our favorite story is about the group of feral youths who were making fun of him at Bethel. Elisha had what today we might call prophet pattern balding. As he came into town, the boys started chanting, "Go away, baldhead! Go away, baldhead!" Maybe Elisha's feet were sore. Maybe it was too hot that day. Matthew 5:9 hadn't been written yet, so maybe Elisha didn't know he was supposed to turn the other cheek. Whatever the case Elisha didn't take having his baldness made fun of very well. So he cursed the boys in the name of the Lord and two she-bears came out of the woods and mauled forty-two of those kids. Yikes.

And what is the moral of this story? Maybe there isn't a moral per se, but one thing is clear—even prophets of the Lord aren't perfect, which is reassuring in a funny way. And kids, one other lesson: next time you're tempted to make fun of your pastor for his "wide part" or his really big forehead remember to make sure there are no bears around.

As we said there are a lot of similarities between Elijah and Elisha. For example:

Similarities	Elijah	Elisha
Both provide unending sustenance for a widow	a jar of meal and jug of oil 1 Kings 17:8-16	a jug of oil 2 Kings 4:1-7
Both raise a widow's son from the dead	in Zarephath 1 Kings 17:17-24	the Shunamite woman 2 Kings 4:8-37
Both work during troubled times in Israel	during a drought 1 Kings 17:1	during a famine 2 Kings 4:38

On top of this Elisha completes the work that Elijah is given to do. In 1 Kings 19:15-16 God says to Elijah, "Go, return on your way to the wilderness of Damascus; when you arrive, you shall anoint Hazael as king over Aram. Also you shall anoint Jehu son of Nimshi as king over Israel; and you shall anoint Elisha son of Shaphat of Abel-meholah as prophet in your place." Before being swept away in the chariot of fire Elijah only got the job one-third of the way done. It was Elisha who anointed Hazael and Jehu (see 2 Kings 8–9).

For all their similarities there are differences too:

- Elijah is a confronter of kings (see 1 Kgs 16:29—19:18; 21; 2 Kgs 1:2—2:17).
- Elisha is a miracle worker (see 2 Kgs 4:38-41; 5:1-19; 6:1-7).
- Elijah is mentioned frequently in the New Testament, most famously when people ask John the Baptist if he is Elijah (Matt 11:13-15), and when Jesus calls out to God from the cross and some folks think he's calling Elijah (Luke 9:1-10; see also Rom 11:1-5; Jas 5:16-17).
- Elisha is mentioned only once in the New Testament, in Luke 4:27, where Jesus is teaching in Galilee and says that he is the fulfillment of Scripture.

In a real sense Elijah and Elisha make up one sustained story. Elijah and Elisha are prophets of action, who stand as examples of trust in and faithfulness to the Lord even in the face of terrible odds and great difficulties. Elijah and Elisha called Israel—and call us—to recognize the power of the one true God to deliver and to save. And they set the stage for another prophet of action who worked miracles and worked salvation to show us his Father.

Key Verse: "When the company of prophets who were at Jericho saw him at a distance, they declared, 'The spirit of Elijah rests on Elisha'" (2 Kgs 2:15; see also 2 Kgs 2–9).

See also: 1 and 2 Kings, Prophets.

Elizabeth \e-LIH-zuh-bihth\

Status:
Elizabeth is happy in her old age.

Profile

Family:	I'm the cousin of Mary, mother of our Lord; married to Zechariah who's a priest at the temple; and mother of John the forerunner and wilderness-path-straightener for Jesus.
Pet Peeve:	When my husband won't answer me (as if he can't)
Favorite Quotation:	"Mmmm. Mmmm. MMMMM!!" My husband Zechariah. I think he wanted me to pass the matzos.

Elizabeth was the mother of John the Baptist (though to be fair the whole family was a little on the evangelical side—filled with the Spirit, prophesying, and so on). Like Sarah (Gen 17:15-21) and Hannah (1 Sam 1:1-20) before her, Elizabeth was unable to have children and was getting on in years. And like Sarah and Hannah, she had prayed for a child, she wanted one more than anything. Out of the blue—or out of the temple actually—the angel Gabriel appeared to her husband Zechariah and said "Prayer answered brother-man. You and Elizabeth will have a son and you will name him John." Zechariah couldn't quite believe it, and so he was made mute until the boy was born. We don't know exactly how Elizabeth responded—the Gospel of Luke doesn't say—but we're guessing Zechariah's muteness tipped her off and, knowing the stories of Sarah and Hannah, she got busy converting the spare room into a nursery.

When she was six months pregnant, Elizabeth entertained her cuz' Mary, who was right at the beginning of her own pregnancy. The unborn baby in Elizabeth's womb started kicking it like the Rockettes at Radio City. Then the Holy Spirit whispered in her ear that Mary's baby was going to be even more special than her own (and just think, Peter usually gets the credit for being the first one to know what a big deal Jesus was going to be).

One woman who had wanted to have a child her whole life, the other who was totally surprised and, let's face it, was pregnant way earlier than she would have planned; both having children who were central (understatement) to God's plan of salvation. Quite a pair.

Key Verse: "When Elizabeth heard Mary's greeting, the child leaped in her womb. And Elizabeth was filled with the Holy Spirit . . ."
(Luke 1:41; see also Luke 1).

See also: John the Baptist, Luke (The Gospel according to), Zechariah (husband of Elizabeth).

Ephesians \ee-FEE-zhunz\

by Paul (New Testament, Letters, six chapters)

Ephesians has something for everybody. You got your epic, over-the-top, poetic hymn of praise for God's almighty work in Jesus Christ (chapters one and two). You got your "gospel in a nutshell" (Eph 2:8-10; worth memorizing). You got your "Christ the cornerstone" (Eph 2:19-22). You got your "one body . . . one Spirit . . . one hope . . . one Lord, one faith, one baptism, one God and Father of all" (Eph 4:4-6). You got your vision for "equipping the saints for the work of the ministry, for the building up of the body of Christ" (Eph 4:11-16). You got your wives and husbands submitting themselves to each other (Eph 5:21-23; read it carefully). And you got your "whole armor of God": belt, breastplate, shoes, shield, helmet, and sword. That is, you got one big, slicin'-'n'-dicin' sword of the Spirit, a.k.a. the word of God. That's what you got. So, again, Ephesians has something for everybody. That's why it was probably crafted for circulation among many congregations, rather than for one specific congregation. One more thing: You also got some language that's similar to the language in letters that were written by Paul, as well as some language that suggests another hand. But if Ephesians was apostolic enough for those early Christians, then it's apostolic enough for us!

See also: Paul (Saul of Tarsus).

Esau \EE-saw\

Status:
Esau used to be hungry, then he was hungry for revenge, now he is just hungering to forgive.

Profile

Vocation:	I'm a skillful hunter and a man of the field—one of the original field-and-stream types.
What's in a name?	Esau means "hairy," nice huh? At least they didn't call me "Curly" or "Shaggy" (I don't even have a dog).
Pet Peeve:	Red-headed, stepchild jokes. I was the firstborn, but the hair, you know?
Least Favorite Quotation:	"See to it that no one becomes like Esau, an immoral and godless person, who sold his birthright for a single meal" (Heb 12:16)—which is a little harsh in my opinion.

Poor Esau gets the short, wet, used, nasty end of the stick. He was the older brother, the one who by tradition was to inherit and carry on the line of his father Isaac. But he was tricked by his little brother not once (shame on Jacob) but twice (shame on Esau) and had what was rightfully his stolen from him. Esau gave up his *birthright* because he was hungry and just couldn't wait to get some stew in his belly (Gen 25:27-34—Esau came in from the field and Jacob was cooking up some red stew, which Esau wanted so bad and that's where he gets the nickname "Edom" which means "red"), and he lost his *blessing* because Jacob tricked their father who was old, blind, and trusting (Gen 27:1-45—Jacob dressed up in an Esau-like disguise and Isaac blessed him instead of Esau).

Esau was not, apparently, the brightest penny in the change purse (we went with penny instead of knife-in-the-drawer or bulb-on-the-tree because... any guesses? Think copper.). But he was clear on one thing—all of his problems started with his little brother. And so Esau did what any red-blooded man might: he decided to kill Jacob after Isaac died. As you can imagine Jacob ran away form home, and Esau didn't get his chance. Not then at least.

One of the things about Esau that tends to get overlooked is that when Jacob finally came back, he fully expected Esau to kill him. If you read Genesis 32 you get the sense that Jacob even thinks he's got it coming. But Esau, seeing his brother for the first time in years, doesn't kill him. Instead he welcomes him home graciously and forgives him, and refuses the bribes that Jacob offers saying, "I have enough... keep what you have for yourself." This from the guy with neither blessing nor birthright. Guess that Esau wasn't all immoral and godless. And maybe we even have something to learn from him.

Key Verse: "Esau said to his father, 'Have you only one blessing, father? Bless me, me also, father!' And Esau lifted up his voice and wept" (Gen 27:38; see also Gen 27, 34).

See also: Genesis, Isaac, Jacob, Rebekah.

Essenes \eh-SEENZ\

A famed group of pottery-making, Torah-observing, isolationist librarians.

The Essenes were a rather strict group of Torah-observing Jews, who were active around the time of Jesus. The Essenes are most famous today because their library—a little collection of documents that we like to call the Dead Sea Scrolls—was discovered by a shepherd boy in 1946. It seems that the Essenes had packed away their library in clay pots, sometime around the year 70 CE—perhaps just prior to being destroyed by an invading Roman army, bent on destruction. At any rate, most of what we know about the Essenes is gleaned either from reading the Dead Sea Scrolls or from what the ancient historian Josephus had to say about them. The Essenes have often been compared to later monks, living in isolated communities, shunning contact with the wider world (which they considered corrupt) and with other Jews (whom they considered spiritually soft).

Esther \EHS-tuhr\ (book)

by Anonymous (Old Testament, Historical Books, ten chapters)

The wise Mordecai sends a message to the beautiful queen Esther, urging her to dare to prevent genocide: "For if you keep silence at such a time as this, relief and deliverance will rise for the Jews from another quarter, but you and your father's family will perish. Who knows? Perhaps you have come to royal dignity for just such a time as this" (Esth 4:14). On this hinge, the plot of the book of Esther turns.

And a wonderful plot it is! A beauty pageant, a rags-to-riches story, political intrigues, an attempted genocide, the actions of a brave few, and a climactic religious celebration.

Some have argued that because the book of Esther does not mention God by name, it doesn't deserve a place in the Bible. (It is the only Old Testament book for which a copy has not been found among the Dead Sea Scrolls, perhaps signaling that some did not consider it Scripture.) But Mordecai has faith that "relief and deliverance will rise for the Jews," signaling the book's subtle witness that God's hands are often unseen and unfelt at the time, but are shaping history nevertheless. The book is also interesting because Mordecai and Esther seem uninterested in Jewish law, and Esther's marriage to a foreigner (forbidden in Ezra and Nehemiah) ironically paves the road by which God delivers the people—a subtle argument that when it comes to saving and delivering, the law does not and cannot tie God's hands.

See also: **Esther, Historical Books.**

Esther \EHS-tuhr\

Status:
Esther is not just another pretty face.

Profile

Vocation:	Beauty Pageant Winner; Queen; Savior of my people
What's in a Name?	My name isn't even Hebrew; it's Persian and means "star." It is closely related to "Ishtar," the Babylonian goddess of love and war (love *and* war, ironic no?).
Favorite God other than Yahweh:	Psych! Don't have one. I'm a committed *Yahwist*. But I bet you thought I was gonna say Ishtar.
Favorite Holiday:	Purim, the Jewish holiday held on the 14-15 of Adar (that's the March of the Jewish calendar, more or less) when we celebrate me saving us from them
Favorite Quotation:	"... 'tis the sport to have the engineer *Hoist with his own petard*; and 't shall go hard But I will delve one yard below their mines And blow them at the moon ..." *Hamlet*

Esther is an interesting character. She's an Israelite with a Persian name. She becomes the queen of Persia because she is beautiful, and saves the Israelites from a vicious plot because she is courageous and smart. She's really the perfect example of a good and faithful Jew living in a foreign land under a foreign power. You might call her a role model of faithfulness, a paradigm of believerhood-ed-ness. And not once does she mention God. Not once. Neither does the book that bears her name. You can read it for yourself and check, but trust us "God" is not mentioned in Esther. Which makes her story unique in the Old Testament.

Esther is caught in the middle of Persian politics and an ancient rivalry between the Israelites and the Amalekites. The historic animosity between the Israelites and the Amalekites becomes the tension in the story of Esther and her people.

Esther is no Cinderella. While she is an orphan who becomes a queen she doesn't have wicked stepsisters. And once she marries the king she doesn't live happily ever after, in fact that's when her troubles really begin. Haman, a powerful official in the court of king Ahasuerus and a descendant of the Amalekites—one of Israel's traditional foes—hated the Israelites and tried to get Mordecai (Esther's cousin and adoptive father) and all of the Jews in Persia hanged. *NOTE*: Haman was not a good dude.

Esther risks the wrath of the king (who had this silly rule that no one should approach him without being summoned, even when genocide is in the air) to stand up for her people. Her story ends with all the bloody flair of a Spaghetti Western. Down and almost out, Esther and Mordecai turn the tables on Haman and his whole crew. Haman, who had built an extremely large gallows (how extremely large you ask? fifty cubits tall that's how) to hang Mordecai, is himself hanged. Talk about getting hoisted on your own petard! All of the "Amalekites" (Haman's sons and everyone else who had plotted against the Jews) are killed. And Esther, Mordecai and the Jews in Persia finally live happily ever after.

One of the subtleties of Esther's story is that she keeps her religious and ethnic identity a secret, even from the king. This maybe explains why God isn't mentioned in her story. When you read Esther you have to look for God with optimistic eyes. Kind of like in your real life. You have to trust that God is working behind the scenes and more importantly through the faithfulness of those who believe and trust that God is there. Kind of like Esther.

Key Verse: "If I have won your favor, O king, and if it pleases the king, let my life be given me—that is my petition—and the lives of my people—that is my request" (Esth 7:3).

See also: Esther (book), Haman.

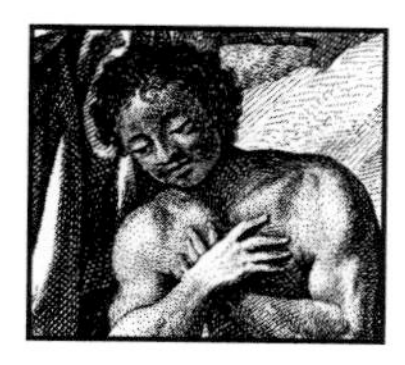

Ethiopian Eunuch, The

\thee-EE-thee-oh-pee-uhn-YOO-nuhk\

Status:
EE has an urgent report for Queen Candace.

Profile

Vocation:	Personal Financial Assistant to Candace, queen of Ethiopia
What's in a Name?	Nobody seems to bother with my name, only my condition.
Alias (or Nickname):	Double-E; Crazy Eights
Fun Fact:	2 out of 3 biblical eunuchs are Ethiopian (Jer 38:7; 2 Kgs 23:11; Acts 8:26-39).
Favorite Book:	Isaiah—I find his poetry very moving

When you read Acts 8:26-30 you might come away with two questions:

1. What is an Ethiopian?

2. What is a eunuch?

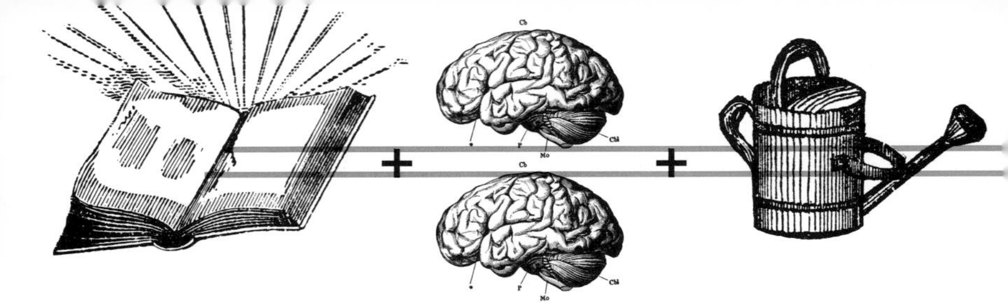

An Ethiopian is somebody who comes from (drum roll) Ethiopia, an African kingdom just south of Egypt (in Biblical times). The whole "eunuch" thing can be difficult for us to understand today. A eunuch is a man who has been . . . um. Well, a eunuch is a guy who has had his . . . ah. That is, a eunuch has had a procedure to remove the. . . . Wow, is this making you as uncomfortable as it is us? Let's just say that a eunuch is a man who is no longer functional in the procreative sense. For this reason eunuchs were often employed among other things as guards for harems, or to work closely with important women (such as Candace) without putting them in a socially awkward situation. Eunuchs also saved a lot of money because they didn't need shaving blades.

Double-E was traveling back to Ethiopia from Jerusalem. He had taken along a little light reading for the chariot ride home—the Prophet Isaiah. Now Crazy Eights was a curious fella. He read Isaiah and was wondering what it meant exactly. One passage in particular caught his eye—Isa 53:7-8 (feel free to take minute to look that up; we'll wait). At just the right time along comes Philip the Evangelist, ready to provide answers. In conversation with Philip, EE asks questions that lead him into a relationship with God, questions like:

How can I understand this Isaiah chap without someone to help me?
[Philip: "Allow me to help."]

Who is this sheep who is led to slaughter, and what is he to me?
[Philip: "That would be Jesus."]

Why should I worry about complicated theological issues such as when to get baptized or who's ready to get baptized or who can do the baptizing; there's some water right there why not get my baptism on?
[Philip: "Good idea—let's get wet."]

And so it was that the Ethiopian Eunuch was converted to faith in Christ—through water and the word and the ministry of Philip. He was curious, humble, and open to God's word—the perfect storm for his rebirth into new life in Jesus.

One last note. There were some who thought less of eunuchs because of their condition. At some points even the Bible seems to exclude them from the community of God's people (cf. Deut 23:1). But what we find here is that God's word is for everyone—the outsider, the imperfect, the broken, the needy. In other words, for us.

Key Verse: "As they were going along the road, they came to some water; and the eunuch said, 'Look, here is water! What is to prevent me from being baptized?' He commanded the chariot to stop, and both of them, Philip and the eunuch, went down into the water, and Philip baptized him" (Acts 8:36-38).

Bonus Key Verse: "For thus says the Lord: To the eunuchs who keep my sabbaths, who choose the things that please me and hold fast my covenant, I will give, in my house and within my walls, a monument and a name better than sons and daughters; I will give them an everlasting name that shall not be cut off" (Isa 56:4-5).

See also: Acts of the Apostles, Philip.

Eve \eev\

Status:
Eve thought that fruit was supposed to be good for you.

Profile

E

Vocation:	Help Mate, the Mother of Life
What's in a Name?	"Eve" is a play on words with "life" in Hebrew; *chavah*=Eve, *chay*=life
Did you know?	The name "Eve" occurs only four times in the whole Bible.
Interests:	Cross stitch with fig leaves; forbidden fruits
Pet Peeves:	Pain in child bearing; men who can't keep their mouths shut when our story will work just fine if we stick to it
Favorite Quotation:	"God created man at the end of the week, when he was tired." —Yiddish proverb

It was all a set-up. Had to be. *You can have the run of the Garden, God says to Eve (and Adam), except for the one tree.* Those poor first people didn't stand a chance. Of course they were going to try it eventually, how could they not? All they needed was the right set of circumstances and a little push in the right direction. Doubt us? Then try an experiment some time. Buy a variety pack of donuts (we'd suggest the standards—powdered, chocolate, and those brown ones that are coated in something that looks like coconut barf). Put the donuts on the counter and tell your kids, "You can have any one you want, just not the chocolates; those are for me." Then sit back and let the temptation build. Later, you'll probably find one of those tasty brown ones with a bite missing. You can then cast the offender out of Eden and eat the rest of the donuts yourself. (This would also work with little brothers or sisters and your toys—you can play with anything except . . . —or with a selection of craft beers and your roommate—you can drink any one except . . . —you get the idea. Sin will win out.)

Just one tree that she shouldn't touch.... After awhile even all the fruits of Paradise must have seemed waxy and bruised next to the ripe produce of the tree of the knowledge of good and evil.

All it took was for the right opportunity, the proper motivation to suggest to Eve that she could give it a try, just this once. Enter the serpent, slithering stage left, telling Eve that she and Adam would be like God if they ate that fruit. Be like God? Ooo, a chocolate donut *filled with pastry creams!*

Most of Eve's story is downhill from there. She and Adam eat. She makes the first line of eco-friendly clothing. She feels guilty. And then Adam runs his mouth and throws her under the bus. If things had been different she might've left him then, but it was a different era and there weren't any better men to choose from (literally). After she and Adam got kicked out of Eden they got down to living their lives. They made a home together, worked through life's joys and heartaches, had a family. Legend tells us that Eve was the first person to prepare snake. Slow-roasted, with an apple in its mouth, and just a hint of rosemary. Yummy.

Eve really is the Mother of all Sinners—she blew it big time, just as all the living do. Eve's story is about mistakes and consequences. We all make them, just as Eve did. And we will all face the consequences for our sin. But like Eve we can take heart in the fact that though we may disappoint God with our disobedience, still, God loves us and cares for us.

Key Verse: "The man named his wife Eve, because she was the mother of all living" (Gen 3:20; see also Gen 2–3).

See also: Adam, Genesis.

Exile \EHK-sil\ or \EHG-zil\

The forty-year (more or less) timeout that God gave the people as a reward for sacrificing children to other gods, oppressing the poor, and so on.

It works for our kids. They hurt each other. They get a timeout. They say, "Sorry." We say, "Love you." And things move forward. That is what the Exile was. In the year 587, after a nice, long, 500-year history of God's children consistently being unfaithful to God, God put them in timeout in Babylon.

What did the children of God do there? According to Psalm 137, they sat, they wept, they didn't sing. Sort of like our kids when they are in timeout.

And again, like our kids in timeout, the timeout doesn't change human nature. So when we say "it works," we only mean that it changes behavior in a small way in the short term—it doesn't permanently change behavior because it can't change human nature.

God said to the people, "You'll always be my children. When you were little, I held you to my cheek. I taught you to walk and carried you when you couldn't walk anymore. I will always love you. We can't go on like this, with you rebelling and me putting you in timeout. We'll find a different way to have a relationship" (see HOSEA). The timeout in Babylon (a.k.a. "Babylonian Captivity") lasted about fifty years, after which many of the people returned to Jerusalem and the surrounding region.

See also: Babylon.

Exodus \EHK-suh-duhs\ or \EHG-zuh-duhs\ (book)

by Anonymous (Old Testament, Pentateuch, forty chapters)

How many stories follow this pattern?

1. People (or person) are enjoying prosperity.
2. A jealous or greedy enemy takes what is theirs.
3. People are oppressed or even enslaved.
4. A hero comes to save them.
5. Enemy is defeated.
6. People are led out of oppression into a future bright with milk and honey (to mix metaphors).

Exodus is no exception. Like a Hollywood hit-writer going back to the well for a clichéd ending to a predictable story, this is exactly what happens in Exodus. At least that is how one might read this story of Israel's origins if Exodus hadn't been written long before this pattern became rote storytelling. In fact it is the author of Exodus who set this pattern, a pattern that can be seen in later biblical writing (not to mention Hollywood screenplays).

Exodus is a plucky David-and-Goliath story with storms, insect plagues, confrontations between national leaders, and a visitation by the angel of death that would inspire even the most jaded Hollywood special-effects technician. The book is made up of two major sections. The first, chapters 1–15, is about Israel's liberation from Egypt. The second, chapters 16–40, deals with Israel's struggle to come to grips with a freedom lived in relationship with God, which struggle is skillfully told in the story of Israel's making an idol and worshipping it instead of the living God.

On the surface Exodus reads like a prizefight between two contestants, Moses (wearing the blue trunks and fighting for Yahweh) and Pharaoh (wearing the lapis lazuli trunks and representing Egypt). At stake in this struggle is not some title-belt but the freedom of the Hebrew people. Small-time underdog Moses delivers a series of body blows to Pharaoh, through ten plagues (or supernatural signs) which left the Egyptian people demoralized and all but beaten. The final knockout punch comes when the entire army of Egypt, pursuing the Israelites into a path made through the sea with water piled up on either side, sees the seas come rushing down upon them and is drowned. Knockout for Moses and the Israelites.

Mr. Anonymous sets the tension for this contest dramatically by having Moses, who would one day be the prophet and savior of Israel, raised as brother to Pharaoh. But this human contest is not the heart of Mr. Anonymous' work. (Frankly, we think that the old movie *The Ten Commandments* gets it wrong by making Moses the center of the story.) The recurring theme of Exodus is its theological claim: that Yahweh is God and no-one/no-thing else is. This point is driven home in many and various ways: in the central event which gives the book its name, in the great poem that celebrates that event (chapter 15), in the covenant that is established between God and God's people on Mt. Sinai, the giving of the Ten Commandments, and even in the incident of the Golden Calf. At each point it is "the LORD (read: Yahweh) as God" that is central to the story.

See also: Pentateuch.

Exodus and Wilderness Period

\EHK-suh-duhs-and-WIHL-duhr-nuhs-PEER-ee-uhd\

The saving event the Israelites groaned for—and once it happened, that they immediately started groaning about. And after it was done, that they looked back fondly upon.

Ever been camping? Ever been full-on wilderness camping? We're talking serious, hard-core, no boat, no plane, no motor car and not a single luxury camping? Like Les Stroud in *Survivorman?* Then maybe you can understand just how long those forty years felt. You too might have been pining for the leeks and onions and garlic of Egypt. Never mind those pesky chains.

The Exodus was not just an event, it was an era—lasting much longer than anyone, maybe even God, had planned. The Exodus and Wilderness time was a full generation's worth of roughing it. Scholars differ about exactly when it happened... because that is what scholars do. We know because we know from scholars. Some date the Exodus to roughly the fifteenth century BCE, while others put it sometime around the year 1280 BCE.* It may be hard to pin point exactly when the Exodus time frame fits into history's larger picture, but one thing is certain, this was a hugely important time for Israel, a time when their relationship with God was tested, and when the nation was transformed by God's saving action.

More importantly, the Exodus offers the essential clue about who God is. In the Old Testament, when you ask the question, "Who is God?" the answer is, "God is the One who brought Israel out of slavery in Egypt." God is a Lord who frees, who delivers people out of bondage.

Immediately following the Exodus, God entered into the covenant relationship with the people at Mt. Sinai. Then spent forty years in the Wilderness with the people, basically teaching them how to be a free people. Although these years of roughing it were, well, rough, the people later looked back fondly on them. The way many married couples look back on those first days of marriage when they had no money, living in a studio apartment, ate low on the food chain, but somehow seemed happier.

See also: Egyptians, Exodus (book), Israelites, Moses.

*Here is a nerdy footnote for those of you who dig such things. There is this little known monument, found in Egypt, called the Merneptah Stele; it's a big rock on which one of the Pharaohs of Egypt (Merneptah) mentions a victory he won over the Israel, which is "laid waist" (apparently for pharaohs, graffiti and trash talking were expected—see the article on Pharaoh). The monument dates to the thirteenth century BCE, which doesn't tell us exactly when the exodus took place, but it might give us a ballpark time before which it had to have happened.

Ezekiel \eh-ZEE-kee-uhl\ or \EE-ZEE-kee-uhl\ (book)

by Ezekiel Ben-Buzi (Old Testament, Prophets, forty-eight chapters)

Perhaps you have had this experience after reading a book: You turn the last page and wonder, "Now what is it, exactly, that I just read?" Many a reader has had that experience after reading all, or even part of, Ezekiel Ben-Buzi's perplexing book with its significant veins of mysticism. As the seventeenth-century Jewish commentator Rabbi Shabbatai HaKohen warned about studying mysticism, "there are those who say that one should wait until the age of forty . . . for it says in the Mishnah . . . 'forty is the age of wisdom.'"

Mr. Ben-Buzi's book consists of messages from and stories about his prophetic ministry, which lasted from 593–571 BCE, from just before the fall of Jerusalem to about halfway through the Babylonian exile. The book describes his strange visions (see 1:1—3:15; 37:1-14), the unfathomable symbolic actions he enacted (see 4:1-3), allegories (see chapters 15–17), and other forms.

As for the theological message of the book, it is risky for a reviewer to oversimplify. But how else can one say anything coherent about such a complex book? Basically, the messages that the Lord sent to Mr. Ben-Buzi prior to the fall of Jerusalem in 587 were words of judgment and warning. After the fall of Jerusalem, most of the messages were promises of hope and restoration. From this, we can deduce that nobody is immune from judgment. But that God is faithful through judgment and on the other side of judgment. Many people assume that God's faithfulness means that we will escape judgment or be rendered immune to judgment. On the contrary, *Ezekiel* seems to say that God's judgment is one movement on the way to faithfulness.

See also: Ezekiel.

Ezekiel

\eh-ZEE-kee-uhl\ or \EE-ZEE-kee-uhl\

Status:

Ezekiel's foot bone is connected to his ankle bone, his ankle bone is connected to his shin bone . . .

Profile

Vocation:	Living Children's Sermon
What's in a Name?	My name means "God Strengthens," but it feels more like "God Uses To Make a Point" or "God Calls A-Not-So-Stuffy Prophet."
Interests:	Baking (Ezek 4:9); a good game of pick-up sticks
Favorite Celebrity:	Herman Munster; he sang my song in season 2, episode 12, "Will Success Spoil Herman Munster?" Classic.
Favorite Song:	"Dry Bones"—I get misty just thinking about it.
Favorite Book:	*Crazy Talk: A Not-So-Stuffy Dictionary of Theological Terms*

The most famous part of Ezekiel's story is, of course, the valley of the dry bones. The story became a traditional spiritual, and has made appearances in countless movies and TV episodes. (If you don't know more than the song part you should really read the whole story —it's in Ezekiel 37.) But this is really only a small part of Ezekiel.

What sort of guy was Ezekiel? Well, if a teacher told him it was time to step up, he would take two strides toward the chalkboard. If a coach told him it was time to show some guts, he would lift his shirt.

Here are some examples of Ezekiel's performances:

1. He made a brick model of Jerusalem surrounded by little green soldiers and Tinker Toy catapults. Symbolic of the punishment of Jerusalem of course (Ezek 4:1-3).

2. He took a sword and used it to shave all the hair from his head. He divided the hair into three piles—burned one pile, chopped up another pile with his sword, and threw the other pile up into the air—symbolic of the announcement that some would be killed in the siege, some would be scattered in the Exile (5:1-4).

3. After the Valley of Dem Dry Bones rock fest he took two sticks. On one he wrote "For Judah" and on the other "For Joseph" (Judah was the southern Israelite kingdom and "Joseph" was a name for the Northern Kingdom). Ezekiel then holds the two sticks together in one hand. All of which symbolizes? The reunion of the kingdom of Israel which God is making happen (37:15-28).

And there is a lot more. He ate a scroll. Kept silent for months (nobody minded). And so on.

Notice what Ezekiel does: he delivers his message with a memorable and sometimes pointed (and sharp edged) illustration. We like to think of Ezekiel as a great teacher. We've all had them (at least we have and hope that you have), those teachers whose way about the classroom was just different—dynamic, interesting, fun and unforgettable. Ezekiel didn't just tell his people things. He didn't just lecture. Ezekiel made his messages interactive, he did them, performed them, and even was the message himself. In fact one of the most important parts of Ezekiel's life was a message for Israel. While he was living in exile his wife died. At the instruction of the Lord, he did not mourn her. He neglected all of the traditional stages of grief and just went about his business. As you can imagine, this caught the attention of his fellow exiles. When they asked him about it he told them what his behavior meant: the temple in Jerusalem would be destroyed and Israel shouldn't mourn a building. The point of this message? Israel had put its pride in the temple and its trappings instead of in right relationship with God (the prophets seem to say this a lot—cf. Amos 5:21-24; Hos 6:6; Mic 6:6-8), and so the "delight of their eyes" was taken away. They would need to find a new way of living.

Ezekiel gave his whole life as an example and as a metaphor for relationship with God. He himself is literally the prophetic message:

Key Verse: "Thus Ezekiel shall be a sign to you; you shall do just as he has done. When this comes, then you shall know that I am the LORD God" (Ezek 24:24; see also the book of Ezekiel).

See also: Ezekial (book), Monarchy.

Ezra–Nehemiah \EHZ-ruh-nee-uh-MI-uh\

by Anonymous (Old Testament, Historical Books, ten chapters)

When a good storyteller arrives at the climax of the story, it is often the case that some dunderheaded listener will ask, "And then what happened?" Well, imagine that you had just finished telling the long and dramatic story that we like to call "First and Second Chronicles." That story ends with the Persian King Cyrus announcing to the Lord's people exiled in Babylon, "Whoever is among you of all his people, may the Lord his God be with him! Let him go up [to Jerusalem]" (2 Chr 36:23). And then imagine that some pumpkinseed said, "And then what happened?"

The answer would be, "The Books of Ezra and Nehemiah." These books continue the story of God's people and tell what happened after the exile. The hand that penned Ezra and Nehemiah is different from the one(s) that wrote 1 and 2 Chronicles. Yet, the concerns and themes of these books are so similar that it seems that authors of all of them were at least similar—probably Levitical priests living in Jerusalem, who had a strong interest in God's promises to David.

But we still haven't answered your question, "And then what happened?" Here are the answers, not in any particular order:

- The people returned from exile.
- They restored worship in all of its rigor and majesty.
- They started to rebuild the Temple (because rigor and majesty require edifices).

- They quarreled with the squatters living in the land, who didn't want the Temple rebuilt.
- They rebuilt the walls of Jerusalem.
- They quarreled with the squatters living in the land, who didn't want the walls rebuilt.
- They quarreled amongst themselves about whether they could marry outside of the family (the final answer was No, but not all agreed with this).
- They opposed oppression, foiled evil plots, signed a covenant, and kept the Sabbath.

And then what happened? We knew you'd ask.
Answer: see the Apocrypha.

See also: Historical Books, Temple.

Flood, The \fluhd\

The great cosmic do-over.

Ever wished you could go back and start all over? Re-write a letter to a loved one or a paper for a class or a sermon for your congregation, that kind of thing? Ever get so frustrated with your kids or your spouse or your coworkers that you wish you could just go back to a time when things were simpler (read: those morons were not around)? All of us, we're betting, have been there. So was God once upon a time.

God took a look at the earth and all the earthlings—God's own beloved and "good" creation—and saw that "the wickedness of humankind was great in the earth, and that every inclination of the thoughts of their hearts was only evil continually" (Gen 6:5). So God picked a couple of the less continually evil folks (read: righteous), and opened the windows of the heavens and washed the whole world clean—forty days and forty nights of rain and a big, big flood. No more wicked sinners; the slate was washed clean; then God started it all over again.

That's the bad news (at least for the folks who were washed away, and maybe for anyone who might meet this God). The good news is that God promised never to do that kind of thing again. There might be times when we want to start over with new kids or friends or spouses. And of course once we do that kind of thing the more likely we are to do it again. And again. And again. But, to borrow from one of our favorite theologians, Lyle Lovett, "that's the difference between God and me." God promised: No more floods that destroy everybody (collective sigh of relief much?). And that, according to the Bible, is why we have the rainbow, to remind us, and even to remind God, of just who God is.

See also: Genesis, Noah.

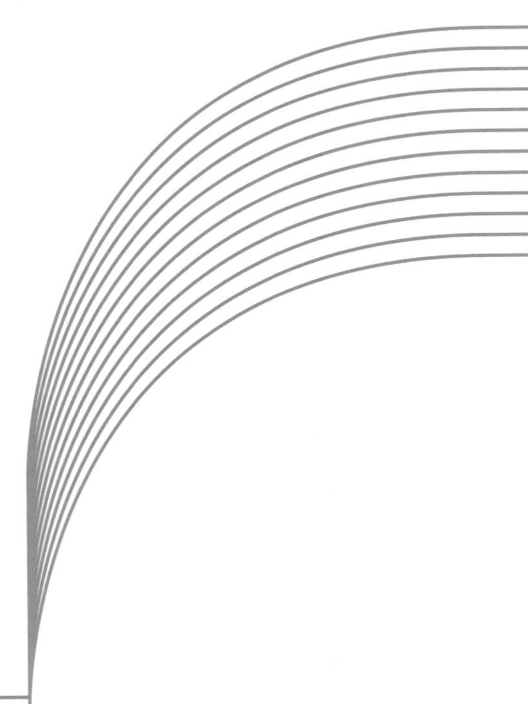

Gabriel \GĀ-bree-uhl\

Status:
Gabriel has never danced on the head of a pin.

Profile

Vocation:	Messenger
What's in a Name?	My name means "Mighty Warrior of God."
Favorite Celebrities:	Christopher Walken, Tilda Swinton, and Andy Whitfield; they all did a nice of job playing me in their movies—especially Tilda, she's money.
Fun Fact:	When I said hello to Mary I didn't say anything like "Hail," as if I was paying homage to her. Who's the angel here? What I said was *chaire*, a Greek word that means "hi," "howdy," "what up."
Favorite Quotation:	"You're handed this precious gift, right? Each one of you granted redemption from the Creator. . . . In all the worlds in all the universe no other creature can make such a boast, save man. It's not fair."—Tilda Swinton as Gabriel in *Constantine*

Although the angel Gabriel's name identifies him as a mighty warrior, a soldier in the hosts of the Most High, that's not how we meet him in the Bible. In both the Old Testament (Daniel 8) and the New Testament (Luke 1) Gabriel is a messenger. In point of fact this is primarily what an angel is, a messenger from God. In the Old Testament, Gabriel brings Daniel a message that helps him understand a dream. In the Gospel of Luke, Gabriel brings two messages. The first is to Zechariah. Gabriel tells him that he and his wife will bear a son, even though they're really old. 'Course, Zechariah didn't believe Gabriel (guess he hadn't read a little story we like to call Genesis 15–17), and was unable to utter a sound until, lo and behold, the wife gave birth to John the Baptist. The second message Gabriel delivers is to Mary, telling her that she will be the mother of Jesus. Mary did believe Gabriel, and the rest as they say is the greatest story ever told.

Key Verse: "I am Gabriel. I stand in the presence of God, and I have been sent to speak to you and to bring you this good news" (Luke 1:19).

See also: **Daniel (book), Luke (The Gospel according to).**

Galatians \guh-LĀ-shuhnz\

By Saul of Tarsus, a.k.a. the Apostle Paul
(New Testament, Letters, six chapters)

What has gotten into the Apostle Paul? Readers familiar with Paul's careful verbiage and measured tone will recognize that Galatians represents a departure for the man from Tarsus. Paul has a point to make and make it he does. One will find no buttery salutation here, no "I-thank-my-God-for-every-time-I-remember-you," as in Paul's letter to the Philippians. Instead, the start of Galatians is all business: "Paul, an Apostle." And then Paul gives them the business.

After spending two entire chapters (re-)establishing his authority and the faithfulness of his preaching, Paul lambastes the Christians in Galatia for turning to another gospel. Paul fires: "You foolish Galatians! Who has bewitched you?" Apparently, there were some folks stirring things up there in the Galatian congregations, teaching that the Gentile (that is, non-Jewish) males had to be circumcised in accordance with the Law of Moses. What's not clear is if the pro-circumcisers in Galatia were at all connected with the circumcision party mentioned in Acts 15:1-5. Party? It doesn't seem like a party to this Gentile reviewer. Anyway, in response to the pro-circumcisers,

Paul cuts to the chase: "If you let yourselves be circumcised, Christ will be of no benefit to you" (Gal 5:2).

Readers will appreciate Galatians' many catchy phrases that are sure to become classics—phrases such as, "I have been crucified with Christ; it is no longer I who live, but it is Christ who lives in me" (2:19-20), "There is no longer Jew or Greek, slave or free, male and female; for all of you are one in Christ Jesus" (Gal 3:28), and this reviewer's favorite, "For freedom Christ has set us free; stand firm, therefore, and do not submit again to a yoke of slavery" (Gal 5:1). (On the other hand, Paul's nine "fruits of the spirit"—"love, joy, peace, patience, kindness, generosity, faithfulness, gentleness, and self-control"—could be improved by the addition of one more fruit, if only to make the list an even ten. How about "humbleness"?)

In the end, the great accomplishment of Paul's Galatians is that it gives Christ his due by giving Moses his due and vice versa. For those who take Paul seriously, it would seem that being able to tell the difference between Moses and Christ, law and gospel, is a good thing.

See also: Paul (Saul of Tarsus).

Galilee \GAL-ih-lee\

A happy way of doing things... such as re-settling a region.

The name Galilee was derived from the Hebrew name meaning, "District of the Nations." Meaning it was where non-chosen-type-people lived. But around 150 BCE, the Judeans conquered the area and started re-settling it—which we are sure they did gay-i-ly. (There are way too few puns in this book, so we felt compelled to insert one here.) The region came to be the home of many Judeans, included a carpenter named Joseph, his wife Mary, and their son—good ol' what's-his-name (he has many names, see the article on Jesus). Galilee was in the northern part of the land, with Lake Galilee at its heart. Its major towns included Nazareth and Capernaum.

See also: Jesus.

Genealogy \jee-nee-AH-luh-jee\

A list detailing the depths of the family gene pool.

Wow, who ever knew that explaining who slept with whom could be this boring!? Don't believe us? Just try to read 1 Chronicles 1–9. We dare you. Just try.

But in truth, the genealogies in the Bible are about much more than the answer to the age-old question, "Who's your daddy?" The genealogies are actually a theological document. They bear witness to God's faithfulness in keeping the promises to Abraham and David (see Gen 12:1-3 and 2 Sam 7:1-17). For example, in Genesis, the last child named in each of genealogy is the child through whom the promise passes. Or, in Matthew 1, the four women mentioned in Jesus' genealogy show that God uses the least likely people to keep the promise of sending a Messiah descended from Abraham and Sarah. The many genealogical lists are just the Bible's way of letting you know that you are barking up the right family tree.

See also: 1 and 2 Chronicles, Matthew (The Gospel according to).

Genesis \JEHN-uh-sihs\

by Anonymous (Old Testament, Pentateuch, fifty chapters)

A brash and engaging history of the early world, Genesis begins, somewhat predictably, at the beginning. Most good stories do the same, starting with what is important for the reader to know in order to follow the story. What makes Genesis such a bold departure from the norm is that it starts with *The* Beginning, the story of the earth's first days and years.

There are some who claim that Mr. Anonymous did not write Genesis and that it was in fact the work of Moses. Yet there is no citation within the book itself to support these claims. The question of authorship is just not addressed in the text of the book of Genesis. Accusations of plagiarism put aside, and Mr. Anonymous' reputation thus made safe, we can turn to the flow of this remarkable story.

In the first major section of Genesis, chapters 1–11, which are often referred to as the "primeval history," Mr. Anonymous recounts the earliest days of the earth including: creation of night and day, water and land, animals, fishes, insects, and birds; and of course people, starting with Adam and Eve; all of which are dubbed "good" by its Creator. Were this the end of the story of the beginning, the reader would surely be left flat and uninspired. But into this idyllic setting Mr. Anonymous introduces the tension of the story—human flaw and failing, which the author frequently calls "sin." Throughout Genesis, and indeed throughout the rest of the writings in the Bible line, this tension, and its recurring pattern of sin-redemption-sin-redemption, is among the most important themes. The primeval history reaches high tide in the Great Flood, which is God's attempt to deal with human failing. In a plot twist sure to shock and offend the modern sensibility, God floods the earth, drowning every living thing—except for one Noah and his family (and their collected menagerie). From this new beginning, God then re-news the creation, starting almost from scratch.

The second major section of Genesis, chapters 12–50, involves the telling of the stories of a particular family—and we're not talking about the Cleaver family. These chapters, which tell the stories of Abraham and Sarah, Isaac, Jacob, Joseph and his brothers among others, read like a collection of family memoirs. But the outsider should not be put off by this very personal material. In these stories Mr. Anonymous seeks to show the love of God for this creation and for its people—people like Abraham and Sarah who are so much like us. Again the problem of human sin comes to the foreground in each of these stories. In fact this theme is revisited so often that one is almost overwhelmed by the flaws and foolishness of Mr. Anonymous' characters. But the reader is not left to labor in this tension unsatisfied. Nor does one turn each page expecting another Noah and another flood. To counter the problem of the human condition reflected in his story Mr. Anonymous turns to the counter-theme of God's grace. Over and over again God meets the problem of human failing with compassion. The promises of homeland, of family, of relationship with their God is issued and uttered anew to each character, to each generation. Each time one of Genesis' heroes (who are in many cases anti-heroes) stumbles into the consequences of sin or doubt, God comes once more to renew the promise of grace and life and hope.

In Genesis, Mr. Anonymous tells the story of creation, of humankind, and of individual people, but above all the story of a God who is intimately involved with and passionately caring for this world and its people. For anyone seeking to make sense of life, the universe, and everything, there may be no better place to begin.

See also: Adam, Ancestral Period, Eve.

Gideon \GIHD-ee-uhn\

Status:
Gideon is coming to a hotel near you.

Profile

Vocation:	Judge, Inspirer of Para-church Organizations
If I was in a Christian Rock band, its name would be . . .	The Winepress Fugitives (see Judg 6:11)
Favorite Movie:	*300*; I can't help but feel that my story is their story, only with a happier ending.
Favorite Quotation:	This German proverb: "Dumb dogs and still water are dangerous." And so are warriors who drink from still waters like dogs! (Judg 7:5-7)

Have you heard the saying, "Even a broken clock is right twice a day"? The problem is that makes it wrong 1438 minutes a day (1498 minutes on the first day of daylight savings). And that's God's people—doing evil in the sight of the Lord roughly 1438 minutes a day.

We meet Gideon when Israel has gotten itself in trouble again. Once again Israel had turned away from God and was paying the price. The Midianites were given victory over Israel and kept destroying Israel's crops and making life all around unpleasant. So the Israelites called out to God to send them a savior—a judge who would lead them to victory over Midian. Enter Gideon. And where do we meet God's judge, God's champion, the chosen savior of the people? Hiding from the Midianites, doing his chores in a winepress.

Gideon is a study in contrasts. On the one hand he probably seems about the least likely type of person to be a hero. A boy trapped in a well *gets rescued*, he doesn't rescue others. Add to that the way God instructs him to wage his war against the Midianites. He's supposed to whittle his army of 32,000 down to 300. And who does he keep as the elite core of his fighting force? A bunch of yokels who drink water like dogs, lapping it up on all fours. Nice. It all probably seemed more like Gideon's foolishness than God's plan. His beginnings and his strategies are hardly the stuff that inspires shock or awe. On the other hand Gideon is trusting and faithful. When the Lord tells him to tear down an altar to Baal (one of the gods the Midianites worshipped) he didn't worry about the consequences, he just yoked up the oxen and tore it down. And adding theological insult to injury in its place he built an altar to Yahweh.

Gideon wasn't much to look at. But he was God's "not much." And in the end his story is really about what God does. It is God who delivers Israel. It is God who uses Gideon—and all the judges for that matter—to get the job done. What makes Gideon stand out is his trust. Gideon trusts in the God who has called him to be of service from unlikely places and in unlikely ways. Ways that work. God's ways.

Key Verse: "Gideon said, 'But sir, how can I deliver Israel? My clan is the weakest in Manasseh, and I am the least in my family.' The LORD said to him, 'But I will be with you, and you shall strike down the Midianites, every one of them'" (Judg 6:15-16; see also Judg 6–8).

See also: Judges.

Goliath \guhl-ɪ-uhth\

Status:
Goliath is trying to get his head on straight.

Profile

Vocation:	Warrior
Home:	I'm from Philistia. That makes me a Philistine, but don't think that means I'm uneducated or unrefined.
Interests:	Me. I am huge—I go a good six cubits, plus a span. For fun, I like to taunt Israelites and polish my bronze armor.
Turn-offs:	Small, smooth stones (don't trust them) and the number five (it's my unlucky number)
Favorite Quotation:	"I am the greatest!"—Muhammad Ali

Here is the deal about Goliath. He was a big, strong foreign warrior who fought against God's people Israel. But neither his size nor the fact that he was a foreign warrior were his real problem (read: his *real sin*). In fact, there were more than a few powerful warriors who fought against Israel who were actually servants of God—for example, Naaman or Cyrus (or even Sennacherib or Nebuchadnezzar, for that matter). No, Goliath's real offense against God was that he thought that he was bigger, better, and stronger than God. His problem was that his religion was himself. He believed in Goliath. He believed in Goliath with such a fierce passion, in fact, that he thought he could challenge God's people.

And who could blame him? For a long time, he got away with it. He was the big dog in the Philistine army. And for forty days in a row, he stood in front of the Israelite army and challenged someone—anyone—to take him on, one-on-one. Nobody dared. Until one day, a young guy named David came out with nothing more than a slingshot, five smooth stones, and his faith in the Lord. And of these, only the faith in the Lord really mattered. As David said,

"You come to me with sword and spear and javelin; but I come to you in the name of the Lord of hosts, the God of the armies of Israel, whom you have defied" (1 Sam 17:45).

So when we talk about a David vs. Goliath battle, it isn't about a little guy with courage taking on a big guy. It's about someone with no meaningful resource, except one—faith in the Lord—being forced to take on someone with every meaningful resource, except one—faith in the Lord.

Key Verse: "The LORD does not save by sword and spear; for the battle is the LORD's" (1 Sam 17:47; see also 1 Sam 17).

See also: David, Philistines, 1 and 2 Samuel.

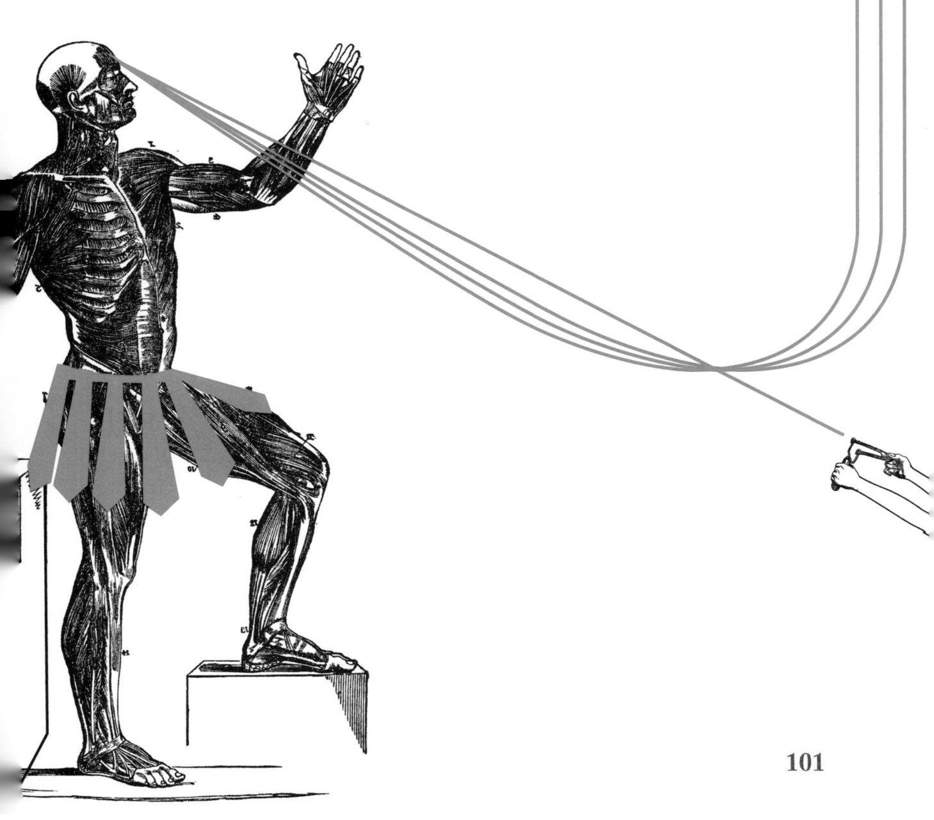

Gomer \GOH-muhr\

Status:
Gomer is ?

Profile

Hometown:

Vocation:

Likes:

Dislikes:

Favorite Quotation:

Favorite Song:

Warning: This article will not attempt to be funny or even slightly light-hearted. While the style of this book lives somewhere between light-hearted humor and sarcastic irreverence, there are some things one just doesn't joke about. And Gomer is one of them. Because the historical Gomer was probably used and abused by many men. And her use and abuse did not stop when she died. Interpreters of the Bible have continued to abuse her, and at times some even suggest that her story supports the heinous idea that men have the right to abuse women. Which is evil.

You have probably noticed that the profile above is blank. That is because we don't know Gomer's story. The Book of Hosea tells *Hosea's story*, but it doesn't tell *Gomer's*. Who was she? Was she happy? Did she love her kids or her husband? What did she think about God's command to Hosea? What did she think about God? Was she a good woman? Was she an abused woman? There are too many blanks in her story.

When people of faith have tried to "fill in the blanks" about Gomer's life, they have usually been utterly sexist about how they have done it. Gomer is called "a wife of harlotry." But what does that mean?

Some have maintained that she was a promiscuous woman. Some that she was a common prostitute. Others that she was a cultic prostitute (meaning one who engages in sex as a part of worship—but we do not even know if cultic prostitutes existed in ancient Israel). But no matter which of these options people have taken, they have too often assumed that it is okay for men to punish, divorce, and even to abuse women "like Gomer." And that is wrong.

Nobody gets to abuse anybody in God's name.

Key Verse: "'Go, take for yourself a wife of whoredom and have children of whoredom, for the land commits great whoredom by forsaking the Lord'" (Hos 1:2; see also Hos 1–3).

See also: Hosea.

Gospel \GAH-spuhl\

A narrative testimony that makes the grand claim that through Jesus' life, death, and resurrection, Jesus is Lord of all.

Writing to the Galatians, Paul advised, "if anyone proclaims to you a gospel contrary to what you received, let that one be accursed!" (Gal 1:9). A different gospel? The Bible has *four* Gospels!! Which one did Paul mean?

The answer: None of them and all of them (duh).

"None of them"— Paul wrote his letter to the Galatians before any of the four Gospels were written or circulating. In the New Testament, the term "gospel" never refers to a genre or a book but only to the "good news" or "good message" that Jesus is Lord. ("Gospel" is an old-timey English word that means "good news.") So when Paul talked about "a different gospel," he didn't mean a different book but a different message.

"All of them"—The Bible contains four Gospels. Although these Gospels are different from each other in some ways, they are also the same in that they bear witness to the life, death, and resurrection of Jesus, the Lord. Together, these four Gospels tell us who Jesus is.

These four Gospels were compiled and written during the first century CE. In the second century CE, some additional "gospels" began circulating, but the consensus was that these documents were not authentic (read: apostolic) and so were ultimately not included in the New Testament. (Sorry, Dan Brown, no conspiracy here.)

As a literary genre, a Gospel is not a biography or a history by modern standards, although there is certainly biographical and historical material in the Gospels. You might ask: How did this type of literature get called "Gospel" in the first place, instead of something like "Christstory" or "Theologic-History"? Maybe the answer is as simple as the beginning of Mark's gospel, which begins with the words, "The beginning of the good news [*gospel*] of Jesus Christ . . ." Put simply, Jesus is what a gospel is all about.

See also: Creation, Jesus.

Gospels, The \GAH-spuhlz\

The story of the life of Jesus, only begotten Son of the living God and the Savior of all humankind and, what's more, of the whole creation, which we naturally try to make all about ourselves.

The Gospels tell the story of Jesus. Lots of different people have parts to play in the Gospels—disciples, mothers, enemies, lepers, priests, governors, kings, emperors, and even Satan—and of course the Gospels are written for people like you and me. But the Gospels are Jesus' story.

It is important to distinguish between Gospel big G and gospel small g. The word *gospel* comes from the Greek *euangelion*, which means "good news." When we talk about good news in general we use the small g, and when we are talking about the story of Jesus—that is, the books that tell Jesus' story—we use the big G.

In the Bible there are four books that bear the name Gospel: Matthew, Mark, Luke, and John. While we know about a lot of other "gospels" that were written back in the day—like the gospels of Judas or Mary or Peter—these were not accepted by the vast majority of the early churches as authoritative or important in the same way as the four biblical Gospels (despite anything you may have heard or read).

As we said, lots of things can *be* gospel—the preaching, teaching and sharing of Jesus that any of us does, that's gospel. The care you show the poor or your next door neighbor or your parents in spite of what you think they might really deserve from you, that's gospel. That you finally get off your duff and mow the lawn or do the dishes, that's gospel. OK, maybe that's just what you should be doing, but you get the point.

But *the* Gospel, told in slightly different ways in each of the four books we call Gospels, is this:

For God so loved the world that he gave his only Son, so that everyone who believes in him may not perish but may have eternal life. Indeed, God did not send the Son into the world to condemn the world, but in order that the world might be saved through him (John 3:16-17).

Sound familiar? We hope so.

See also: Matthew (The Gospel according to), Mark (The Gospel according to), Luke (The Gospel according to), John (The Gospel according to).

Habakkuk \huh-BAK-uhk\ or \HAB-uh-kuhk\

by Habakkuk (Old Testament, Prophets, three chapters)

Mr. Habakkuk is to be congratulated on this insightful, important, and above all creative little book. Mr. Habakkuk's argument, that God is indeed just and that God works both through the nations and the situations that plague Israel and also works to visit vengeance and justice upon those same nations, is presented in an engaging style. Habakkuk is an autobiographical dialogue between the prophet/author and the Almighty.

Mr. Habakkuk presents his case to God as a prayer of lament, asking why the chosen people suffer and arguing both the injustice and inconsistency of it. God responds, "Okay, I'll send the Babylonian army to punish the people for their sins." "Whoa," says Mr. Habakkuk, "bringing in an enemy who is pretty sinful in its own right is strange."

But God does not simply answer Mr. Habakkuk's questions. God takes it a step further and commands the prophet to become the utterer of that answer. Mr. Habakkuk both hears and is told to go tell; he is both answered and the answerer. "Write my answer big. Really big." God says. "Write my response so big, so absolutely huge, that even someone who is out for a jog could read it as they pass by." And that answer, that large-print message which summarizes God's word and Mr. Habakkuk's book, is this:

"The righteous live by their faith" (Hab 2:4).

What does this mean in Habakkuk? It means that even though you can't see what God is doing, the righteous will trust that God is in it, God is active, and that God will win out. Mr. Habakkuk even says that this means we can thank God when the orchards produce no fruit, when the barns hold no grain, and the pastures have no flocks. Now there is a trusting faith indeed!

See also: Prophets.

Hagar \HĀ-gahr\

Status:
Hagar is looking for a new employer—one that offers child care.

Profile

Homeland:	Egypt
Turn-offs:	Jealous, manipulative, insecure bosses and wimpy, cowardly husbands of manipulative, insecure bosses
Favorite Quotation:	"You're not the boss of me!"
Did you know that . . .	. . . I have absolutely nothing to do with the "Hagar" comic strip?
Thing I would most like to change about me:	My look-that-could-kill glare. Don't get me wrong, I'm proud of it, but it can be counter-productive at times.

If you want to know about Hagar, you've got to do two things. First, you've got to start with Abraham and Sarah. Second, you've got to wrap your mind around the whole concept of God's promises. Especially you've got to cozy up to the truth that God keeps promises, but not always in the ways we think we want or according to our timetables.

God had promised Abraham that his descendants would become a great nation and that this nation would be blessed in order to be a blessing to the other nations of the earth (see Gen 12:1-3). But Abraham and his wife Sarah grew old, and they had no children. Frustrated with God's timing, Sarah decided that she would help God keep the divine promise. She sent her husband Abraham to her Egyptian slave-girl Hagar with orders to get her pregnant so that Sarah could "obtain children by her" (Gen 16:2). Abraham did. And Hagar did. And the baby boy was named Ishmael.

But here is the deal. The Bible doesn't say whether Hagar wanted to have Abraham's baby. Since she was a slave, she probably didn't have a vote. But you do the math: Abraham was like eighty-five years old. Get the picture?

After Ishmael was born, one day Hagar fixed her best, most contemptuous glare on Sarah. It felt good at the time. A way to get back at Sarah for making her have the baby. But it wasn't the most "strategical" move. Sarah saw the look and proceeded to make Hagar miserable.

Fast-forward a little less than fifteen years. God kept the promise that Sarah would have a child: Isaac was born. And then Sarah, in what we can only say was not her best moment, made Abraham send Hagar and Ishmael away. The mother and child wandered into the desert, where they ran out of water and lay down under a bush to die. And then God did one of those amazing God-things. God kept the promise to be faithful to Abraham's descendants—even the descendant that came into being thanks to Sarah's maneuverings. God rescued Hagar and Ishmael and made Ishmael the father of a great nation.

Key Verse: "As for the son of the slave woman, I will make a nation of him also, because he is your offspring" (Gen 21:13; see also Gen 16–21).

See also: Abraham, Ishmael, Sarah.

Haggai \HAG-i\

by Haggai (Old Testament, Minor Prophets, two chapters)

Similar to later public figures such as Madonna, Wynona, and Prince, the prophet whose ministry is recounted in this book went by only the one name: Haggai. And similar to earlier prophets such as Amos and Isaiah—who named their children funny names in order to make a prophetic point—Haggai probably gave himself a funny name in order to make his prophetic point. That's because the very name Haggai, which means "My Festivals," is a summary of the prophet's message.

Mr. My-Festivals' ministry can be located precisely during the second half of the year 520 BCE, shortly after the exiled Judeans had begun to return to the promised land. When they returned, they started to rebuild the Temple, but then someone yelled, "Oh my goodness, I forgot to rake the lawn." So everyone went to rake the lawn, and the work on rebuilding the Temple was forgotten.

So along came Mr. My-Festivals, who said, "How can we claim to be God's people if we don't worship God on the big festival days of the year (Passover, Pentecost, and Booths—in case you didn't know)? And how can we worship if we don't have a temple? And how can God bless us if we don't worship?" So, they hired a professional fund-raising consultant, had an appeal, did an every-member visit, and low-and-behold, work on the Temple started up again.

See also: Prophets, Temple.

Haman \HĀ-muhn\

Status:
Haman will be celebrating Purim this year.

Profile

Hometown:	Susa (capital of the Persian Empire)
Vocation:	Prime Minister to King Ahasuerus (bless you!) of Persia
If there's One Thing I've Learned . . .	King Saul once spared my ancestor Agag and was rewarded for this act of mercy by being removed from the throne—I don't plan ever to make Saul's mistake of being merciful.
Favorite Quotation:	"There are only two things I can't stand in this world. People who are intolerant of other peoples' cultures. And the Judeans." —Me (with apologies to Nigel Powers, who said something similar about the Dutch in *Austin Powers in Goldmember*)

A wise soul once noted that one of the first things that dictators do when they come into power is shut down the theaters. Why? Because dictators cannot stand to be laughed at. Dictators are very serious people. They take oppressing people seriously. They take themselves seriously. And above all, they take any joking about themselves very, very, very seriously. For example, it was reported that Hitler was not pleased with *The Great Dictator*, Charlie Chaplin's satirical send-up of Naziism.

When the Jewish counselor Mordecai refused to bow in homage to Haman, Haman convinced the Persian king to order the extermination of all the Jews in the empire. He cast lots and determined that the extermination was to occur on the thirteenth day of the month of *Adar*.

13

But the Jewish Queen Esther intervened. And when the thirteenth of *Adar* rolled around, rather than destroy, Haman and his henchmen were themselves destroyed. And on the next day, the Jews celebrated their triumph over their enemies.

In fact, to this day, Jewish people still celebrate the feast of *Purim* (because *pur* was the ancient word for "lot") on the fourteenth of *Adar* every year. On *Purim*, the book of Esther is read, which tells of the story of Haman, Mordecai, and Esther. The festival is a joyful party, full of downright un-religious fun. At each of the fifty-four mentions of Haman's name, the faithful boo, hiss, stomp, rattle, guffaw, and make a joyful noise on their noisemakers. What a perfect way to remember the evil that Haman intended. After all, evil-doing dictators hate laughter.

Key Verse: "Haman plotted to do away with all of the Jews . . . throughout the kingdom of Ahasuerus" (Esth 3:6).

See also: Esther, Esther (book).

Hebrews \HEE-brooz\

By Anonymous (New Testament, Letters, thirteen chapters)

Hebrews is a theological treatise disguised as a letter. Like Paul in his letter to the Romans, Mr. Anonymous makes a carefully developed argument for the good news of Jesus Christ. Like Romans—perhaps even more so—the argument of Hebrews is based in the interpretation of the Old Testament (that is, the Hebrew scriptures) in light of God's new revelation in Jesus Christ. It's called "Hebrews," presumably, because you pretty much have to be familiar with all things Hebrew to appreciate its full meaning. The very first phrase—"Long ago, God spoke to *our* ancestors"—assumes that the reader will at least know who those ancestors are. But Hebrews is not a closed book, for insiders only, it is also written with the world in mind: it was originally written in Greek and all of its many Old Testament quotations are taken directly from the Greek version of the Hebrew Scriptures (called the *Septuagint*).

Hebrews wants to make one thing perfectly clear: Jesus is Lord. Okay, so that's not very original; many of the New Testament writings want to make that one thing perfectly clear. However, Hebrews is original in its sustained testimony that Christ is both the ultimate sacrifice *and* the ultimate high priest making the sacrifice. Hebrews lauds the heroes and priests of Israel's religion. Even a non-Hebrew, the obscure King Melchizedek of Salem, gets some unexpected props (chapter seven). But in the end, Christ—the Great High Priest—trumps them all.

Hebrews has a lot going for it, including some memorization-worthy passages: "Faith is the assurance of things hoped for, the conviction of things not seen" (Heb 11:1) and "Since we are surrounded by so great a cloud of witnesses... let us run with perseverance the race that is set before us looking to Jesus, the pioneer and perfecter of our faith" (Heb 12:1-2). Hebrews is a solid addition to your New Testament collection.

See also: Letters (or Epistles).

Herod Antipas

\HEH-ruhd-AN-tih-puhs\

Status:

Herod Antipas is keeping his head while all about him are losing theirs.

Profile

Vocation:	To the Romans, I'm a Tetrarch (not to be confused with the video game); to the Judeans, I am a king. It's good to be the king.
What's in a Name?	My family sort of likes the name Herod; my dad, Herod the Great, went George Foreman on the bit and named me and three of my brothers Herod.
Alias (or Nickname):	The Fox
Turn-offs:	Honey-eating, camel-hair wearing, desert-dwelling, God's-law-quoting, sinner-baptizing prophets
Fun Fact:	I'm the "Herod" most frequently mentioned in the Bible. Yea, Me!
Favorite Film:	*Jesus Christ Superstar*—my song (creatively titled, "King Herod's Song") is the highlight of the movie! Prove me wrong!

Herod Antipas set out to out-do his dad in the area of dastardly deeds, and that is saying something, since his daddy was quite the dastard himself (see Herod the Great). In order to top his dad, Herod Antipas came up with a three-step action plan.

Step One. Herod married his niece, Herodias. Which might not have been that big of a deal, except that both Herod and Herodias were already married: Herod to the daughter of another king, and Herodias to—get this—Herod's brother, Philip. This little scandal made for, like, a decade's worth of cover stories for the Galilean Enquirer. It also drew the attention of John the Baptist, who thought the whole sordid affair was a royal offense to God.

Step Two. When John the Baptist wouldn't make like a good, obedient little prophet and shut his yapper, Herod threw the bigmouth in jail. Then, at Herod's birthday party, the daughter of Herodias danced such a dance that Herod promised her anything she wanted. Herodias instructed her daughter to ask for John the Baptist's head on a platter. Herod didn't want to kill John, but he felt he owed it to him, so he "reluctantly" granted the mother/daughter duo's request.

Step Three. Since his dad had acted so despicably at the birth of Jesus, it seemed like good symmetry for Herod Antipas to act despicably at the end of Jesus' life. At Jesus' trial, Herod pressed the would-be Messiah to perform some miracles. But when Jesus wouldn't oblige, Herod laid on the verbal abuse. He dressed Jesus up like a mock king, and handed him over to the Roman Governor, Pontius Pilate.

Nevertheless, despite the above action plan, it's not clear that Herod Antipas out-stunk his dad, Herod the Great. On the other hand, Herod Antipas was bad enough to tick-off the insane and debauched Emperor Caligula. So he had that going for him. Which was nice.

Key Verse: "Some Pharisees came and said to Jesus, 'Get away from here, for Herod wants to kill you.' He said to them, 'Go and tell that fox for me . . . "you will not see me until the time comes when you say, 'Blessed is the one who comes in the name of the Lord'" (Luke 13:31-35; see also Mark 6:14-29; Luke 23:6-12).

See also: Jesus, John the Baptist, Luke (The Gospel according to).

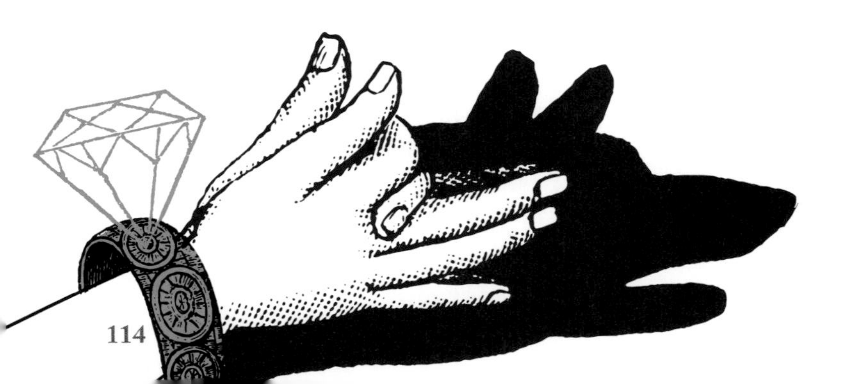

Herod the Great

\HEH-ruhd-thuh-GRĀT\

Status:
Herod the Great is still looking for those magi who had mentioned something about a newborn king; if you hear anything from them, let me know.

Profile

Vocation:	I am the king of the Jews, and just because I am not descended from King David, don't think for a second that I won't be king long after you are gone.
Family (and Friends):	Lots of sons, three of whom I ordered executed, and even more wives (one of whom I ordered executed)
Likes:	Building projects (harbors, temples, cities)
Dislikes:	The terrible twos
Favorite Song:	"Bad to the Bone" by George Thorogood and the Destroyers
Favorite Quotation:	"It's better to be Herod's dog than one of his children."—Augustus Caesar (I take it as a compliment.)

Herod had accomplished a lot in his life, but he had the bad luck to live and reign mostly in the "intertestamental period"—the time between the Old Testament and the New Testament. He earned the right to call himself King of the Jews by teaming up with the Romans, who were the new bully on the block. Herod helped the Romans drive the old bullies out of Galilee and Jerusalem in the years 40–37 BCE. Near the end of his life in 4 BCE, Herod realized that if he didn't do something spectacular, he wasn't going to get his name in the Bible. And that just wasn't fair. It wasn't his fault that he was born between the Testaments, after all.

So Herod did two things to get noticed. First, he decided to remodel the Temple in Jerusalem. Solomon had built the thing the first time. And the second Temple was rebuilt by people like Ezra following the Exile. But it was pretty shabby, so starting in 20 BCE, Herod went nuts with a massive expansion and remodeling. He had had plenty of practice, since he had also rebuilt Samaria (once the capital of Israel) and had built a new tourist destination on the sea called, Caesaria Maritima. The Temple remodel wasn't finished until long after his death, but it got him some good press.

But it still wasn't enough to get him into the Bible. As you know, only the worst news gets you into the paper, so Herod did something really, really bad. Just before he died, he got the chance. Some wise guys came and told him that a new kid had been born and was being called "The King of the Jews." "WHAT?!" old man Herod shouted, "You mean the Messiah is going to be born now?! Go kill him. And just to be sure, kill all of the other children around Bethlehem under the age of two. That'll teach them to start the New Testament without me."

Herod "the Great" made it into the Bible all right, forever remembered as a murdering despot and one of scripture's greatest villains. Incidentally, the young victims of Herod's crime are remembered each Christmas season on "Holy Innocents Day"—an observance that dates back to the fifth century.

Key Verse: "In the time of King Herod . . . Jesus was born in Bethlehem of Judea" (Matt 2:1; see also Matt 2).

See also: Jesus, Matthew (The Gospel according to).

Hezekiah \HEHZ-uh-KI-uh\

Status:
Hezekiah is wondering what those Assyrians beyond the border are up to.

Profile

Vocation:	King of Judah and Religious Reformer
What's in a Name?	My name means "God strengthens," which is what happened to me.
About My Family:	I don't like to talk about it, because my dad was a bad man, very bad. He worshiped false gods and even sacrificed a few of my brothers to his wicked false gods. No, I'm not making this up.
Interests:	Worship, God's word, trashing pagan worship sites, hanging out with prophets, invasion preparation
A Place I'd Like to Visit:	New York City, 'cause I would like to see the Holland and Lincoln tunnels
Favorite Celebrity:	Gimli, son of Gloin of the Lonely Mountain Dwarves
Favorite Quotation:	"No! No! That's not true! That's impossible!"—Luke Skywalker to Darth Vader (after Vader said, "*I* am your father.").

When sportswriters named the 400th anniversary Kings of Judah dream team, five kings were at the top: David, Solomon (although we think he only got in because his mom was famous), Jehoshaphat, Josiah, and, of course, Hezekiah. We say "of course," because you already know that this entry is about Hezekiah . . . duh.

So what was so great about Hezekiah? Well, a few things. First, he sort of had the Gerald Ford role—he took over from a king who was pretty corrupt. It so happened that the corrupt king was Hezekiah's father, Ahaz. When Hezekiah took over, he went all Elliott Ness-Martin Luther-John the Baptist on the bit and cleaned up the city.

Clean-up project number one: the Temple. Hezekiah threw out all of the foreign-god stuff that had gotten into the Lord's house. He even threw out the bronze snake-on-a-stick that Moses had made (see Num 21:4-9), because people were treating it like a false god.

He reorganized and reformed the priests, trying to whip some discipline and faithfulness into them (whip being just a turn of phrase here, he didn't literally whip them, although we bet that he wanted to, especially when the sermons went too long). Hezekiah got worship going the right way, making sure that the important days of the year were celebrated right. And making sure that there were donuts after services and that every kid could have two donuts, even if the old ladies told them they couldn't.

Clean-up project number two: the religion. Hezekiah burned and destroyed all of the shrines and altars where people were worshiping the false gods of the land of Canaan. Now this might seem a bit harsh. After all, aren't we supposed to have separation of church and state and religious tolerance and all that? Well, yes, today we are. But back then, there was no separation of King and Temple. And more to the point, do you know what those people were doing at their "high places? They were sacrificing babies. "Passing their sons through the fire" is what they called it, as if that made it any better. Hezekiah himself had lost a couple of brothers that way.

Clean-up project number three: the military. Finally, Hezekiah reformed his military. He knew that the Assyrian army was on its way to drop unholy smack down on the Kingdom of Judah, because Hezekiah refused to treat the Assyrian emperor like he was a god. So Hezekiah fortified as many of Judah's cities as possible and strengthened Jerusalem's defenses. He even had a long tunnel dug, called the Siloam Tunnel, in order that the city could have water during a siege (you can tour this underground water way—or one like it—when you visit Jerusalem today). And that water proved pretty helpful, as the Assyrian emperor Sennacherib destroyed all of Judah's cities, but he couldn't capture Jerusalem. Through Hezekiah's preparations, God saved the city. Or, as Hezekiah's name means, "The Lord strengthened" its defenses.

Key Verse: "Thus says the Lord concerning the king of Assyria: He shall not come into this city. . . For I will defend this city to save it, for my own sake and for the sake of my servant David" (2 Kgs 19:32, 34; see also 2 Kgs 18–20; 2 Chr 29–32).

See also: Assyria, Assyrians, Temple.

Historical Books \hih-STOHR-ih-kuhl-BUX\

The Encyclopedia Israelica, these books chronicle the sordid details of the birth, life, death, and rebirth of the kingdom of Israel.

Starting with the book of Joshua and running for twelve volumes (up through Esther), the second major portion of the Old Testament is a lengthy survey of Israel's history from the days when there was no king in Israel (Judg 21:25), through the struggles of Israelites living under the rule of the king of Persia (Esth 1:1). The historical books begin with the conquest of the Promised Land, led by Joshua. At the end of Joshua, the people promise to worship God faithfully but, as with most human promises, this promise is, if not hollow, then at least fleeting. In Judges the people live primarily in the lands allotted to their respective tribes (that is the twelve tribes descended from the twelve sons of Jacob that make up Israel). In the stories of the judges, the people constantly revert to their default orientation: pointed away from God and towards sin. In Samuel, Kings, and Chronicles the stories of the Israelite kings are told; there we learn that even with a king, each person (including the king!) did as they pleased. In Ezra and Nehemiah the return from the Exile and the rebuilding of Israel is begun, but there again the problem of sin and conflict rears its misshapen head.

The constant theme of biblical history is the failure of people—be they kings, citizens, the occasional prophet or judge, and in fact the nation as a whole—to be faithful to God. But the good news is the counter-theme that God's faithfulness is constant—in the face of sin and wrongheadedness God remains committed to God's people. And that, in the end, is really the subject of Israel's history. Israel's history is in fact God's history, the history of God's faithfulness, the history of God's saving work, for God's people who need saving.

See also: Old Testament.

Holy Week \HOH-lee-week\

(Covering the Triumphal Entry, Last Supper, Arrest, Trial, Crucifixion, and Burial of Jesus)

It is the week that changed everything.

Please refer to PASSION NARRATIVE, THE.

See also: Jesus, Passion Narrative.

Hosea \hoh-ZĀ-uh\ (book)

by Hosea Ben-Beeri (Old Testament, Minor Prophets, fourteen chapters)

Well! Whichever editor let this "Hosea" manuscript slip through the cracks of the book proposal process is surely looking for work picking figs and crushing olives. Imagine God actually commanding a prophet, the erstwhile Hosea Ben-Beeri, to marry a "wife of whoredom" (1:2). This is in the Bible? The Bible, we believe, is a family book. For use in building up family values (no whores, thank you very much), respectful citizenship, red-blooded patriotism, and obedient faith.

Mr. Ben-Beeri, whose words and actions are presented in this book, was none of the above. He chastises priests and prophets for their wickedness (not obedient!). He compares his nation to a heifer and a wanton woman (not patriotic!). He criticizes kings (not respectful!). While Mr. Ben-Beeri does point to a promising future in a few places (1:10—2:1; 2:16-23; 11:1-9), we must state that this sarcastic and disrespectful book does not live up to the high standards of family values and citizenship that we have come to expect from this line of imprints.

See also: Gomer, Hosea, Prophets.

Hosea \hoh-zā-uh\

Status:
Hosea is wondering why other families don't like to hang out with us much.

Profile

Profession:	Prophet
Family:	My wife is Gomer—a story in and of itself. We have three kids, a boy named "The-Lord-Sows," a girl named "Not-Shown-Mercy," and a boy named "Not-My-People." Are they family names? They are now!
Dislikes:	Corrupt prophets, lazy priests, and incompetent rulers

Tip for readers: This article is better if you read it out loud (preferably in front of a skittish aunt or prudish school teacher).

For all-out, full-blast, biblical fun . . . there is nothing like the prophets. There is nothing they won't do to get their point across. Take Hosea. (And most of the people who knew him would have said, "Please! Take him!"). God appointed Hosea to deliver the news to Israel that they were being unfaithful to God. But Hosea didn't just speak this message. He put the *live* in de-live-ry.

First, Hosea got married. A man came to him, saying, "Hey Hosea, I hear that you finally settled down, tell me about your new wife." "Oh," said the prophet, "She's not a faithful woman. In fact, she is a whore. Just like you, sir, ARE A WHORE IN GOD'S SIGHT!! In the same way that my wife is always unfaithful to me, so, sir, are you always UNFAITHFUL TO GOD!!" Obviously, Hosea wasn't in it to make friends. (Note to reader: If the foregoing has offended you, please do not write our bishop or complain to the publisher. We didn't make this stuff up. If you don't like it, take it up with God.)

Second, Hosea had a baby boy. The nice young woman selling olives at the marketplace cooed, "He's so *cute*, what's his name?" "His name is 'God-Sows' [Hebrew: *Jezreel*] because just as the king of Israel shed blood at the valley God-Sows [*Jezreel*], so God is going to put an end to the kingdom of Israel. Do you like the name?"

Third, Hosea had a baby girl. Gomer couldn't make it to the couples' shower (she was off for a long weekend in Vegas), so people were sort of uncomfortable. To break the ice, someone asked, "So what is the baby's name going to be?" Someone quickly tried to change the subject, but Hosea piped up, "Her name will be 'Not-Shown-Mercy' [*Lo-ruhamah*] because YOU ARE SO UNFAITHFUL THAT GOD WILL NO LONGER SHOW YOU MERCY!!!" (Have you noticed that Hosea spoke with a lot of exclamation points? What's up with that?)

Fourth, Hosea had another baby boy. By this point, nobody dared asked about the kids' names. So Hosea taught the kid to do the speech for him. "Hi, my name's 'Not-My-People' [*Lo-ammi*]. It is an unfortunate name, you will agree, but my dad is a prophet and he says YOU ARE SO UNFAITHFUL THAT YOU ARE NO LONGER GOD'S PEOPLE!!!" (Even the kids started doing that !!!!! thing!)

But here is the amazing thing. God's judgment did arrive, just as Hosea announced. But judgment was not God's final word. Once it became clear that judgment was inevitable, Hosea also announced that on the other side of judgment—after the people *passed through* judgment—God would be there for the people again.

And Hosea lived that message, too. He stayed faithful to his unfaithful wife. He changed the interpretation of his first son's name: "God is sowing the seeds of your future, and it will be great." And he changed the names of his other children to "Shown-Mercy" and "My-People."

Key Verse: "Say to your brother, My-People, and to your sister, Shown-Mercy" (Hos 2:1; see the Book of Hosea).

See also: Gomer, Hosea (book), Prophets.

Isaac \ɪ-zihk\

Status:
Isaac is laughing.

Profile

Vocation:	Rancher (I own a lot of livestock and manage the large amount of land that I inherited from my father.)
Family:	Father: Abraham; Mother: Sarah
Likes:	Rams (as in the animals, not the football team); blessings
Dislikes:	Mountain-top altars; father-and-son outings; tests
Favorite Quotation:	"The Lord will provide."—My dad, Abraham, after the Lord provided. And I said, "Whew!!"

When Sarah finally conceived a child, everyone agreed that the baby's name would be Isaac—which means *laughter*. It was a pretty happy moment. The first of, well, the first of not too many happy moments for Isaac.

The name *laughter* fit his mother better than it fit the boy. Because his life was pretty far from fun. When he was just a boy, his older brother Ishmael was sent away. Not too long after that, Isaac's mother died. Losing your mom is never easy, and for Isaac it was especially rough, because he hadn't found a wife of his own yet. And later still, at the end of his life, there was the time when his wife, Rebekah, and his youngest son, Jacob, played him for a fool. The result of that episode was two estranged sons. No, there wasn't much laughter for Isaac.

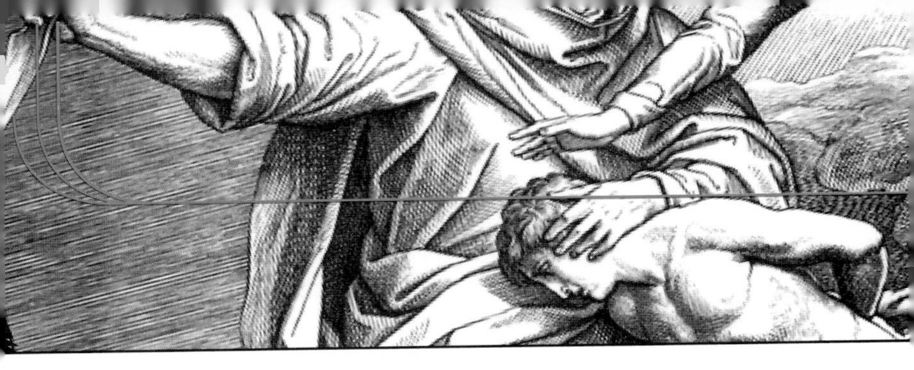

But perhaps the saddest, scariest, hardest moment of all came when Isaac was still a boy. What happened is that God put Abraham to the test. Why did God test Abraham? Nobody knows. Why would an all-knowing God need to test a human being to see what he would do? Humans can't know the mind of God. But test Abraham is what God did. God commanded Abraham to sacrifice Isaac, in order to test whether Abraham really *feared God*. One thing is for certain, Isaac *feared*. He feared with every fiber of his being. He feared dying. He feared his father. And he feared God. And maybe this wasn't even the good kind of fear, the kind that shows a loving respect. Maybe Isaac just flat out feared. We can imagine Isaac, bound up there on the altar: "Uh, you s-s-sure about this, Dad?"

And then God provided. God provided a ram. Just as the blow was about to fall, a ram appeared, with its horns caught in a bush. Later, both Abraham and Isaac swore that the ram wasn't there one second, and then in the next it was. And God said, "Do not lay your hand on the boy or do anything to him; for now I know that you fear God, since you have not withheld your son, your only son, from me" (Gen 22:12). And Isaac and Abraham both laughed. In fact, for the rest of his life, the sight of a ram would bring a smile to Isaac's face.

Key Verse: "I will indeed bless you, and I will make your offspring as numerous as the stars of heaven and as the sand that is on the seashore" (Gen 22:17; see also Gen 21:1-7; 22:1-19; 24:1-67).

See also: **Abraham, Jacob, Rebekah, Sarah.**

Isaiah \i-zā-uh\ (book)

by Isaiah Ben-Amoz, with others
(Old Testament, Major Prophets, sixty-six chapters)

Isaiah Ben-Amoz, a prophet of Jerusalem, began the ambitious project that eventually grew into this volume in response to a command he received from the Lord: "Go now, write it before them on a tablet, and inscribe it in a book, so that it may be for the time to come as a witness forever. For they are a rebellious people, faithless children, children who will not hear the instruction of the Lord" (Isa 30:8-9). Mr. Ben-Amoz started collecting his teachings sometime around 730 BCE. The project was only completed more than two centuries after Mr. Ben-Amoz's death, by those who chose to leave their own identities secret. Our best guess is that the ghostwriter (or writers) lived sometime around the year 540 BCE.

The first part of the book, chapters 1–35, mainly features many of the messages that the Lord delivered to the people of Judah through Mr. Ben-Amoz. The messages promise God's presence with the people through peril (such as Isaiah 7), but also sternly demand that the people prove worthy of God's presence (such as Isaiah 1). Many of the messages promise that in the future, the Lord will send a perfect king, whom some call the Messiah. Chapters 36–39 are borrowed almost verbatim from 2 Kings—not that we are accusing anyone of plagiarism!

The second half of the book, chapters 40–66, contains messages of hope from a much later prophet, who lived during and immediately after the Exile. It is a shame that we do not know the author's name, but most likely he or she had to remain anonymous, for legitimate fear of the Babylonians. This splendid author promised that the Lord would bring the people home from Babylon. The prophet also voiced strident condemnations of Babylonian idol worship. These chapters mention "God's servant." Some believe this servant represents the entire people of Israel; others understand that the servant is the perfect king—"wonderful counselor, mighty God, everlasting father, prince of peace" (Isa 9:6)—announced in the earlier chapters. Whatever the case, this compilation of prophetic voices is not the easiest read, but it will profit all who are up to the challenge.

See also: Babylonians, Isaiah, Prophets.

Isaiah \i-zā-uh\

Status:
Isaiah is getting a little tired of that song that goes, "Here I am, Lord. Is it I, Lord? . . ."

Profile

Vocation:	Prophet
Hometown:	Jerusalem, the City of Zion, the highest mountain in the world (spiritually speaking)
Family:	My wife's a prophet, too. And we have a thing for fun names. Nothing average like Mark, John, or Dave! To read more, check out Isaiah 7:1-6 and 8:1-4 (and if you are an overachiever, 7:14-17).
Dislike:	Angels wielding tongue scorching hot coals
Fun Fact:	You know Handel's *Messiah*? I wrote the lyrics for some of those songs.

The prophet Isaiah was minding his own business, sleeping through Sabbath worship, when suddenly he heard a voice, "HOLY, HOLY, HOLY IS THE LORD OF HOSTS!" At first he thought it was his cousin Deane, screwing around in the balcony again. But Deane was asleep, too. It was a couple of angels, screaming out praise of God. They had to scream their praise and cover their faces, because being in God's holy presence actually *hurt* them.

And the Lord said, "You in the sandals and dirty robes. Yeah, you! Go tell my people that I am faithful. And that being faithful means that I love each and every one of them so very, very much, that I cannot stand it when the rich oppress the poor, when the strong cause the weak to suffer, or when the powerful make life hell for the powerless. So at the moment, being faithful means that I am more than a little angry with the people."

Isaiah responded, "Word. I can say that. How long should I keep it up?"

The Lord answered, "Good question. You should know in advance that the people won't listen to you. Well, they might listen, but they aren't gonna understand, agree, or 'get it.' See, people just want to have a nice, cuddly god. One who protects them but requires nothing of them, one who ignores their sins rather than one who *forgives* their sins. So, you are going to have to spend your life giving my word to the people knowing that they just won't listen."

"So why bother?"

"Why bother? Because I'll give you some eager students who will write down whatever you say. They'll put your words in a book and call it by your name. And in the future, the words will still be there for people of faith to study. They still mostly won't get it, but my word has power and it will accomplish what I want it to accomplish. Oh, yes. It will."

Key Verse: "Go now, write it before them on a tablet, and inscribe it in a book, so that it may be for the time to come as a witness forever. For they are a rebellious people, faithless children, children who will not hear the instruction of the Lord" (Isa 30:8-9; see also especially Isa 1 and 6).

See also: Babylonians, Isaiah (book), Prophets.

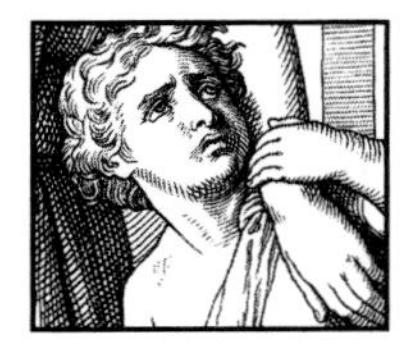

Ishmael \IHSH-māl\

Status:
Ishmael is thinking of visiting Mecca and Islam's holiest shrine—a shrine that they say was built by me and my father, Ibrahim.

Profile

What's in a Name?	Ishmael means "God hears," which in my story is good news, because God heard my crying (Gen 21:17).
Least Favorite Bible Verse:	Gn 21:9-10 "But Sarah saw the son of Hagar the Egyptian, whom she had borne to Abraham, playing with her son Isaac. So she said to Abraham, 'Cast out this slave woman with her son; for the son of this slave woman shall not inherit along with my son Isaac.'" Never liked my step-monster much, as you can imagine.
Favorite Book:	*Moby Dick* by Melville (Gotta love that opening sentence.)
Favorite Song:	"Call Me" by Blondie
Favorite Quotation:	"Come, lift up the boy and hold him fast with your hand, for I will make a great nation of him." An angel of the Lord said that to my mom. Kind of made up for the whole Sarah-kicking-us-out thing.

Please refer to HAGAR.

Key Verse: "And God was with the child [Ishmael], and he grew and dwelt in the wilderness, and became an archer" (Gen 21:20).

See also: Abraham, Hagar, Sarah.

Israelites \IHZ-ree-uhl-īts\

Descendants of Jacob and ancestors of both Jews and Christians (and Samaritans).

Residents of the Northern Kingdom (c. 900–722 BCE).

Originally, all of the Hebrew people were considered Israelites. Every descendant of Jacob (to whom God gave the name Israel when Jacob was returning from the witness protection program; see Gen 32). Later, when the twelve tribes split into two kingdoms, the south got to keep the capital city and the Temple, and the north got to keep the name Israel.

The Old Testament is neither a Christian book or a Jewish book—it is a book of Israelite religion (for example, neither Christianity nor Judaism practice animal sacrifice in worship or have hereditary priesthoods, but both of these are features of Old Testament religion). Christianity and Judaism both *evolved from* Israelite religion. So the Israelites are the spiritual ancestors of both Christians and Jews.

See also: Babylonians, Egyptians, -ites, Monarchy.

-ites \-īts\

The peoples who lived in or around the promised land, before, during, and after Israel.

In a tried-and-tested Hebrew way of looking at the universe, there are two types of peoples. There is the chosen people and there is everyone else. The chosen people is Israel, the one nation blessed to be a blessing to the other nations. The "everyone else" are the Goys or Goyim (from the Hebrew word *goyim*, meaning "the nations" or "the peoples").

Some of these "peoples" lived in, with, around, and among the chosen people. These people have funny names, often ending with the suffix "-ite." Some of these people sound like wicked infections, or birth defects, or creepy bacteria, or tasty malt beverages: Canaanites, Hittites, Amorites, Perizzites, Hivites, Jebusites, Millerlites, electric-lights, and so on. On the other hand, there were the peoples who had their own nations, living around Israel: Ammonites, Moabites, Edomites, Hittites (different than the Hittites above), and so on.

Throughout the Old Testament, the peoples cause trouble for Israel (and in truth, Israel often caused trouble for the peoples). These peoples often posed the dual threats of military oppression (see Judg 3:7-11) and religious corruption (especially the temptation to engage in violent pagan acts of worship such as child sacrifice; see 1 Kgs 16:31-34).

See also: Israelites, Prophets.

Jacob \JĀ-kuhb\

Status:
Jacob is going to see the doc about a sore hip he thinks is related to an old wrestling injury.

Profile

Vocation:	Cheater, Hired Hand, Wrestler
What's in a Name?	One morning, after wrestling with some strange dude all night long, God gave me a new name: "Israel." It means "Wrestles with God." Talk about a name that stuck (see Gen 32:28).
Family (and Friends):	Isaac and Rebekah (parents); Esau (my hairy, older twin brother); Leah and Rachel (my wives); Joseph (my favorite son; the others aren't worth mentioning)
Dislikes:	Camping, family reunions (between my dad, my mother, my brother, my uncle, my wives, and my sons, things can get sort of tense)
Favorite Quotation:	"I put the funk in dysfunctional family"—Me (I say that about myself because it pretty much is true)

If you research your family tree far back enough, you'll discover that at least one of your relatives was a complete disappointment, an utter embarrassment, a rotten scoundrel. The same thing goes for your spiritual family tree—those people who are your ancestors and elders according to the faith. And if you don't believe us, look no further than Jacob. Jacob's name means both "heel" (as in the tough, bony extrusion that stomps on people and things) and "usurper" (as in one who doesn't mind taking what is yours and claiming it as his own). And Jacob was both.

Here are a few highlights from his resume. When he was young, Jacob cheated his older twin brother out of both his birthright (his share of the inheritance) and his blessing. Stealing Esau's blessing was maybe Jacob's lowest act. It involved having their mother Rebekah dress him up as Esau so that their blind, old father Isaac thought he was giving the blessing to Esau. When Esau found out about it, the older brother flew into such a murderous rage that Jacob had to flee the country, to live with his Uncle Laban.

On his way to Laban's place, Jacob was forced to camp out at a place called Bethel, with nothing but a rock for a pillow. As he slept, the Lord sent a vision of a ladder that stretched up to heaven, with angels cruising up and down the thing, as if it were a giant, two-way escalator. Now before going any further, imagine Jacob's state of mind. He had just stolen his brother's divine Blessing and was running for his life. And then God appeared. Jacob expected the smack to be dropped straight down on his head, like the rock on which he slept. But God did something that we have come to expect, but only because we live after Jacob. God was gracious! God repeated the promise to Jacob that had been made to Abraham: "I will be your God; you'll have the land, many descendants, and through you all the earth will be blessed." Isn't that crazy? Not only was the blessing-thief *not* going to be punished, he was to be the means through which God worked to bless the entire world!! (So take heart, if God can work through a scoundrel like Jacob, God can work through anyone, including you.)

Jacob's adventures were only getting going. As you read the stories about Jacob, you get the sense that the old sinner never really improved. He never learned to stop manipulating people or stop treating them as objects. If you want to learn a bit more about Jacob, check out the entries on Leah, Rachel, Esau, and Joseph. When Jacob finally died, they buried him in the same place as his grandpa Abraham. We don't know if they wrote anything on his tombstone, but if it were up to us, it would have said: "Here lies Jacob, a thief and sinner claimed by God in order that God might bless the entire world."

Key Verse: "All the families of the earth shall be blessed in you and in your offspring" (Gen 28:14; see also Gen 27–35).

See also: **Esau, Genesis, Isaac, Rebekah.**

James \jāmz\

by James the brother of Jesus (New Testament, Letters, five chapters)

You've seen the *Where's Waldo?* books? The reader of James may want to know, "Where's Jesus?" Jesus is mentioned only twice in James, including once in the opening address. If there is something to the ancient tradition that "James" refers to the same James who was the brother of Jesus (Matt 13:55, Gal 1:19), then we can postulate that this James was not as enthusiastic about glorifying his brother when compared to, oh, the whole rest of the New Testament. James does offer some strong exhortation and rules for Christian living. Still, some (like Martin Luther) have wondered if James didn't have a problem with Paul's idea of justification by faith apart from works—or at least with those who used the idea as a license for sin. Whatever the case, Mr. James makes an important point, namely that much will be expected of those who claim faith in Christ. Faith *will*, to borrow from Paul, produce good fruit. In other words, faith cannot *not* produce good fruit. Therefore, faith without works is not only dead, it's not even faith.

See also: **Letters (or Epistles).**

Jeremiah \JEHR-uh-MI-uh\ (book)

by Jeremiah Ben-Hilkiah, with Baruch Ben-Neriah
(Old Testament, Major Prophets, fifty-two chapters)

The literary world owes a great debt to Baruch Ben-Neriah, the personal secretary of the prophet Jeremiah Ben-Hilkiah (his ministry began in 627 BCE), for pulling together the voluminous material to make this book possible. What a wearisome labor it must have been for poor Mr. Ben-Neriah! Indeed, he had finished an earlier edition of the volume, only to have the irksome Judean King Jehoiakim burn it. Not to be daunted, the faithful scribe set to work again transcribing his master's words. (That is not to say, of course, that the book of Jeremiah did not undergo editorial corrections—some major and some minor—after Mr. Ben-Neriah's death.)

The first portion of the book, chapters 1–25, are mostly rain with no sunshine. They consist of the messages of warning and judgment that the Lord sent through his prophet, Mr. Ben-Hilkiah (a.k.a. Jeremiah). As the Lord said to the young boy when he was called to bear the prophetic burden: "Gird up your loins [an old colloquial phrase that can be roughly translated, "Hike up your diaper!"]; stand up and tell them everything that I command you" (Jer 1:17). Some people may be turned off by the constant calls to repent, amend their evil ways, and shape up. But one must remember, when one person causes another to suffer, *it is precisely because God loves the one who is suffering* that God calls for repentance.

The second portion of the book, chapters 26–45 consists mainly of stories that recount incidents in the life of Mr. Ben-Hilkiah. Especially worth noting is Mr. Ben-Hilkiah's promise that the Lord will form a new covenant (Jer 31:31). The last section, chapters 46–52, consists mainly of messages concerning the future of those nations who vexed and annoyed Judah during Mr. Ben-Hilkiah's life. If you like a book filled with warnings and promises in the face of impending doom, then Jeremiah is for you.

See also: Jeremiah, Prophets.

Jeremiah \JEHR-uh-MI-uh\

Status:
Jeremiah is crying.

Profile

Hometown:	Jerusalem
Vocation:	Chief Information Officer, Yahweh-or-the-Highway, Ltd.
Places I would least like to visit:	Rome, Canterbury, Salt Lake City, the Taj Mahal, Green Bay (Wisconsin)—basically any place with a big, temple-like building that people worship, instead of worshiping God
Turn-offs:	Yes-men prophets and the kings who hire them
Favorite Song:	"Crying" by Roy Orbison
Not-so-fun Fact:	I didn't really like being a prophet. In fact, I tried to resign my call a couple of times and really let God know how miserable the whole gig was.

Jeremiah lived during an age when the people of God were served mostly by faithless preachers, prophets, and priests. While Jeremiah was still too young to have a driver's license, the Lord called him: "Jeremiah, are you a faithless preacher? Or are you a mean, Torah-quotin' servant of the Lord?" And it turned out that Jeremiah was, indeed, a mean, Torah-quotin' servant of the Lord.

Jeremiah had to be tough. Because he was God's press secretary during one of the most down, bear-market times in the history of the Lord's stock. During Jeremiah's life, the Kingdom of Judah went through kings faster than Liz Taylor went through husbands. After Josiah died in 609 BCE, guys like Jehoahaz, Jehoiakim, Jehoiachin, and Zedekiah, all took their turns sitting on the throne. In 586 BCE, the kingdom was finally overrun by the Babylonians, who destroyed the temple and took Judah's leaders and citizens into captivity. Throughout the years that led up to the fall of the kingdom, Jeremiah was God's chief spokesperson. And because times were tough, Jeremiah cried a lot.

Jeremiah's most famous press release was probably the one about the Temple. All of the priests, prophets, and preachers were there. With one voice, they announced that God would protect the city from the Babylonian army, because God would not let the holy Temple be destroyed. Jeremiah's retort was as sarcastic as it was simple: "Do not trust in these lying words: 'This is the temple of the LORD, the temple of the LORD, the temple of the LORD.' For if you truly amend your ways and your doings, if you truly act justly with one another, if you do not oppress the alien, the orphan, and the widow, or shed innocent blood . . . then I will dwell with you in this place." (Jer 7:4-7). The leaders didn't like being mocked in this way, so they did things like throw Jeremiah down a well, put him in the stockades, and keep him in jail.

Then the end came. In the form of the Babylonian army.

And then Jeremiah did a strange thing. He invested in real estate. He promised that God would still be faithful to the people on the other side of exile in Babylon. Sitting in jail, with the Babylonian army surrounding the city, Jeremiah purchased the land on which the Babylonians were camped. He said, "It may look like it's over, but it isn't over until God says it's over. And God says, 'My people will one day buy houses, plant fields, and harvest vineyards again.'" Thereby proving once again that the best time to buy property is when the market's down.

Key Verse: "The days are surely coming, says the LORD, when I will make a new covenant with the house of Israel and the house of Judah" (Jer 31:31).

See also: Babylonians, Jeremiah (book), Prophets.

J

Jericho \JEHR-ih-koh\

A fortress town near the Jordon River, known for its poorly-constructed, sound-sensitive city wall. Beautiful panoramic views of the Promised Land. Beware bandits and Samaritans.

Some archaeologists call Jericho "the oldest continuously inhabited city in the world." In New Testament times, if you were going from Galilee to Jerusalem, you'd follow the road that ran down along Jordan River. Jericho was where you'd hang a right and head up the hill for Jerusalem. In the Old Testament, Jericho was the place where, as the old spiritual has it, "Joshua fit de battle. . . ." After crossing Jordan into the Promised Land, the ancient Israelites discovered that, hey, other people were already living there! Jericho was the first city taken by Joshua and his army after crossing the Jordan. You know the story (in Joshua 6): March around the city for seven days, blow the horns, shout out loud, watch the wall come a-tumblin' down, slaughter the inhabitants (except for Rahab), move in. On the other hand, Jericho was the place where Jesus met Zacchaeus and "Blind Bartimaeus"—so nice things happened in Jericho, too.

See also: Israelites, Joshua.

Jerusalem \jeh-ROO-suh-lehm

God's hizzle fo' shizzle, so wipe your feet before entering. Jerusalem is the place where God dwells and where God may be worshipped, and therefore a place people fight over like rabid squirrels over a half-eaten corndog.

Ever heard of the "Big Apple" (New York, right?), or the "Windy City" (that's Chicago)? How about the LCW—Lutefisk Capital of the World (what, you've never heard of Madison, MN?)? Pretty nifty nicknames, right? Well, Jerusalem, the capital city of the nation of Israel, has one too—Jerusalem the Golden.

David made Jerusalem the center of the Israelite nation, both in terms of ruling his kingdom and worshipping God. He had the Ark of the Covenant (which contained the broken tablets of the Ten Commandments and which God would sit on from time to time) moved there permanently, making Jerusalem *the* dwelling place of God on earth. (On the dwelling place of God see Psalms 74:7; 76:2; 84:1; 90:1; 91:9; 132:7.) Jerusalem is also sometimes called "Mt. Zion," the holy mountain around which the city is settled and on which the Temple was built.

Today Jerusalem remains the place for which the hearts of many Jews pine. At the end of the Passover supper it is traditional to say, "Next year in Jerusalem," which means that next year they will celebrate the Passover there. This comes from longing for home, as well as the return to dwelling near to God. After Israel was conquered by the Babylonians, the capital city became even more important, especially to Jews living in the Diaspora (meaning spread all around the world, "dispersed" among neighboring nations).

Psalm 137 is a good illustration of how important Jerusalem was:

> "By the rivers of Babylon—
> there we sat down and there we wept
> when we remembered Zion.
>
> If I forget you, O Jerusalem,
> let my right hand wither!
> Let my tongue cling to the roof of my mouth . . ."
> (Ps 137 1, 5-6).

Or as Matisyahu (the Hasidic Jewish hip hop artist) says it,

> "Jerusalem, if I forget you,
> fire not gwan come from me tongue.
> Jerusalem, if I forget you,
> let my right hand forget what it's supposed to do."

The New Testament also picks up on the importance of Jerusalem, talking about the City of God, heaven, as the "New Jerusalem" (Rev 21:1-4). It is the idea of Jerusalem as the place where God meets humankind, dwells among them—us—and calls us to live with God, that makes it Golden indeed. "See, the home of God is among mortals. He will dwell with them; they will be his peoples, and God himself will be with them!"

See also: David, Revelation to John, Zion.

Jesus \JEE-zuhs\

Status:
Jesus is sitting at the right hand of the Father.

Profile

Vocation:	Savior
Also Known As...	Adam (new, second, last), Advocate, Almighty, Alpha and Omega, Apostle of our Profession, Atoning Sacrifice, Author (of Life, Salvation), Blessed Ruler, Bread of Life, Bridegroom, Capstone, Cornerstone, Christ, Creator, Deliverer, Everlasting Father, Faithful Witness, Firstborn from the Dead, Gate, God, Good Shepherd, Head of the Church, Heir of All Things, High Priest, Holy One, Hope, Horn of Salvation, I Am, Image of God, Immanuel, Judge, King (of the Jews, of kings, of the ages), Lamb of God, Life, Light of the World, Lion of the Tribe of Judah, Living Stone, Lord (of all, of glory, of lords), Mediator, Mighty God, Morning Star, Offspring of David, Only Begotten Son of God, Our (Great God and Savior, Holiness, Husband, Protection, Redemption, Righteousness), Prince of Peace, Prophet, Rabbi, Resurrection and Life, Righteous Branch, Righteous One, Rock, Root of David, Savior, Son (of Abraham, of David, of God, of Man, of Mary), Truth, Vine, Way, Wisdom of God, Wonderful Counselor, Word—have we left anything out?
Networks:	Heaven and Earth
Interests:	Reconciliation, redemption, atonement, forgiveness, salvation

See *Crazy Talk: A Not-So-Stuffy Dictionary of Theological Terms*, pp. 98-99.

Key Verse: "There is salvation in no one else, for there is no other name under heaven given among mortals by which we must be saved" (Acts 4:12; see also Matt 1:1; Rev 22:21; a little something that we like to call the New Testament).

See also: Creation, Gospel.

J

Jews/Judaism

\jooz\ \JOO-dā-ih-zuhm\ or \joo-DĀ-ih-zuhm\

Probably not who you think they are—but probably either the descendants or ancestors of who you think they are.

In the Bible, when you read about a "Jew" (31 times in the NRSV) or "Jews" (220 times), you're working in the world of what we pointed-headed academic types like to call "Second Temple Judaism." That is, the Jews you meet in the Bible are neither the "Rabbinical Jews" of today, nor are they the "Israelites" of the First Temple period. [Reminder: the First Temple lasted from about 922 to 586 BCE; the Second Temple from about 520 BCE to 70 CE.]
Here is a little chart:

Descendants	First Temple, Israelite Religion	Post-Temple, Rabbinic Judaism
The people are . . .	. . . a nation living in one area, with tribal distinctions, ruled by a king.	. . . dispersed throughout the world, with no single leader.
The worship is . . .	. . . centralized in the Temple, with animal sacrifice.	. . . dispersed in local synagogues, with purely spiritual worship.
The religious leaders are . . .	. . . priests, who are born into a family or tribe of priests.	. . . rabbis, who are trained according to the standards of the religion.
The holy books are . . .	. . . under development.	. . . the Bible is developed and canonized, and the Talmud and Mishnah augment it.

So what is Second Temple Judaism? Think of it as the midway point between First Temple Israelite religion and Post-Temple Rabbinic Judaism.

But if Second Temple Judaism were a feast, it would be a buffet with many options, rather than one set menu. In Jesus' day, for example, many competing groups were trying to figure out what it meant for the Jewish people to live faithfully as God's people in a changing world. To explore some of the options, check out the articles on: ISRAELITES, JUDEANS, SAMARITANS, ESSENES, PHARISEES, SADDUCEES, ZEALOTS, PRIESTS.

See also: Second Temple Period.

Jezebel \JEHZ-uh-behl\

Status:

Jezebel is wishing she could get her hands around Elijah's scrawny little neck.

Profile

Hometown:	Sidon
Family Stuff:	My dad was king of Sidon and he married me off to Ahab, the king of Israel.
What's in a Name?	It ticks me off that my name has become a slang term for a loose woman. I may be a little corrupt, but I'm no tart!
Turn-offs:	Prophets that are not on my payroll
Favorite Quotation:	"What's yours is mine, and what's mine is mine."

We think that Ethbaal, Jezebel's father, was perfectly happy to pack Jezebel off to the court of Ahab, the king of Israel. See, she was always rather a pain in the neck (or about two feet lower). When she moved into Ahab's palace, along with the new silver and china that they got as wedding presents, Jezebel brought her god Baal with her. She also brought along a bunch of prophets who worshiped her god.

Truth be told, there was already quite a lot of Baal worship going on in Israel, but she got a temple built for Baal in the capital city. And practices like child sacrifice didn't seem to bother her. In the eyes of many Baal worshipers, you couldn't really dedicate the cornerstone of a building without spilling a little blood. (Don't believe us? Just read 1 Kings 16:34).

As soon as she moved in, Jezebel started making plans to improve the menu at the king's table. Ahab was still living like a bachelor, always serving red meat. She decided to plant some veggies and came to the conclusion that the cute little vineyard next to the palace would be a perfect spot. But the owner, Naboth, wouldn't sell. No problem for a queen. She just arranged to have him killed. And then named a salad dressing after him. (Not really.)

The Lord's prophets, especially Elijah, started blogging about Jezebel —her corruption, her bloodshed, her tendency to wear too much makeup. Being a bit sensitive to criticism, Jezebel wanted to serve up for those prophets a big helping of what Naboth had received. Pretty soon, it wasn't safe to be a prophet of the Lord in Israel. But as 1 Kings 18:40 shows, it wasn't safe to be prophet of Baal either.

Key Verse: "There was no one like Ahab, who sold himself to do what was evil in the sight of the LORD, urged on by his wife Jezebel" (1 Kgs 21:25; see also 1 Kgs 16-21).

J

See also: Ahab, Baal.

Job \johb\ (book)

by Anonymous (Old Testament, Poetry, forty-two chapters)

You may have heard it said that "the road to hell is paved with good intentions." For the story of Job this could not be more apropos, as most if not all of the characters in Job's story do seem to wish him well, and hellish suffering is where Job spends most of his story.

Job is a well-to-do man in every sense—healthy, wealthy and theologically wise. He is blessed with family and happiness. Everyone thinks well of Job, even the one who might be considered the pickiest of critics, the Almighty, who says of Job, "There is no one like him on the earth, a blameless and upright man who fears God and turns away from evil." Enter "The Satan" (satan is a Hebrew word that means something like "opponent" or "accuser"). The Satan challenges Job's faithfulness and suggests that if things were not so rosy, Job might not be so blameless and upright—and here the tension of the story builds.

Job is tested, attacked, afflicted and generally made miserable, unto but not quite at the point of death. His faith is challenged and his hope is all but stripped away. Enter Job's wife and friends. The Satan is not the only one to test Job. Job's wife tells him to curse God and die. His friends Eliphaz, Bildad, and Zophar chastise him constantly for his poor attitude. By their good intentions, the friends defend against the idea that God is ultimately the source of all of Job's struggles. Certainly, part of Job's trial is to suffer through good intentions and bad theologies. In the end, Job gets to hear from God who got him into the mess in the first place. Job got an answer from God, but not the one Job was looking for. The book does end like the proverbial country record played backwards—with Job getting back his health, his fortunes, seven sons and three daughters and, one presumes, his dog, and his ATM card.

To be perfectly frank, there are not many likeable characters in this latest of Mr. Anonymous' books, God included. But this difficult book is worth the read. Job wrestles with serious questions of faith in the face of struggle, and where God is when we suffer. This reviewer is confident that when you read Mr. Anonymous' "search for meaning," you will find help for those times when you are frustrated, struggle, doubt, and yet believe.

See also: Job, Poetry.

Job \johb\

Status:
Job is not giving up on God, although for the life of him, he can't figure out why not.

Profile

Hometown:	Uz (not to be confused with Oz)
Interested in:	Making new friends
Turn-offs:	Gambling, Sabeans, lightning, Chaldeans, tornadoes, skin diseases, ash heaps, the day I was born
Favorite Song:	"Patience," by Guns 'n Roses
Turn-ons:	A good, old fashioned argument
Favorite Quotation:	"I'm gonna yell at you, 'cuz I'm mad at you! I CAN'T TAKE IT! Gimme a sign or something! Blow this pain out of me!"—Robert Duvall as Sonny in *The Apostle*.

Job was watching poker on TV when some Texan with a cowboy hat lost all of his chips to a Canadian with a bad haircut, because three 2's came off the deck. One of the Texan's friends said, "That's okay, there must be a reason you lost. When God closes a door, he opens a window."

Job observed this and said to nobody in particular, "I've been there, that's been me." Someone asked, "Which one was you?" Job answered, "I've been the winner. I've been the loser. I've even been the chips. The only one I haven't been is the idiot friend who said it happened for a reason."

Job had won his share of pots. He was the richest guy around, with a great wife and family. And he was holy. He was so holy, in fact, that when his kids threw a party, the next day Job would make a big donation to church in the name of each of his kids, just in case one of his kids had sinned after having one too many.

So, naturally, Job became the chips in a game of poker between God and God's chief prosecuting officer. And just for the record, it isn't fun to be the chips.

And then Job hit the worst run of bad luck a poker player ever had. Between the Sabeans, lightning, the Chaldeans, a tornado, and a nasty skin rash, Job lost his property, his kids, and finally his health.

Job's wife gave him some advice: "Job, curse God and then die."

Job's three friends—Eli, Bill, and Zoey—came over and they gave him some advice: "Job, everything happens for a reason. You must have sinned. So get right with the Man Upstairs and God will give you back your pickup, your fishin' boat, your kids, and your dog."

Job said, "I don't feel like repenting. I feel like arguing."

And so for the next 39 chapters, Job argues with those "friends"—Eli, Bill, and Zoey—plus he argues with another friend (in chapter 32). Finally, Job argues with the Lord God Almighty. It's quite the argument. But in the end, God plays the "I'm All-Powerful and All-Knowing" card and kind of wins the argument. Kind of.

Then God said, "Eli, Bill, and Zoey. Job did the right thing. You guys only talked *about me*. Job talked *to me*. Do you see the difference? True, Job was arguing with me. True, Job came pretty close to smearing my name. But he never gave up on me. And so for the sake of Job, I'll forget how stupid you have been."

"Hey," said Zoey, "We don't say stupid!"

And God thought, *Stupid is as stupid does.* Job's fortunes turned around and he started taking down pots again at the poker table of life.

Key Verse: "I will accept his prayer not to deal with you according to your folly; for you have not spoken to me as is right, as my servant Job has done" (Job 42:8 [our translation]).

See also: Job (book), Poetry.

Joel \johl\ (book)

by Joel Ben-Pethuel (Minor Prophets, three chapters)

"Like a virgin," the ancient prophet known as Joel Ben-Pethuel sang. But don't be confused, Madonna did not plagiarize Mr. Ben-Pethuel. The prophet sang these words: "Lament like a virgin dressed in sackcloth . . . The fields are devastated, the ground mourns" (Joel 1:8, 10). This was no call for men to cross-dress! Instead, Mr. Ben-Pethuel was calling for all the people to join in a worship service of repentance. The land and the people were suffering a desperate crisis. The service of repentance was in the hope of moving the Lord to have mercy on the land and on the people.

Mr. Ben-Pethuel announced that "a great and powerful army" would come, and that by the time it had left, it will have eaten "what the swarming locust left, the hopping locust." Was he announcing the invasion of an army of locusts? (Locusts are the swarming phase of short-horned grasshopper, don't you know.) Or was Mr. B-P announcing the invasion of an army of humans who would be as numerous and devastating as locusts? Flip a coin. We don't know. We wish he were around to ask. If he were, we would also ask him when he lived, because his book doesn't say. Perhaps it was before the exile in 587, or perhaps long after.

But this much is clear. Unlike the prophets Isaiah, Amos, or Micah, Joel Ben-Pethuel had a very high opinion of worship. For him, the act of repenting and the act of worshiping go hand-in-hand. True repentance requires turning to God, ideally in public worship.

One startling aspect of Mr. Ben-Pethuel's work is the promise he delivers—a promise straight from the Lord: "I will pour out my spirit on all flesh; your sons and your daughters shall prophesy . . . Even on the male and female slave, in those days, I will pour out my spirit" (2:28-29). Who knew that the Spirit of the living God could be poured out upon on all people, even those who don't occupy the positions of privilege.

See also: Prophets.

John (The Gospel according to) \jahn\ (book)

By John* (New Testament, Gospels, twenty-one chapters)

Readers looking to get a better glimpse into the mind and heart of Jesus of Nazareth will want to check out The Gospel According to John. When compared to the other three Gospels, John is sparse in terms of relating the details of Jesus' birth, his many miracles, and the content of his public sermons. However, John more than makes up for any perceived shortcomings by offering readers:

- A magnificent prologue about Jesus as co-Creator with God of all things—literally the "Word" by which God spoke existence into being.
- Seven miracles—make that "signs"—rich with messianic meaning.
- Seven theologically autobiographical "I Am" sayings.
- A powerful foot-washing scene.
- A four-chapters-long speech representing Jesus' last words to his followers.
- Along with additional insight into Jesus' arrest, trial, and crucifixion.
- Not to mention some fresh resurrection stories, including one where Jesus cooks up some fish for breakfast!

While it may be true that John's story of Jesus was the last to appear on the literary scene, it is safe to say that John, though last, is certainly not least. Martin Luther was just one of many who have held John in high esteem, claiming that "John's Gospel is one, fine, true, and chief gospel, and far, far to be preferred over the other three . . ."* Luther had good reason to appreciate this Gospel. The "long goodbye" speech (which comes just after the Last Supper) alone is worth the price of admission. The serious reader (and disciple) will find much to chew on here—a veritable feast of tasty teachings about Christ's relationship to the Father, the promised Holy Spirit, and the challenge of the Christian life.

*LW 35:362.

Still, no matter how good this "farewell discourse," even better are the dramatic closing scenes, including a showdown of sorts between Pilate and Jesus: "What is Truth?" versus "I Am the Way, and the Truth, and the Life." John intends the truth about Jesus to appeal to all people everywhere. For example, the inscription above the crucified Christ declares Jesus to be king not only with words written in Hebrew (or Aramaic), but in Latin and Greek as well. Still, no matter how broad the appeal of this gospel, John's intention is focused and personal: "These things are written so that you may come to believe that Jesus is the Messiah, the Son of God, and that through believing you may have life in his name" (John 20:31).

* As with the other Gospels, the author is not identified by name within the text. However, John 21:24 speaks of a disciple "who is testifying to these things and has written them, and we know that his testimony is true." The wording suggests that the Gospel stems from reports originating from the disciple in question. The earliest tradition held that John, son of Zebedee and brother of James, was that disciple.

See also: Jesus.

1, 2, and 3 John

\FUHRST-SEH-kihnd-and-THURHD-JAHN\ (books)

By John (New Testament, Letters, seven chapters)

Readers looking for a solid sermon on Christian community and the commandment to love one another will appreciate 1 John. In addition, readers will find themselves wondering, "Now where have I heard that before?" when they read passages that begin "If we say we have no sin we deceive ourselves" (1 John 1:8) and "Beloved, let us love one another" (1 John 4:7). Readers of 2 and 3 John will appreciate the fact that together they add up to a mere twenty-eight verses.

These three letters form a sort of chronicle of controversy within the Johannine churches—so-called for the popularity of Mr. John's writings there. 1 and 2 John reflect some struggle over the nature of the Christian life, the nature of confession of Christ, and the nature of Jesus' Christ-ship. 3 John deals with the proper and improper response to "prophets" or emissaries sent by "the Elder." While reading these letters may well feel like a stroll through your neighbor's backyard, they provide helpful follow-up material to John's Gospel, and the questions that present themselves as we live life in the wake of Christ's resurrection, and by the power of his Lordship.

See also: Letters (or Epistles).

John the Baptist

\JAHN-thuh-BAP-tihst\

Status:
John is wondering what they're serving up in Herod's palace tonight.

Profile

Hometown:	I live in a desert! You know what this is? Sand! You know what it's gonna be a hundred years from now? It's gonna be sand!!
Political Views:	Anti-monarch ("divine right," my camel!)
Turn-offs:	Dancing, silver tableware, prisons
Turn-ons:	Baths (if you lived in a desert, you would understand)
Job I Would Most Like:	I would love to be the highway-construction guy that holds up the signs that show people when and where to go.
Nickname:	Wingman

Sometimes, the best role for a particular person is the supporting actor rather than the lead. After all, think of the great lines that some of the supporting actors have had over the years. Cuba Gooding Jr. in *Jerry Maguire*: "Show me the money!!" Claude Rains in *Casablanca*: "I'm shocked, shocked to find out gambling is going on in here!" and "Round up the usual suspects." Ted Knight in *Caddyshack*: "The world needs ditch diggers, too."

And, of course, the best supporting actor of them all: John the Baptist. Think of his great lines:

"You brood of vipers! Who warned you to flee from the wrath to come?"

"The one who is more powerful than I is coming after me; I am not worthy to stoop down and untie the thong of his sandals. I have baptized you with water, but he will baptize you with the Holy Spirit."

"Behold the lamb of God who takes away the sin of the world . . . He must increase, but I must decrease."

"I'll take a camel-hair jacket in a 42-long, that black leather belt, and a small bag of locust bon-bons soaked in honey."

John's role was pretty simple. He was to point away from himself and toward Jesus. In the last verses of the Old Testament, God promised that before the "great and terrible day of the LORD," the prophet Elijah would be sent to prepare the way (see Mic 4:5-6). John played Elijah's role (that is why he wore the same funny camel-and-leather clothes as Elijah and ate a prophet's locust-based diet).

And like many-a-good supporting role, John had to go offstage before the end, so that the leading actor would be the focus. So John railed against King Herod's sins. As a reward, Herod threw him in prison and then had his head served up on a silver platter.

But John played his part to perfection. Looking back, he played Elijah's role. Looking ahead, he pointed to Jesus. Who took the sin of the world away.

Key Verse: "John testified to him and cried out, 'He who comes after me ranks ahead of me'" (John 1:15; see also Matt 3:1-17; 9:1-17; John 1:1-34; 3:22-36).

See also: Elizabeth, Herod Antipas, Zechariah.

Jonah \JOH-nuh\ (book)

by Anonymous (Old Testament, Minor Prophets, four chapters)

Although this fishy tale is found amongst the minor prophets, the book is unlike most other prophetic books, because it is not a collection of a prophet's messages. Instead, it is a short story about a disobedient prophet who becomes successful, even though he doesn't want to be successful. The book is inside-out and upside-down. When the main character, Jonah, should be obedient, he runs away. When he should try to save his skin, he sleeps. When he should be praying for rescue, he sings praise. When he should sing praise, he curses God's faithfulness. When he should be happy, he is mad. And then there's chapter two and the ultimate *deus ex machina*: a big fish and an oddly-placed psalm.

Since the book ends with a question, so will we: Does the runaway prophet learn the lesson that God wants him to learn? Make that two questions: Do you learn the lesson that God wants you to learn?

See also: Jonah, Prophets.

Jonah \JOH-nuh\

Status:
Jonah is trying to figure out what a bush has to do with the most evil city on the face of the world.

Profile

Profession:	Prophet (after some convincing)
Turnoffs:	Foreigners, the Assyrian empire, the ocean, fish guts, lack of shade
Favorite Song:	"Runaway" by Del Shannon: ". . . run run run run runaway . . ."
Favorite Show:	*Mission Impossible*

J

So, Jonah opened up the envelope that spelled out his super-secret mission from God. And the tape recorder started playing: "Your mission, Jonah, should you choose to accept it, is to preach to the evil city of Nineveh, the capital of the Assyrian Empire, so that they may repent and then I won't destroy them. As always, if you are captured. . . ." Then the tape recorder self-destructed. And Jonah? He chose not to accept his mission.

And then Jonah ran. Nineveh was due east, so Jonah caught the first ship toward the west—running away from God, from God's mission, and from Nineveh. Why? Because Jonah hated Nineveh on account of the great evil that Nineveh had done. He didn't want them to repent, because he did the math like this: If Nineveh is destroyed, there will be less evil in the world. And if there is less evil, fewer people will suffer and be murdered. Besides, Ninevah had it coming.

To make a long story short, God pulled a few strings (a fish story in itself). The next thing Jonah knew, he was standing a few clicks from Nineveh. And God said, "Your mission, Jonah—and *you will* accept it!—is to preach to the evil city of Nineveh, so that they may repent and then I won't destroy them." Jonah preached. The City repented. And God didn't destroy them.

And was Jonah ever FURIOUS!! He said, "See God, this is why I ran away. I knew you would do this. I knew that you are a forgiving God, and that's just what I don't like about you. How can you forgive such an evil city? Grace is all good and fine, but forgiving Nineveh is a little too much grace." Then Jonah sat down beneath a little desert bush and, when the bush wilted and died, Jonah felt sad.

And God said, "Jonah, Jonah, Jonah. You love that little bush. Shouldn't I love Nineveh, which has 150,000 people—not to mention all the livestock?" Jonah got the point. But that didn't mean he had to like it.

Key Verse: "That is why I fled to Tarshish at the beginning; for I knew that you are a gracious God and merciful, slow to anger, and abounding in steadfast love, and ready to relent from punishing" (Jonah 4:3).

See also: **Jonah (book), Prophets.**

Jordan River \JOHR-duhn-RIH-vuhr\

A good place to raise up your Ebenezer, or to see a baptism.

The Jordan River runs from a little lake north of the Sea of Galilee, called Lake Huleh, south to the Dead Sea, and marks the boundary of Israel. It was the site of the reenactment of the Red Sea parting, when Joshua—taking over for Moses—led the people of Israel into the Promised Land. After passing through with miraculously dry feet, the Israelites piled up twelve stones there as a monument to God's help (called an "ebenezer"; see Josh 4:9). This second parting of the waters moment brought the Israelites full circle—the waters had parted in the Exodus allowing them to escape the land of slavery, and parted again as the first act of Israel's entry into the Promised Land.

The Jordan was also the site of another miraculous event. It was in the Jordan that Jesus was baptized by John. In that event it was the heavens that parted and God said of Jesus, "This is my Son, the Beloved, with whom I am well pleased" (Matt 3:17). The significance of the Jordan for us is that it was in that moment that we were united with Jesus—in a baptism like his and a new life like his (Rom 6:3-4). It was in the Jordan River that our exodus from the land of sin and death and our entry into the promised land of life everlasting was begun—and ended. Who knew that a river so far away could mean so much?

Extra! Extra! Read All About It!!!—In spirituals, the Jordan River is described as "deep and wide." Not so much in real life, where it is more like shallow and narrow. But the artistic license is cool, because in those songs, the Jordan River functions artistically as a spiritual boundary between life and death. And crossing *that* boundary is indeed a deep and wide happening.

See also: Jesus, John the Baptist, Mark (The Gospel according to), Naaman.

Joseph (husband of Mary)

\JOH-sihf\

Status: Joseph is tired of everybody snickering behind his back when he's walking around with his pregnant fiancée.

Profile

Hometown:	Bethlehem, originally, then Nazareth, then Egypt, then Nazareth again
Turn-offs:	Kings, divine messengers
If the world were perfect . . .	. . . door-to-door salesmen would not try to sell you something, they would just give you gifts. Like gold or frankincense.
Favorite Song:	"If I Were a Carpenter and You Were a Lady" (I like the rustic Johnny and June Carter Cash version)

One night, a dream interrupted a perfectly good night of sleep: "Joseph, you may already be a winner! Just click on 'yes,' to learn what you've won." Joseph knew that he shouldn't click yes in response to unwanted spam, but it was a dream, so he didn't have a choice. And besides, the dream came from God. So he really didn't have a choice. "Your wife will bear a child, who will save his people from their sins! Name him Jesus, which will fulfill the old promise that a virgin shall give birth to a son who will be named Emmanuel."

"Wait," said Joseph, "I don't get it. How will naming a child Jesus fulfill the promise that a child will be named Emmanuel? That makes no sense!"

"Yes, it does, because Emmanuel means, 'God is with us," and your son Jesus will be God-in-the-flesh. He will save all people from their sins."

"You're right, I have already won."

"Well," said the messenger from God, "It won't all be donuts and apple juice. The kings of the world, like Herod, won't really dig someone who will contest their rule. So you'll have to hide out in Egypt for a while, but I'll send some wise guys with some gifts to help you pay for the trip."

Key Verse: "'Look, the virgin shall conceive and bear a son, and they shall name him Emmanuel,' which means, 'God with us'" (Matt 1:23; see also Matt 1:18—2:23).

See also: Bethlehem, Gabriel, Jesus.

Joseph (son of Jacob) \JOH-sihf\

Status:
Joseph is looking for his coat.

Profile

Family:	Too many. I mean that I have too many brothers and sisters to mention—and, for my taste, just flat out too many brothers. I guess Benjamin is okay.
Aliases:	Where I come from, they call me the Dreamer. In Egypt, Pharaoh calls me Zaphenath-paneah (I don't know what it means, but the fact he gave me a name is a good sign).
Turn-offs:	Brothers, pits, slave-traders, other people's wives
Turn-ons:	Andrew Lloyd Webber musicals
Favorite Quotation:	"Be fearful when others are greedy. Be greedy when others are fearful."—Warren Buffet
Favorite TV show:	*CSI*

Joseph was a jerk: full of himself, arrogant, self-important, special... and a tattle-tale to boot. Although he had eleven brothers, Joseph was his father's favorite. And he never let his brothers forget it. He would flaunt the special gifts that his father gave him—like the professionally tailored sport coat he would wear to Sabbath dinner, while his brothers had to settle for discount suits they bought over the Internet. And he would go on and on about the dreams he had—the one where his brother's wheat bundles all bowed down to his own wheat bundle. Rubbing it in, Joseph explained how his wheat bundle hovered in the air to receive the brothers' adoring worship. And one time, Joseph narc'd on his brothers, telling daddy when they lost a sheep.

So one day, when the brothers got him alone out in the field, one said, "Hey, here comes the Dreamer with his special sport coat!" Another said, "Let's kill him and throw him in a pit." Then Judah said, "We could, but we'll make more money if we sell him. Hey, check it out! Slave traders!" To cover their tracks, they planted some false evidence, which fooled their dad. Next stop for Joseph: Egypt.

After being sold to an Egyptian named Potiphar, everything Joseph touched turned to gold (not literally; that would be King Midas, whose story isn't in the Bible). Potiphar liked Joseph, but so did Potiphar's wife. When Joseph wouldn't sleep with her, she planted some false evidence on him, which fooled Potiphar. Next stop: Prison.

In prison, everything Joseph touched turned to gold (not literally, it was a prison). Joseph even set up a little micro-business interpreting dreams for the other prisoners. His dream-interpreting skills eventually brought him to the attention of Pharaoh, who was having dreams about seven fat cows being eaten by seven skinny cows. Joseph said to Pharaoh, "There will be seven years of bull market, followed by seven years of bear market. Invest wisely, grasshopper." Pharaoh replied, "My dream was about cows, not bulls, bears, or grasshoppers . . . you do the investing for me." Next stop: the Penthouse!

Meanwhile, back in the Promised Land . . . a famine. Joseph's brothers were starving (having sold into slavery the one person who might have known a drought was coming and planned ahead). They hitchhiked down to Egypt, and tried to get a loan from the famed financial planner, Zaphenath-paneah (they didn't know it was Joseph, since he wasn't wearing the sport coat). So Joseph planted some false evidence on them and had them arrested.

Joseph said, "Just kidding. It was all God's plan. Group hug! How 'bout a Fresca?"

So the whole family moved to Egypt. Which is (literally) where the book of Genesis ends.

Key Verse: "Even though you intended to do harm to me, God intended it for good" (Gen 50:20a; see also Gen 37, 39–50).

See also: Jacob, Egyptians, Pharaoh.

Joshua \JAH-shoo-wuh\ (book)

by Anonymous (Old Testament, History, thirty-four chapters)

An epic tale of swashbuckling conquests, daring spies, unlikely victories, and a hooker with a heart (and faith) of gold, Joshua is a book sure to stir the imagination and delight both the eyes and the soul of the reader.

On the surface, Joshua is the story of Moses' successor. Following the Exodus from Egypt and disheartening years of wilderness wandering, we find the Israelites on the verge of having their dream-cum-nightmare-cum-dream at long last come true. They stand on the brink of the Promised Land. They sit poised to taste honey and drink deep draughts of refreshing milk. And yet they find themselves leaderless, a flock without a shepherd to borrow the biblical metaphor. Into the breach is thrust the title character, Joshua son of Nun—hero of the battle of Amalek, espier of the land of Canaan, Moses' own chosen, appointed and anointed heir.

The book of Joshua, which some consider the sixth installment of the much vaunted Pentateuch series, lays out the fulfillment of God's promises to Israel—the Promised Land is conquered town by town, people by people, and the tribes of Israel are allotted their share of territory. The victory Joshua won at Jericho, a victory sounded and in fact achieved by the novel means of the trumpet blast (a device that is normally a small-scale instrument of torture in the hands of teenagers rather than an instrument of mass destruction in the hands of priests), and after his spies had escaped their reconnoiter of the city with the help of the prostitute Rahab, is in many regards the climactic story in the book, even though it occurs in the sixth chapter. Jericho is captured and destroyed according to God's instructions, and ultimately by God's doing. This serves to highlight the primary claim of the book, which is not that Joshua is the finest of leaders because of his many virtues, but that all he achieves is on account of his God, who grants him the victory.

The postmodern reader of this pre-modern (okay, pre- pre- pre- pre- pre-modern) tale might well be caught up by this story—either swept away by the graphic and larger-than-life scale of the stories or turned off by what may appear to be its cavalier presentation of Israel's chosen-ness—and miss the point that drives Mr. Anonymous' gripping narrative. At every turn it is God who is working on Joshua's and Israel's behalf. And at every turn the promise that begins Joshua's work is well kept in mind: "I will be with you," God says to Joshua, "I will not fail you or forsake you."

While Mr. Anonymous does not write in a style that is easily described as "feel good" or particularly "family friendly" (were Joshua's tale made into a movie it would surely be rated NC17), the work does accomplish its purpose, and ably. Joshua presents a picture of a life (both of a man and of a people) lived in relationship with God—God who is there for Joshua, there for Israel, and there for you. Joshua is a wonderful read, highly recommended.

See also: Exodus and Wilderness Period, Jericho, Joshua.

Joshua \JAH-shoo-wuh\

Status:
Joshua is trying to forget what went down at Gibeath-haaraloth (see Josh 5:2-8).

Profile

Hometown:	Bethlehem of Judea
What's in a name?	My name means, "The Lord saves." I actually share the name with a guy who is a little more famous—"Jesus" is the Greek form of my name.
Hardest Thing That I Ever Had to Learn:	That being "strong and courageous" actually sometimes means doing things that don't look strong or courageous
Favorite Album:	*The Wall* by Pink Floyd
Favorite Song:	"Serve Somebody" by Bob Dylan
People I Admire:	Saint Peter, Philip Melanchthon, Harry Truman, Aaron Rodgers—people who had to follow in the footsteps of a legend

It was late at night, and Joshua limped up to the campfire. Out of respect, the younger men made room for him. After he settled his bones on a rock, one of them asked, "Joshua, what was the greatest moment of your life?"

"It must have been when you took over for Moses?" suggested one.

"I'll bet it was when you led the people into the promised land," said another.

"No, I'll bet it was when you captured the city of Jericho—tell us again about how Rahab the prostitute helped out!" interjected a third.

"What about conquering the land and setting up the twelve tribes each in their own area?"

Joshua was quiet for a while before he spoke.

"None of those things. And all of them," he began. "You have to decide who you are going to serve in this life. You can serve yourself.

Or money. Or fame. Or a nice, lean piece of roast mutton." His listeners gave him a courtesy laugh for the lame movie quote reference before Joshua continued. "Or you can serve God. When God called me to replace Moses, I was told: 'Be strong and courageous.' I thought that meant I was supposed to fight with the sword and defend the people. But instead of attacking Jericho, God made me march around the city seven days in a row with a bunch of priests blowing on horns and singing the Sabbath liturgy. And let me tell you, those priests weren't exactly trained at Juilliard, if you know what I mean.

"But God was teaching a lesson. Not to trust in sword, or bow, or chariot, or in myself. None of these things is God. Only the Lord is God. So you have to know who you gonna serve." (Cue Bob Dylan tune.)

Key Verse: "Now fear the LORD and serve him with all faithfulness. Throw away the gods your forefathers worshiped beyond the River and in Egypt, and serve the LORD. . . . As for me and my household, we will serve the LORD" (Josh 24:14-15; see the book of Joshua).

See also: Exodus and Wilderness Period, Jericho, Joshua (book).

Judah \joo-duh\

Status:

Judah has changed from being unrighteously angry to being righteously embarrassed.

Profile

Fun Fact:	From me the tribe of Judah descended . . . which became the Kingdom of Judea . . . which became the province of Judea . . . from which the Jewish faith takes its name.
Favorite Quotation:	"Happiness is having a large, loving, caring, close-knit family in another city."—George Burns

See TAMAR.

Judas \joo-duhs\

Status:
Judas is wondering why nobody calls their child Judas, what with the popularity of Bible names and all.

Profile

Profession:	Treasurer
Pet Peeve:	Wishy-washy, do-nothing, ride-the-fence type people
Places I would like to visit:	The Ford Theater, the Roman Senate
Favorite Musical:	*Jesus Christ Superstar*—at least I get some sympathy in that piece, not to mention the title song!

Talk about a bad career move. Betraying the Lord and Savior, Jesus Christ, for thirty silver pieces. Even when Judas wanted to do something good—like giving money to the poor—it came off as a slimy, rotten, bad move. The story goes like this: in the weeks before the crucifixion, a woman anointed Jesus for death by pouring expensive oil on his head. Judas objected, "Why wasn't this perfume sold and the money given to the poor?"*

But why did Judas do it—betray Jesus? Well, nobody knows, but here is a guess: Judas didn't really think that Jesus would die. Judas knew that Jesus was the Son of God. And he knew that if he wanted, Jesus could simply "appeal to my Father, and he [would] send more than twelve legions of angels" to rescue him. We think that Judas wanted Jesus to be a drop-the-smack-on-the-Romans kind of Messiah, rather than a forgive-your-enemies-and-pray-for-them Messiah. We think that Judas wanted to join a kingdom-of-God-on-earth church, rather than a thy-kingdom-come-thy-will-be-done kind of church. Even though Jesus had announced three times that he was

---

*This story doesn't really fit here, but Jesus said, "Wherever the gospel is preached throughout the world, what she has done will also be told, in memory of her"—so we put this story in, in memory of that unnamed woman, who showed-up Judas and anointed Jesus for death.

going to be arrested, crucified, and raised from the dead, Judas just could not find any way to see a dead guy on a tree as God's right-hand man. Here's our theory: Judas grew tired of waiting for Jesus to be the kind of Messiah that Judas wanted, so he figured that he would force Jesus to be that kind of Messiah by putting Jesus in the position where Jesus just *had to* use a little power and might.

But Jesus didn't do what Judas wanted. Because that's not the kind of God Jesus is.

Sadly, Judas didn't stick around to see how the whole thing ended. Once he realized that Jesus wasn't going to do his Harry Houdini act and escape and overthrow the Romans, Judas called it quits by hanging himself. Although it was the end of Judas, maybe it didn't have to be. As Paul wrote, "For I am convinced that neither death, nor life, nor angels, nor rulers, nor things present, nor things to come, nor powers, nor height, nor depth, nor anything else in all creation, will be able to separate us from the love of God in Christ Jesus our Lord" (Rom 8:38-39).

Key Verse: "[Judas] went up to [Jesus] at once and said, 'Rabbi!' and kissed him" (Mark 14:45).

See also: Jesus, Holy Week, Mark (The Gospel according to).

Jude \jood\

By Jude Josephson (New Testament, Letters, one chapter)

You know how a town can be so small that they'll say "Don't blink, or you'll miss it"? That's Jude. This is a little tract warning about certain false teachers and their libertine ways. Mr. Josephson addresses those who deny that Jesus is indeed the promised Messiah. He urges those who share in salvation to persevere in the face of slander, false teaching, and the temptation to abandon the gospel. Mr. Josephson uses examples from Israel's history to make and strengthen his argument, most notably the Exodus of which he writes, "I desire to remind you, though you are fully informed, that the Lord, who once and for all saved a people out of the land of Egypt, afterward destroyed those who did not believe." To summarize Mr. Josephson's argument: you are saved in Christ, but you can be un-saved (or is it de-saved?) if you turn from Christ; so don't, and, while you're at it, help keep others saved, too.

There may be more to say in review of Mr. Josephson's little letter Jude, but we must leave off here, lest we write a review longer than the letter itself.

See also: Letters (or Epistles).

Judeans \joo-DEE-unz\ or \joo-DĀ-uhnz\

Residents of the southern part of the promised land (a.k.a.—the only patch of desert in the entire Middle East with no oil under it).

After the Exodus and that long, forty-year hike without directions in the desert, when the Israelites settled in the promised land, the Tribe of Judah was assigned the seat at the back of the classroom, where the air was musty and the seat was uncomfortable. The region assigned to Judah was a mountainous area, with poorer agricultural ground and still poorer access to trade routes. But its boundaries included Jerusalem. So call it even.

After the kingdom was split into two about 922 BCE, the Kingdom of Judah (a.k.a. the Southern Kingdom) managed to survive under a number of less than adequate kings. That all ended in 587 BCE when the Judeans were carted off to Babylon. About fifty years later many returned to Jerusalem. Jewish people today trace their lineage back to these Judeans.

See also: Israelites, Monarchy.

Judges \JUHJ-ihz\ (book)

by Anonymous (Old Testament, History, twenty-one chapters)

With a title that might seem to imply that a history of Supreme Court justices (or of mothers-in-law) is in the offing, the book of Judges will not excite the interest of every potential reader. The use of the title "Judges" may prove troubling to some because of the way we often use this word in our day-to-day parlance. What is important to know is that in the genre of biblical literature a "judge" is less a somber person armed with a gavel and wearing black robes—flowing, graceful, striking—and more a heroic leader, a dynamic, charismatic, military and spiritual leader armed with faith in the Almighty. "Judges" may present some initial confusion; one ought not, however, be dissuaded by the somewhat lifeless heading of this robust and engaging collection.

The book of Judges is just this—a collection of short stories all of which follow a similar and, after reading just a few of them, predictable pattern. Set in the days when Israel was a loosely organized confederation of tribes with no king, these short stories, collected by the prolific Mr. Anonymous, struck this reviewer as similar to the regional tales of heroic figures that one might find in any area (for example John Henry the "steel driving man" in West Virginia, Paul Bunyan the great lumberjack of the Midwest, or cowboy Pecos Bill from Texas). While Mr. Anonymous does not explicitly credit the oral traditions of the twelve tribes of Israel, it is clear that his heroes and heroines are assembled from a variety of tribal sources—Othniel is from the tribe of Judah, Ehud from Benjamin, Deborah from Naphtali, Gideon from Manasseh, and Samson is a Danite. This anthology of heroic tales serves as a reservoir of paradigmatic and inspirational figures meant to move and unite the people of Israel. These are shared stories, then, recalling a time before Israel was truly united, form a patch-work quilt of communal identity, which Mr. Anonymous has masterfully joined together into a united whole. The characters are paradigms but not necessarily role models—they teach us who we are, but necessarily who we should be.

The means of this joining is the pattern that Mr. Anonymous employs for each of the stories he retells. The pattern is as follows: Israel is disobedient, doing "evil in the sight of the Lord"; Israel is handed over to a foreign power; Israel cries for help; God appoints a judge; Israel is delivered; Israel has peace (usually for about forty years). The reader of the Judges collection is confronted with this continuing problem of sin and its consequences, and is at once warned against sin, and promised that God will deliver him/her from sin's wages. A must-read for any student of the Old Testament, and indeed of the Bible.

See also: Judges (Period of).

Judges \JUHJ-ihz\ (Period of)

The time in Israel's history when God experimented with the herding of cats.

"In those days there was no king in Israel; all the people did what was right in their own eyes" (Jgs 21:25). That's how the book of Judges judges this time in the life of Israel. This summary, the very last verse in the book of Judges, is reached after Israel has endured and/or endorsed constant warfare, idolatry, banditry, treachery, rape, sanctioned kidnapping, the sacrifice of a virgin daughter as a burnt offering, and some seriously messed up family systems. Sounds like the most wonderful kind of nation, doesn't it?

The real problem is this: God is king of Israel. The Psalms (like Psalm 97) say this and God says this (in 1 Sam 8:7). But people don't usually see it that way. And in Judges the people are constantly giving their loyalty, worship and love to other "gods." So at least in the eyes of the Israelites, they have no king. Just like Judges 21:25 says.

"Nature abhors a vacuum," Spock says to Lt. Valeris in *Star Trek VI*. And so when there is no visible king, everyone tries to act as if they are king. It's a little bit like the "king of my own castle" idea common to all of us. And so all of Israel's problems, according to the book of Judges, are because "in those days Israel had no king."

One story in Judges makes this point more clearly than any other. In Judges 9, you can read about Abimelech who was so into doing what was right in his own eyes (that is, pursuing his own "best life now") that he decided to make himself king. In the end his quest for kingship got him a millstone dropped on his head (and not just any millstone—an *upper*-millstone). So, let that be a lesson to you.

The stories that are set during the period of the Judges set the stage for Israel's push for a king. They want a king so that they can be like the other nations. Perhaps not coincidentally, the book of Judges is followed by the book of Ruth, which is set during the period of the Judges, and introduces the great grandmother of Israel's dynastic king David.

See also: Judges (book).

Junia \joo-nee-uh\

Status:
Junia is prominent among the apostles, thank you very much.

Profile

Married:	To Andronicus
Profession:	Apostle
Fun Fact:	My husband and I were "in Christ" before Paul was. Not that I'm bragging about it, but Paul's the one who made a big deal about it.
Favorite Song:	"You Never Knew Me" by Mark Gruebel
Turn offs:	Prisons, sexist pigs

Junia is mentioned only once in all of Scripture. So what did she do to deserve her own entry in this little biblical dictionary? It isn't so much what she did, but who she was, what was done to her during her life by enemies of the faith, and what was done to her after her death by the faithful.

Who was she? An apostle. It says so right there in Rom 16:7. That's right. She (a woman) was an apostle. A leader of the early church. And not just any leader but a prominent and early leader. It is a safe guess that Paul became a Christian sometime around the year 35 CE (Jesus may have been crucified and raised around 30 CE). This means that Junia was among the earliest apostles. And, as Paul says, she was a prominent apostle. So, without a doubt, women could be apostles in the early church. And thus women can be deacons, teachers, pastors, and bishops.

What was done to her during her life by enemies of the faith? Along with Paul and her husband, she was imprisoned for her faith.

What was done to her after her life by the faithful? They tried to give Junia a virtual sex-change operation. If you read some translations—such as the Revised Standard Version or New International Version—they refer to her as "Junias" (which is a male name). That is because after the New Testament was completed, in both later Greek and Latin versions, Junia's name was changed to Junius (a male name). Why? Well, because people just assumed that a woman couldn't be an apostle.

But in the best and oldest copies of the Greek New Testament that we have, Junia is a female. And she is an apostle. A prominent one.

Key Verse: "Greet Andronicus and Junia, my relatives who were in prison with me; they are prominent among the apostles, and they were in Christ before I was" (Rom 16:7).

See also: **Paul (Saul of Tarsus), Romans.**

Kingdom of Judah

\KEENG-duhm-uhv-JOO-duh\ (period of)

Judah, the fourth-born son of Jacob and Leah, would have been proud—proud!—to learn that a kingdom had been named after him and his tribe. Also known as the "Southern Kingdom," the Kingdom of Judah followed on the heels of the United Monarchy. The United Monarchy became the Non-United Monarchy when, around 922 BCE, ten of Israel's twelve tribes seceded from the Union as it were (see 1 Kgs 12). The secessionists formed the Kingdom of Israel, a.k.a. the Northern Kingdom, while the tribes of Judah and Benjamin continued to control Jerusalem and the territory to the south. The ensuing "civil war" lasted about sixty years. The Kingdom of Judah hung around for about 350 years or so, until around 587 BCE, when it became the Babylonian Province formerly known as the Kingdom of Judah.

See also: Monarchy.

1 and 2 Kings \FUHRST-and-SEH-kihnd-KEENGZ\ (books)

by Anonymous (Old Testament, History, forty-seven chapters)

Kings reads like a series of editorials written by as biased, aggressive, and critical of an editor as one can imagine. Mr. Anonymous, the author of the Kings duology, is ruthless in his evaluations of the kings of both the Northern (Israel) and the Southern (Judah) Kingdoms. It is as though he were writing for the Jerusalem Press

Times Gazette, taking every opportunity to lambast and otherwise dress-down the current administration in his column. But Mr. Anonymous' tone seems justified. In a stinging rebuke, this master of the theological press' voice characterizes one unlucky monarch as doing "what was evil in the sight of the LORD, following the abominable practices of the nations that the LORD drove out before the people of Israel" (2 Kgs 21:2). No ruler is safe from the righteous judgments of Mr. Anonymous' history, and precious few (Asa, Josiah, and Hezekiah are examples) receive a favorable evaluation.

The body of Kings is made up of abbreviated stories about the two kingdoms, which were gathered from oral tradition or from older sources that unfortunately have not been preserved (that means they were burned like your old flame burned your old love letters . . . you hope). While reading Kings as a book—that is, chapter by chapter trying to follow a story-line or plot—may prove difficult because of the abrupt narrative style of the work, most of the vignettes are brief enough to read as one's morning coffee cools. And this is often the best strategy—read individual stories and think about them. Kings also covers a number of important events in Israel's history—the building of the Temple by Solomon, the confrontation of Elijah with the 450 prophets of Baal, the appearance of the prophet Isaiah during Hezekiah's illness, and of course the defeats of both Israel and Judah.

As with other of Mr. Anonymous' writings, the title "Kings" may be questioned. In these volumes it is more the recurring appearance, intervention, and importance of prophetic figures that ties the stories of disparate kings together. In fact the stories of Elijah and Elisha (which span 1 Kings 17 through 2 Kings 9) are the glue that holds the two volumes together. For this reason, religious bloggers throughout generations have called these books (along with Joshua–Samuel) the "former prophets."

See also: Monarchy.

Lamentations \LAM-ihn-TĀ-shuhnz\

by Anonymous (Old Testament, Major Prophets, five chapters)

"How lonely sits the city that once was full of people! How like a widow she has become, she that was great among the nations!" Thus begins the sorrowful book of Lamentations. The book contains five poems that weep over the destruction of Jerusalem and her people in 587 BCE. The first four poems are alphabetic acrostics—each verse begins with a successive letter of the Hebrew alphabet. The last poem is a poignant prayer for restoration. Little is known of Mr. Anonymous, but he must have been a survivor of the destruction who wrote sometime before the end of the exile (c. 539 BCE). Lamentations is the perfect book for cheerful people looking for a reason to feel down. Lamentations also demonstrates that, for the believer, things like sadness, mourning, and grief, as well a sense of abandonment by God, coupled with a trusting hope in God, are all within the range of normal.

See also: Prophets.

Law \law\

Depending on your perspective, either a realistic list of behaviors that God rightfully expects of your neighbor, or a demanding list of ideals that God somewhat unrealistically expects you to fulfill.

Can you count to two? Good. The concept of "two" is helpful when considering the law.

There are two types of law in the Bible. *Absolute* (rules that apply at all times and in all places—things "never" or "always" to do) and *casuistic* (rules that apply in certain circumstances—"if" this happens, "then" do this).

These laws are expressed in two ways. *Positive* laws tell us what we should do; *negative* laws tell us what we should not do.

These laws govern two sets of relationship. The *vertical* laws govern our relationship with God; the *horizontal* laws govern our relationship with our neighbors.

L

These Biblical laws have two uses. The *civil* use of the law functions to show people how to live civilly with each other; the *theological* use of the law shows us (when we fail to live up to demands of the law) that we need God's mercy, forgiveness, and love. [Note: Some Christians understand that there is a "third use of the law" for believers only, but it seems to us that such a "third use" is merely the first use dressed up in churchy clothes. Besides, if we added a third use here, it would wreck the whole "two" structure that we have going.]

See also: Gospel.

Lazarus \LAZ-uh-ruhs\

Status:
Lazarus is wondering about this bill from the funeral home.

Profile

Hometown:	Bethany
Pet Peeve:	People who are late. It's called a watch, people! Be on time! Someone may be depending on you.
Family:	I've got two sisters, Mary and Martha, who are great, even though they sometimes get into it with each other about doing chores.
Favorite Movie Line:	"I'm Back"—Arnold Schwarzenegger in *The Terminator*
If I had another life . . .	Well, funny you should ask, but I think I would be a funeral director. I've got a feel for it, you know?

One of the harshest verses in the Bible is this: "Though Jesus loved Martha and her sister [Mary] and Lazarus, after having heard that Lazarus was ill, he stayed two days longer in the place where he was" (John 11:5-6). Wait a minute. What? Lazarus was really sick, so why couldn't Jesus—who made the lame walk, the blind see, the deaf hear, and turned lepers into walking advertisements for skin care products—put a wiggle on it to heal his beloved friend?

When Lazarus died, his sisters were on hand, but his friend Jesus was not. Perhaps one of the last things that Lazarus heard before going all rigor mortis was one of his sisters saying, "What's keeping Jesus?" The next thing Lazarus heard was this: "Lazarus, come out!" It was Jesus. Four days late. But right on time.

John's Gospel doesn't report Lazarus's words as he came out of the tomb. But you can imagine he may have gone something like this: "Who put me in this tomb? I feel like a mummy! Mary! Martha! This is a terrible trick to play on a guy who's sick in bed!" But his sisters were too busy crying and hugging him to argue. They probably didn't even mind the smell.

Key Verse: "I am the resurrection and the life. Those who believe in me, even though they die, will live, and everyone who lives and believes in me will never die" (John 11:25-26; see also John 11).

See also: **Jesus, John (The Gospel according to), Martha.**

Leah \LEE-uh\

Status:
Leah is loved by God.

Profile

Family:	The family members most important to me are my sons, Reuben, Simeon, Levi, and Judah.
Fun Fact:	My son, Levi, became the ancestor of Israel's priests, while Judah became the ancestor of Israel's kings. Not bad for a wife that wasn't really wanted.

Poor Leah. Never loved as much as her sister Rachel, never wanted as much as her sister, never valued as much as her sister. Except by God, who blessed her. Always treated poorly and used. Except by God, who blessed her.

Leah's father, Laban, used her as a chip in a game of high stakes poker with Jacob. Jacob worked for Laban for seven years so that he could marry Rachel, but Laban played bait and switch. Rachel was the bait; Leah was the switch. After the seven years were up, Jacob married Laban's daughter, but only found out after the pastor had said "man and wife" that Laban had swapped Leah for Rachel. So Jacob worked seven more years, and then married Rachel.

Leah was a second-class citizen in her own house, with Jacob loving Rachel more than Jacob loved her.

But she wasn't a second-class citizen in God's eyes. God saw her suffering. And as God is wont to do, God blessed her. She became the mother of four sons, each of whom led a tribe of Israel.

Key Verse: "When the Lord saw that Leah was unloved, he opened her womb . . ." (Gen 29:31; see also Gen 29).

See also: Jacob, Rachel.

Letters (or Epistles) \LEHD-uhrz\ \ee-PIH-suhlz\

What your mom is really wishing you would send her (not via e-mail or text message, thank you, dear), and one way that God still speaks to us through the apostles.

A big chunk of the New Testament is made up of letters; letters written by Paul, letters written by someone like Paul, letters by James and John... letters to congregations (in Thessalonica and Rome), letters to groups of folks (like the troublemakers in Corinth), letters to individuals (like Timothy, Titus and Philemon), and even letters to a group of churches (like Galatians). Letters, letters, letters.

The letters in the New Testament are also the best source we have about life in the early church, right after the time of Jesus. Some of these letters were the first parts of the New Testament to be written—written before the Gospels, even though the Gospels talk about Jesus, who lived before the letters were written. The letters in the New Testament were originally written to specific congregations or individuals but, because of their subject matter (and in some cases because of their author), these letters were circulated to others and before long built up a good bit of steam in the influence and authority department. The New Testament letters deal with matters of faith, life together, the gospel, conflicts about true and false doctrine, vocation, and the promise of the world to come. We who read these letters now are a part of this circulation that has continued for centuries. While we were not the intended recipients of Paul's letter to the Christians in Rome, or of James's letter to the "twelve tribes in the dispersion," these letters have been handed down to us as important witnesses to the gospel and sources for our own struggles with faith, life together, and the meaning of relationship with Jesus.

So here's what we suggest. Open up your Bible to Romans 1:7 and right after the words "To all God's beloved in Rome," pencil in the place where you live. Then turn to 1 Timothy 1:2 and right after the words "To Timothy, my loyal child in the faith," write in your name. 'Cause these letters are for you too.

See also: Paul (Saul of Tarsus).

Levites \LEE-vīts\

Israelite priests, who preferred to dress soul-ly in denim.

You may have a rather narrow view of what a priest is and how one becomes a priest. Back in Old Testament times, you didn't become a priest; you were born one. If you were born into the Tribe of Levi, you became a priest. And when God published the assigned-seating chart of the Holy Land, unlike other tribes, the Levites weren't given a patch of ground. Instead, "The Lord" was their assigned seat. As one Levite wrote, "The LORD is my chosen portion . . . The boundary lines have fallen for me in pleasant places" (Ps 16:5-6).

To mix our metaphors, the Levites were like salt. They were sprinkled around, acting as priests throughout the land, wherever people needed their religious care. They led rituals, played musical instruments for worship festival, presided at sacrifices, they taught and interpreted God's law, and they made denim jeans (not really).

After the Romans destroyed the Second Temple around 70 CE, the Levites eventually disappeared. In Judaism, rabbis took over the spiritual reins. In Christianity, pastors and monks.

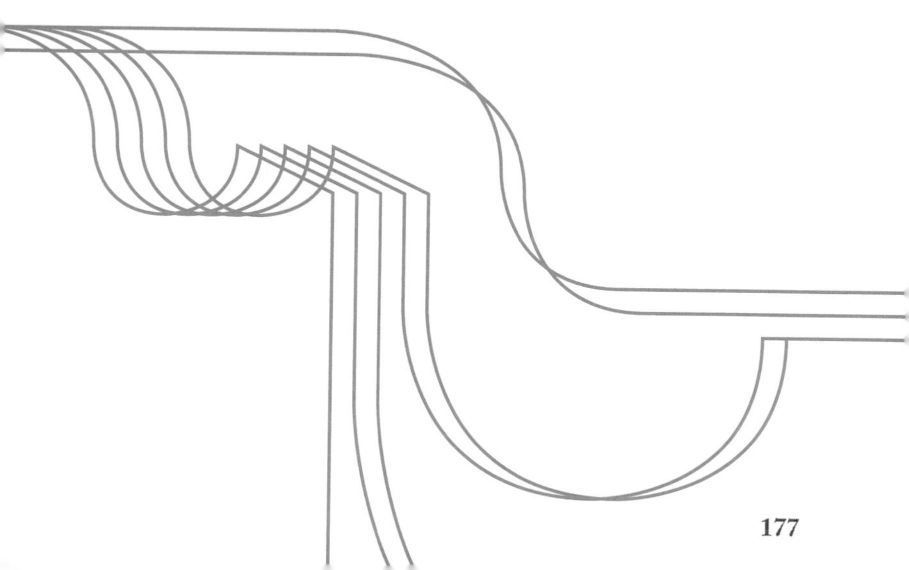

Leviticus \luh-VIHD-ih-kuhs\

by Anonymous (Old Testament, Pentateuch, twenty-seven chapters)

Leviticus might be characterized as the DIY book of the Old Testament, if by "do-it-yourself" you mean "do-it-right-or-you'll-need-to-make-sin-offerings-so-here's-a-list-of-things-to-help-you-get-it-right." Leviticus is a collection of rules and regulations for just about any occasion, occasions as divergent as going to court (Lev 19:15-16), going to the barber (19:26-27), going to bed (18), or going to worship (26:2). While there is some narrative material in the book—stories about the priest Aaron and his sons—for the most part Leviticus is a listing of dos and don'ts.

Leviticus can be roughly divided into two parts. Chapters 1–16 deal with proper procedures for sacrifice and worship, and purity law—largely for those conducting worship. In other words these are rules and instructions that apply specifically (and primarily) to priests. It was with this first section in mind that early rabbinic reviewers of Leviticus called it *torat kohanim*, "Instructions for priests."

Chapters 17–27 deal with holiness in general, rules and instruction for all people. Here the issues that Mr. Anonymous addresses have to do with living together in community, and with Sabbath and festival observance—largely for those attending worship. The modern reviewer might call this section of Leviticus the "Sabbath-go-to-meeting" handbook.

Any book that uses the word "nakedness" thirty times is bound to arch the proverbial eyebrow, but the issue is not that Mr. Anonymous is "working blue"; rather the issue is the perceived disconnect between a holiness code established in the distant past and its application in the present age. Speaking of readability, some might be inclined to think that Leviticus is only worth reading if you are a Levitical priest or an ancient Israelite, but there is something here for the modern reader. Many readers unfamiliar with Leviticus may be surprised to find this chestnut of a law nestled in the middle of this section: "You shall love your neighbor as yourself" (19:18).

Or: "You shall love the alien as yourself" (19:34).

The book can be difficult to work through—and this reviewer would not suggest you try to read it cover to cover in one sitting—but it is important at least as a reference. Of all of Mr. Anonymous' works, statistically, it is Leviticus that is most likely to be quoted to you as you make your way out of a tattoo parlor (19:28), or from shopping for the latest in ephod-wear (8:1ff). And Mr. Anonymous' controversial work is cited over 100 times in the New Testament and is critical to Israel's self-understanding, identity, and relationship with God when Israel is no longer free, and the Temple is no longer standing. This work, then, while often controversial and sometimes difficult to read, is important to understand as it was read shortly after its publication—as a resource for Israel as its people struggled with their identity and worried about their future.

See also: Law, Pentateuch.

Luke (The Gospel according to) \look\

By Luke* (New Testament, Gospels, twenty-four chapters)

Have you ever wondered what became of that little baby born in the manger in that story they tell on the night Santa comes down the chimney? If so, you will be interested in picking up a copy of The Gospel According to Luke, which you can find in an anthology called "The Bible" (on sale now at fine booksellers). Luke begins with the familiar nativity story but includes some details that the corner church probably doesn't include in the stage version. Luke also shares a story from when the child was an early adolescent—yup, teenage Jesus! Nevertheless, most of the chapters in Luke's book are from the last years of Jesus' life—a life that was cut tragically short.

Things start out nice enough. There's a scene in which Jesus holds his own against a devil who offers him the world, followed by a scene in which Jesus announces that he has been anointed "to bring good news to the poor . . . to proclaim release to the captives and recovery of sight to the blind, to let the oppressed go free, and to proclaim the year of the Lord's favor" (Luke 4:18-19). Before long, however, Jesus is running into some resistance from the powers that be—resistance that begins when Jesus starts hanging out with sinners and escalates when he moves on to forgiving sins.

In Luke, Jesus does a lot of teaching with "parables," including one about a negligent shepherd who ditches the entire flock to chase after just one, stupid, lost sheep (see Luke 15:3-6). Another parable tells of a dishonest manager who seems to get a pat on the back for short-changing his boss (Luke 16:1-11) and another parable identifies a venture capitalist who rewards his most reckless investors but punishes the one who plays it safe (Luke 19:12-27). While some may find these parables compelling, in this reviewer's humble opinion, giving people what they *don't* deserve is no way to run things; it's foolish, and offensive.

Teachings aside, it's what happens to Jesus in the end that made the biggest impression on this reviewer. Luke presents Jesus as someone who is concerned for those who are the least and the lowest in his society. Ironically, by the end of the story, it is Jesus who is found to be the least and the lowest. In a bizarre reversal of fortune that can only be described as stunning, this good man, Jesus, finds himself on trial before a hostile crowd yelling, "Crucify him!" In the end, he is stripped of his clothes, nailed to a cross, and left to die. Talk about least and lowest. Fortunately, Luke has one more reversal up his sleeve, but far be it from this reviewer to tell you what it is.

* Irenaeus, an early Christian leader who knew people who knew people who knew Jesus, explained that the author of Luke (as well as Acts) may have been the same Luke that once accompanied the Apostle Paul (see Phlm 1:21).

See also: Acts of the Apostles, Elizabeth, Jesus, Simeon.

Malachi \MAL-uh-ki\ (book)

by Malachi (Minor Prophets, four chapters)

A certain curmudgeonly Old Testament preacher famously declared, "Of making many books there is no end" (Ecc 12:12). But he was wrong! At least as far as the Old Testament goes, Malachi is the end. The curtain call. The fat lady singing. (Unless, of course, you are Roman Catholic or Eastern Orthodox, in which case you have a few more hours of show still to go on in your Old Testament—see entry on Apocrypha).

Similar to the name of the prophet Haggai, Malachi is probably a self-chosen name. It means "My Messenger"—which is sort of like changing your name to your job title. We're sure this made for interesting introductions. "Nice to meet you, Mr. My-Messenger. What do you do for a living? Oh, duh, you're a messenger. Shoulda guessed. Well then who is the 'my' in 'My-Messenger'? The Lord God? You're the Lord God's messenger? [*Awkward pause.*] Hey, how about this weather we're having?"

Anyway, here is Mr. My-Messenger's message to the people living in Jerusalem around the year 465 BCE: The priesthood is corrupt; shape up! You are wrecking the covenant; stop it! Quit leaving your first spouse for a trophy spouse; marriage is about commitment! The final message in the book, and thus in the Old Testament, is: The day of the Lord is coming. Until then, keep my laws. Oh, and one other thing: before the day of the Lord, I'll send the prophet Elijah.

And that's all he wrote.

See also: Prophets.

Mark (The Gospel according to) \mahrk\

By Mark* (New Testament, Gospels, sixteen chapters)

The Gospel According to Mark does not beat around the bush. Unlike other books that share its genre (cf. Matthew, Luke and John), Mark does not bother to begin with a beginning (with, say genealogies or birth account or creation itself). Mark instead favors a concise statement: "The beginning of the good news of Jesus Christ, the Son of God." With this Mark establishes the premise of his Gospel as well as its pace. In the beginning, Mark manages to describe Jesus getting baptized, being tempted, gathering disciples, teaching in the synagogue, casting out a demon, healing a follower's mother-in-law, praying, proclaiming, cleansing a leper, healing some more, proclaiming some more, and gathering crowds everywhere he went. And that's just chapter one.

Although Mark is written in a style that is straightforward, even simple, readers may find themselves puzzled by one particular aspect of the narrative: the so-called "messianic secret." What, the reader may ask, is the deal with the hush-hush demeanor Jesus exhibits whenever anyone—be they demon or disciple—identifies Jesus as the Christ, the Son of God? Take for example a scene in the middle of the story, where Jesus asks his followers, "Who do you say that I am?" One of them, Peter, says, "You are the Christ." Here you'd expect Jesus to say, "Bing! Right Answer! Now go tell the whole world!" Instead, Jesus "sternly ordered them not to tell anyone about him" (Mark 8:30). *Sternly*, it says! Nevertheless, readers will find themselves drawn to Mark's furtive Messiah. That is to say, you will not only want to find out his fate, you will want to find out if the rest of the world ever gets let in on the secret.

As Mark's story speeds toward its dramatic conclusion, the events that Jesus predicts—that he will "undergo great suffering, and be rejected by the elders, the chief priests, and the scribes, and be killed" (Mark 8:31)—actually come to pass. Here, the reader may become so absorbed in Mark's description of the betrayal, arrest, trial, beating, and execution of Jesus that she will forget to ask, "Hey, I thought this was supposed to be the Messiah? What kind of Messiah let's himself get crucified?!" Indeed, in Mark's dark telling, the only thing that this Messiah manages to blurt out in his dying moments is, "My God, My God! Why have you forsaken me?!" Once dead, Jesus is removed from his cross and laid to rest in a borrowed tomb. To be sure, a dead Messiah does not make for a particularly satisfying ending. The astute reader, therefore, will discern in Mark's concluding scenes not an ending but a new beginning—a new beginning that includes the reader.

* The author of this Gospel is not identified in the text itself. One report dating to the second century, explains that "Mark, who had been Peter's interpreter, wrote down carefully, but not in order, all that he remembered of the Lord's sayings and doings."*

See also: Jesus, John the Baptist.

* Eusibius, *History of the Church from Christ to Constantine*, trans. G.A. Williamson (New York: Penguin Classics,1989) 103.

Martha \MAHR-thuh\

Status:
Martha is keeping her nose to the grindstone.

Profile

Profession:	Home-maker, Busy-body
Hometown:	Bethany
Family:	Mary (sister) and Lazarus (brother)
Interests:	Cooking, hosting
Favorite Celebrity:	Martha Stewart
Turn-offs:	Lazy people, holier-than-thou people, tardy people, clutter
Favorite Quote:	"Cleanliness is next to godliness"—an old proverb

Have you ever had the feeling that you were doing all the work while others were just lying around doing absolutely nothing? Martha can relate. Luke's Gospel tells about the time that Jesus was welcomed into Martha's home. Also present was Martha's sister, Mary. While Martha was busy with many things—preparing dinner, dusting furniture, stashing clutter in the cabinet drawers—sister Mary just sat there! Just sat there listening to Jesus speak. Martha complained to Jesus: "Hey! Jesus! I'm working my fingers to the bone here while Miss Ooh-It's-The-Messiah is sitting around as usual! What is up with that!?" Jesus' response: "Chill!" (Or something like that.) As a result, Martha has earned a reputation over the centuries for preferring household tasks to hearing the word of God in person.

Truth be told, we've always been Martha people rather than Mary people. So we're glad when Martha gets her own private audience with Jesus. It happens in the aftermath of the death of her brother, Lazarus. After Lazarus was good and dead and buried, Jesus showed up. While Mary stayed home (wouldn't you know it?), Martha went out to meet Jesus on the road. She was glad to see him, but perhaps also a bit annoyed. "Hey! Jesus! Had you arrived a few days earlier, you could have healed my brother, and I wouldn't be wearing this black dress!" Here is where Jesus had a good word for Martha (a word that Mary wasn't around to hear): "I am the resurrection and the life. Those who believe in me, even though they die, will live... Do you believe this?" And in response, Martha had a pretty good word too. Check out Martha's key verse:

Key Verse: "Yes, Lord, I believe that you are the Messiah, the Son of God, the one coming into the world" (John 11:27; see also Luke 10:38-42 and John 11:1-44).

See also: Jesus, John (The Gospel according to), Lazarus.

Mary (Mother of Jesus) \MEHR-ee\

Status:
Mary is called *blessed* by all generations.

Profile

Interests:	Dreams, singing, songwriting, painting barnyard scenes
Favorite Song:	"Let it Be" by the Beatles
Favorite Saying:	"If momma ain't happy, ain't nobody happy—even if you are the Son of God!"
My business card says:	Mary—Mother of God

What more can be said about Mary? She's the mother of God. Her heart soared to the top when she gave birth to the savior of the world. Her heart shattered when she watched them crucify her son on the cross. All the pieces were put together again when God raised him from the dead. Maybe we can't say anything more about her. But maybe we can learn from something that she said:

"Here am I, the servant of the Lord; let it be with me according to your word" (Luke 1:38).

She spoke these words when the angel Gabriel announced, "Hey, good news! You are going to give birth to the Savior! And don't worry about being a virgin. Your fiancé won't be the father, the Holy Spirit will. I suppose Joseph won't be happy, but don't worry, I'll talk to him. What do you say?"

What would *you* say to such an offer?

Martin Luther speculated that Mary was pretty low on Gabriel's list of prospective mother's for God's Son. Luther imagined that Gabriel first went to the daughters of all the uppity crowd—the daughters of priests, Levites, prophets, public leaders, kings, and so on. And they all said, "Thanks for thinking of me, but I'll pass. Leave my life just the way it is. I've got plans to attend the prom, get into a good college, and have a career."

But Mary humbled herself. She let go of herself. She said, "Let it be with me according to your word." Maybe there's a lesson there.

Key Verse: "God has looked with favor on the lowliness of his servant. Surely, from now on all generations shall call me blessed" (Luke 1:48; see especially Luke 1–2).

See also: Bethlehem, Gabriel, Jesus.

Mary Magdalene

\MEHR-ee-MAG-duh-lihn\

Status:
Mary wants her reputation back!

Profile

Vocation:	My calling is "Apostle to the Apostles"; my calling is not, nor has it ever been, the "oldest profession," no matter what people tell you.
Hometown:	Magdala—that's why they call me "The Magdalene"; someone tried to call me Maggie, once. Once. He's been wearing an orthopedic toga ever since.
Family:	None. Never married. Thank you very much. (Dan Brown can take a hike.)
Pet Peeve:	Artists who paint pictures of me as "that kind of woman"

It has happened to a lot of women over the years, but it isn't funny. They get a bad reputation: slut, whore, easy, loose, prostitute. That kind of thing. Usually, they've done nothing to deserve it. But even when they have, they still don't deserve the reputation. What ever happened to, "Thou shall not bear false witness against your neighbor"?!

Other than in the descriptions of Jesus' crucifixion and resurrection, the only time Mary is mentioned in the Gospel is when Luke reports that Jesus had healed her and that she seemed to be one of the people closer to Jesus. She was there to take care of his body after he was dead. (Where were the men, we ask you?) She went out after the Sabbath was over, bringing spices to anoint Jesus' body. (Where were the men, we ask you?) She was the first person to whom the risen Jesus appeared. More on that in a minute.

So what wrecked her reputation? In a sermon preached in 591 CE, Pope Gregory I (yes, a pope!) explained that Mary Magdalene and an unnamed "sinner" woman who anointed Jesus' feet with her hair were the same woman. (Trivia: Because of this, when painters depict Mary, they usually give her long hair.) And if a woman is a sinner, she must be a prostitute, right? (Wrong! But you see how this line of thinking went.) In the Eastern Orthodox Church, by the way, Mary Magdalene was never seen as a sinner or prostitute but was always understood as a woman of virtue. Sort of.

So who was Mary Magdalene really? She was the Apostle to the Apostles. The first person to whom the resurrected Christ appeared. And the first person to be sent by Christ to proclaim (to the other apostles) the good news that he was risen. For that fact, she deserves our honor and respect. Not a reputation.

Key Verse: "Mary Magdalene went to the disciples with the news: 'I have seen the Lord!'" (John 20:18; see also Luke 8:2; Mark 15:43-47; Mark 18:1-8; John 20:1-18).

See also: Jesus, John (The Gospel according to), Mark (The Gospel according to), Luke (The Gospel according to).

Matthew (The Gospel according to)

\MATH-yoo\

By Matthew* (New Testament, Gospels,twenty-eight chapters)

M

The Gospel According to Matthew may not start with a bang but it certainly finishes with one. Between the admittedly slow beginning (which includes phrases like "Aram [was] the father of Aminadab, and Aminadab the father of Nahshon, and Nahshon the father of Salmon") and a great surprise ending, the reader can't help but get caught up in the story of "Jesus the Messiah, the Son of David." Although Matthew was clearly written for an audience familiar with the Hebrew Scriptures, this Gospel has something for everybody. That something of course is a someone: Jesus of Nazareth, crucified and (spoiler alert!) risen.

Frankly, this reviewer was a bit surprised that the author would begin the story with a long chapter delineating the protagonist's genealogy. On the other hand, there are some interesting women named in that family tree—their back stories are definitely worth checking out. Things kick into gear with some mysterious magi who show up in Bethlehem bearing gifts for a newborn king. Indeed, the Jesus-as-royalty note is one that is played often from beginning to end. After some intrigue involving the newborn king and a certain pretender named Herod, Matthew fast-forwards to the grown-up Jesus. Here, the Nazarene is portrayed as a provocative and knowledgeable teacher in the best rabbinical tradition, and much, much more. Jesus is a healer, a miracle-worker, and, perhaps most significantly, a man who stands up to the "The Man"—namely, the religious authorities. "You're like whitewashed tombs," Jesus says, "nice-looking on the outside, but full of bones and rot on the inside" (Matt 23:27). Those are strong words—strong enough to get a would-be Messiah killed.

Almost a full third of Matthew's story recounts events that take place during the last week of Jesus' life. By giving this much papyrus to an otherwise brief period in his subject's life, Matthew obviously wants to communicate that when it comes to understanding Jesus of Nazareth, this final week is the crux of the matter (pun intended). Not to give away too much, but—beginning with a royal entrance into Jerusalem, climaxing in a most unusual coronation, and concluding with the beginning of a new "reign of heaven"—Matthew expertly reveals Jesus to be the Christ, the Messiah, the Anointed One, the King that nobody expected, nobody recognized, and everybody needs.

* Although the work was anonymously written, early church leaders like Irenaeus, Papias, and Origen attribute its content to Matthew, an original follower of Jesus.

See also: Genealogy, Jesus.

Mediterranean Sea \MEHD-ih-tuhr-Ā-nee-uhn-SEE\

A big body of water without which it would have taken the Apostle Paul a lot longer to spread the Good News of Jesus, in which case many of us would probably still be worshipping Odin, or Isis, or Amaterasu, or Tepoxtecatl—and it hasn't been easy letting go of Tepoxtecatl.

The Sea of Galilee is really more of a lake. The Mediterranean Sea on the other hand—now that's a sea! Bustling ports, big water, ships on the horizon, sea monsters. Sea monsters? Yeah, sea monsters (see, for instance, Job 41:1 or Isa 21:1). In the ancient world, the Sea represented chaos and the great unknown. Truth be told, the Mediterranean Sea only plays a major role in two narratives: Jonah and Acts. Jonah's mode of sea transport is a big fish, while the seafarers in Acts cross the "Middle-Land" Sea by boat. In Acts, it's the impulse to "make disciples of all nations" that gets the Mediterranean Sea involved in the action. Thanks in large part to the Apostle Paul and his willingness to take a boat once in a while, towns all round the northeastern Mediterranean seaboard were hit with the Good News of Jesus. And if it's a tale of at-sea adventure you're looking for, try the last two chapters of Acts. It's no *Moby Dick*, but it's got sailors and a shipwreck scene.

See also: Acts of the Apostles, Jonah (book).

Micah \MI-cuh\ (book)

M

by Micah Ham-Morashthi (Minor Prophets, seven chapters)

In Micah the prophet of the same name announces a surprisingly severe condemnation of all that was sacred to the people of Judah—especially its Temple, capital city, and religiosity. The message of the book might be summed up best in this startling opening salvo: "What is the transgression of Jacob? Is it not Samaria? And what is the high place of Judah? Is it not Jerusalem?" (Mic 1.5).

As with many of the prophetic books, one needs to crack the outer shell of the ancient metaphor in order to digest the nut inside. Mr. Ham-Morashthi (which means "The Man from Moresheth") was a prophet around the years 725–700 BCE. During this time, the northern kingdom of Israel was destroyed when its capital city, Samaria, was sacked in 722. The southern kingdom, Judah, always believed that the sin of the northern kingdom was pulling them away from Jerusalem—where God's one and only temple was located. When the northern kingdom went all Jefferson Davis and seceded from the nation, they set up their own religious institutions, building up "high places" for worship rituals that did not please the Lord—some of which were in Samaria.

So when Mr. Ham-Morashthi asks, "What is the transgression of Jacob? Is it not Samaria?" his Judean audience would have thought, "Most definitely, dude! Preach it, brother man!" And so he did preach it: "And what is the high place of Judah? Is it not Jerusalem?" To which his Judean audience would have said nothing because they would have been choking on their tongues—in shock, anger, and outrage. Our sacred Temple in Jerusalem no better than a high place? The nerve!

Mr. Ham-Morashthi's point here, and throughout this collected volume of his sermons, is rather direct: God is not pleased with meaningless, go-through-the-motions-and-then-hurry-home-so-that-you-don't-miss-the-start-of-the-game worship. God demands that the people live out their faith in God every day. Or, as Mr. Ham-Morashthi said so pithily, "Do justice, love kindness, and walk humbly with your God" (6:8).

We do believe that we could not have put it better ourselves. (And we wish to point out that the we fulfilled the rule in the ELCA constitution that says every document published by the church or its publishing house must cite Mic 6:8 at least once.)

See also: Prophets.

Ministry of Jesus \MIHN-uh-stree-uhv-JEE-zuhs\

Think about the most productive three years of your life—think about the "good" that you did during those years. They can't be anywhere near as productive or as good as the three years (at most) that Jesus "ministered" publicly. (The word "minister," by the way comes from a Latin word for "servant.") In just three years, Jesus went from relative obscurity to being paraded into Jerusalem as a king. In between, there were well-attended sermons, miraculous healings, signs, wonders, adoring crowds, and annoyed religious leaders. Ironically, it's those annoyed religious leaders who, in the end, brought the earth-bound ministry of Jesus to a screeching halt—or perhaps a resounding climax.

If the ministry of Jesus teaches us anything, it's this: "No good deed goes unpunished." Okay, that's the cynical view. But there is something to it. Helping out at the food kitchen once in a while is okay, and we even tolerate people who are unusually committed to their family, community, work, and/or church. But do too much good, and tick-off the religious leaders in the process, and there will be hell to pay. Need proof? When did the religious leaders decide that Jesus needed to be eliminated? According to John's Gospel it was when they heard that Jesus raised Lazarus from the dead (John 11:46-53). See? Recycling your empties is one thing, raising the dead is quite another.

Don't feel bad, though, if no three-year period (or indeed your whole life!) measure up to those three years when Jesus was doing his thing. After all, he had something going for him that people like us don't—he was the Son of God. Then again, because he is the Son of God, and we are his sisters and brothers, we *do* have that whole Child of God thing going for us. And that can make all the difference in the world when it comes to what we say, do, preach, teach and achieve. To borrow from another sibling and fellow underachiever: "By the grace of God I am what I am, and his grace toward me has not been in vain. On the contrary, I worked harder than any of them—though it was not I, but the grace of God that is with me" (1 Cor 15:10). So we've got that going for us, which is nice.

See also: John (The Gospel according to), Mark (The Gospel according to), Matthew (The Gospel according to), Luke (The Gospel according to).

Monarchy \MAH-nuhr-kee\

A system of ruling a nation, in which people give up their rights and their wealth—in exchange, the ruler usually gives up responsibility and accountability.

When God rescued the Israelites from the king of Egypt (a.k.a. Pharaoh), God said, "You are my chosen nation. You don't ever have to have any king other than me." Flash forward about 200 years. The people, like a bunch of insecure adolescents, said, "Hey, the other nations have kings and skateboards and tattoos! We want a king, a skateboard, and a tattoo, too!!" God said, "The Assyrians will laugh if you wear a tutu." The Israelites rolled their eyes, "Very funny. We want a king." God said, "OK, but first my prophet Samuel will tell you what kings are good for."

So Sammy said, "Kings are good for taxes, armies, harems, and oppression. And for the odd bit of idolatry and bad foreign policy."

"Where do we sign?" they asked (See 1 Samuel 8).

For the next 425 years or so Israel was ruled by kings. From about 1000 to 922 B.C.E. the twelve tribes were united under one king—we like to call this period the "United Monarchy." (Clever, huh?) After 922, the northern tribes seceded from the union. Their grievances? "Taxes, armies, harems, oppression, the odd bit of idolatry, and bad foreign policy."

The resulting Northern Kingdom (a.k.a. Kingdom of Israel), lasted from 922 to 722 B.C.E. Because of royal mismanagement, they were destroyed by the Assyrians. The Southern Kingdom (a.k.a. the Kingdom of Judah), lasted from 922 to 587 B.C.E. Because of royal mismanagement, they were destroyed by Babylon.

But something good came out of all of this. God promised that one day, God would send the perfect king, who would rule by serving others and in love. We like to call this king the Messiah. Otherwise known as Jesus.

See also: David, 1 and 2 Kings, 1 and 2 Samuel, Saul.

Moses \mō-zehz\

Status:
Moses would, at this point, rather have two tablets of ibuprofen than two tablets of stone.

Profile

Vocation:	Deliverer, Law Giver, Wilderness Guide
Favorite Celebrity:	Who else? Charlton Heston—Peace be upon him!
Favorite Movies:	What else? *The Ten Commandments*! *Prince of Egypt*!

Your image of Moses may have been distorted by Cecil B. DeMille's movie, *The Ten Commandments*. For instance, half of *The Ten Commandments* is spent depicting Moses' growing-up years. The Bible only spends five verses (Exod 2:11-15) on those years!!

If you want the skinny on Moses, put the young, strapping, shirtless Charlton Heston out of your mind and read Exodus, Leviticus, Numbers, and Deuteronomy. Here, Moses is the poster child for the idea that God chooses the least likely persons to do God's work. Moses was wanted for murder in Egypt, so he was hesitant to return there to deliver Israel. But God prevailed and Moses found himself staring down Pharaoh (played by a young, strapping, shirtless Yul Brynner—delete that image, too). Ten plagues later, the Israelites were mucking through the Red Sea.

Most of Exodus deals with Moses' frustrations "leading" Israel around the desert. A favorite exploit is when an aggravated Moses asks to see the face of this God who's been telling him what to do. But beholding God's face would kill a mortal, so God deigns to show Moses the Divine Backside. That's a great story! One (of many) that DeMille left out. Read Exodus yourself, and see how God is faithful—even while using the least likely helpers.

Key Verse: "Let my people go!" (Exod 5:1; see also Exodus–Deuteronomy).

See also: Exodus (book), Exodus and Wilderness Period, Israelites.

Naaman \NĀ-muhn\

Status:
Naaman is bummed about the zit on his forehead.

Profile

Profession:	Army General
Nationality:	Aramean
Interests:	Skin care
Favorite TV Shows:	All of those skin care infomercials
Did you know . . .	. . . that I'm obsessed with skin care?

Naaman's story (in 2 Kgs 5) is a bit involved, so here it is quick: A foreigner (read: "outsider") is cured by a Prophet of God and, as a result, confesses that there's no other God but Israel's God. Here's the slightly longer version: Naaman, a military commander who'd battled Israel, had a really bad case of acne. Really bad. That or leprosy. Either way, lucky for Naaman, his wife had a slave who knew a good dermatologist. The slave—a young girl from Israel—remembered that back home there was this holy man named Elisha. On the slave girl's recommendation, Naaman set out for Samaria, where Elisha was hanging out. Elisha's servant met Naaman and told him to "go and wash in the Jordan. Not once but several times." After a bit of balking at this advice—there were bigger and better rivers up north, after all—Naaman took a dip in the Jordan river and came out with skin as smooth as a baby's bottom. Naaman was converted; he told Elisha, "Listen, your God is the only god for me." But Naaman's new religion presented a problem: "When I get home," Naaman told Elisha, "my king is gonna make me worship those no-account gods we have up in Aram. Would your God mind so much if I played along, just this once, as long as I didn't really mean it?" Elisha responded graciously: "Go in peace."

Centuries afterward, Jesus remembered Naaman as an example of how sometimes God's gracious blessing is withheld from those "insiders" who think they are deserving and, instead, given to "outsiders" who the insiders think don't deserve squat (Luke 4:27).

Key Verse: "Elisha sent a messenger to him, saying, 'Go, wash in the Jordan seven times, and your flesh shall be restored and you shall be clean'" (2 Kgs 5:10; see all of 2 Kings 5).

See also: Elisha, Jordan River.

Nahum \NĀ-uhm\

by Nahum of Elkosh (Old Testament, Prophets, three chapters)

Mr. Nahum's book is not for the squeamish, the touchy, or the subtle. Mr. Nahum provides a stark departure from the general tone of the biblical genre, with pointed diatribe and a relentless thirst for the harshest of justice to be visited on Israel's enemies.

Based on what you know about other books in the biblical collection, finish this phrase: "*The Lord is slow to anger and*____________." If you want to check the standard non-deviated answer, you might consult some of Mr. Nahum's contemporaries (see Joel 2:13 and/or Jonah 4:2). For Mr. Nahum the second piece of this phrase is unique. Nahum 1:3 reads: "The LORD is slow to anger, *but great in power, and the LORD will by no means clear the guilty*." Mr. Nahum's message is cutting and harsh. But for his intended audience, the people of Israel, it would have been welcome. His ruthless invective is directed at the city of Nineveh, the capital of the Assyrian empire. The Assyrians were the bully super power of the day and, if Mr. Nahum's sample can be taken as any sort of representation of the *zeitgeist* (a German word that means "spirit of the times"), most folks would have joined the Israelites in wishing Nineveh ill.

The third chapter of Nahum is the epitome of another German word, the *schadenfreude*—the joy taken in the suffering of others—of the author in the prediction and graphic description of Nineveh's downfall. For Mr. Nahum Nineveh's collapse, disgrace, and ultimate ruin includes the city's streets being heaped with corpses, the city being described as a woman ravaged following battle while "filth" is thrown at her. At these last we can only shake our heads and wonder at the depths of Mr. Nahum's passionate hatred.

But basically Mr. Nahum got it right that Nineveh had it coming, and got what it had coming not long after Mr. Nahum penned his sometimes shrill, sometimes offensive, but sometimes entertaining little booklet. While this little book cannot be called a "must read" per se and is certainly no easy read, it does provide a valuable insight into the mindset of a small nation caught in the grips of a much greater and deeply hated enemy.

See also: Israelites, Prophets.

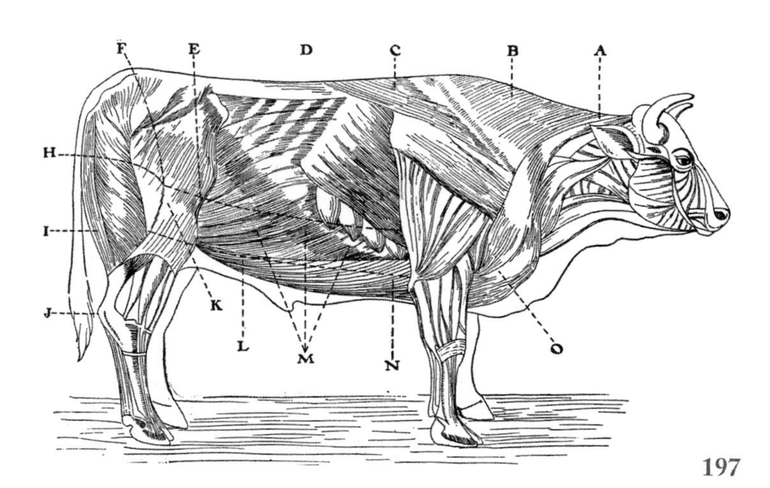

Marriage License.
—State of— —County of—
The people of the State of ... You are hereby author...
Marriage, GREETING: ... to celebrate the rites and ceremonies of Marriage, ...
and M... , and you are required ...
the celebration of such Marriage, with a Certific...
under the penalty of One Hundred Dollars.
Witness, ... our said Court and the ... in said County, this d...
Seal.
State of ... County. } ss.
... day ... the ...
Mr. ...
authority given in the above License, ...
Given under my hand and seal, this ...

169
FIRST NATIONAL BANK
OF DE KALB. ILLINOIS.
10
CAPITAL STOCK FIFTY THOUSAND DOLLARS
This certifies that James M. Cameron is the owner of Ten Shares of the Capital Stock of FIRST NATIONAL BANK of the par value of ONE HUNDRED DOLLARS each; transferable only on the Books of the Bank in person or by Attorney on the surrender of this Certificate.
In Witness Whereof the President and Cashier have hereunto subscribed their names and caused the seal of the Bank to be affixed at De Kalb Ill. this First day of ...
John C. Otis Cashier
President

Naomi \nā-oh-mee\ or \nah-oh-mee\

Status:
Naomi is happy to be back in Bethlehem.

Profile

Vocation:	Matchmaker, Landowner, Wheeler-dealer
Hometown:	Bethlehem (I lived in Moab for a time, but we don't talk about that; those more difficult times.)
Fun Fact:	Did you know that King David is my great, great grandson-in-law?
Favorite Quote:	"Where you go, I will go; where you lodge, I will lodge; your people shall be my people, and your God my God. Where you die, I will die— there will I be buried." My daughter-in-law Ruth said that, after my sons died. I was so touched!

We meet Naomi in the book of Ruth (that's her daughter-in-law). But an argument could be made that Naomi plays such an important role that the book should have been titled "Ruth *and* Naomi," or maybe even "*Naomi* and Ruth." But that would have meant splitting the royalties. Anyway, we meet Naomi in the middle of tough times.

Her husband and two sons had died and all that she had left were two foreign-born daughters-in-law and some property in Bethlehem. To keep the property in the family, she had to resort to a bit of strategic match-making that would have made Emma Woodhouse proud (that's for you Jane Austen fans). Naomi gets her kinsman, Boaz, to hook up with her daughter-in-law, Ruth, and gets him to buy the land. To top it all off, Ruth and Boaz give Naomi her first grandson, Obed, who became the father of Jesse, who became the father of King David. In a system that could be especially tough on husband-less women, Naomi knew how to work the system.

Key Verse: "Then the women said to Naomi, 'Blessed be the LORD, who has not left you this day without next-of-kin; and may his name [Obed] be renowned in Israel! He shall be to you a restorer of life and a nourisher of your old age; for your daughter-in-law who loves you, who is more to you than seven sons, has borne him'" (Ruth 4:14-15; see also the book of Ruth).

See also: Ruth.

Nathan \NĀ-thuhn\

Status:
Nathan took a bit of a risk, but thinks it came out pretty well, thank you very much.

N

Profile

Vocation:	Prophet, Advisor to the kings
Fun Fact:	The King and Queen have a son named Nathan. I like to think they named him after me!
Dark Secret:	That story I told King David—you know, that one about the poor guy with the one little lamb? I totally made it up!
Favorite Celebrity:	Dr. Phil (I just love how he confronts people with the truth!)

The prophet Nathan's "fifteen minutes of fame" came in the wake of King David's affair with Bathsheba, wife of Uriah. (For the dish on this scandal, check out the entry for Bathsheba and/or Uriah.) The Lord was shocked and appalled (yes, shocked *and* appalled) by what

David had done. So the Lord sent the prophet Nathan to confront the king and speak some truth to power. Nathan approached David with a story that went something like this: "There was this rich guy who owned all kinds of livestock. There was also this poor guy and the only animal he owned was this cute, cuddly little lamb. The poor guy loved the lamb with all his heart. One day, the rich guy had a guest and wanted to serve the guest some dinner. So—get this!—rich guy takes poor guy's little lamb and serves it to the guest." King David, fixin' to blow a gasket on hearing this, goes: "I promise you that rich guy will pay for what he did! In fact, he deserves to die!" Nathan, in a classic bit of bait-and-switch, goes: "You da man!" (But not in the good way; he meant "You're the dude that done did it!") When David heard this he recognized his mistake (*read*: sin), repented, and wrote Psalm 51. (Or at least he should have.)

Key Verse: "Then David said to Nathan, 'I have sinned against the Lord.' Nathan replied, 'The Lord has taken away your sin. You are not going to die'" (2 Sam 12:13; see also 2 Sam 12, Ps 51).

See also: David, 1 and 2 Samuel, Uriah the Hittite.

Nazareth \NA-zuh-rihth\

Wide spot in the camel track; back-water refuge of carpenters, prematurely pregnant wives, and their semi-legitimate children; a "wretched hive of scum and villainy."

"Can anything good come from Nazareth?" That's Nathanael's famous wise-guy question. He may have had Obi Wan Kenobi's (played by Alec Guinness) great line from *Star Wars* in mind when he said it. He asked it when a buddy told him that the Messiah was from Nazareth (John 1:45-46). Nathanael's question suggests that Nazareth had a reputation for producing people who were not Messiah-quality. Nazareth is where Joseph, Mary, and Jesus settled after fleeing Bethlehem and detouring through Egypt (Matt 2:19-23). It would have taken Jesus about half a day to walk to Lake Galilee, with its sunny beaches and great fishing. It would have taken him another hour or so to walk *across* the lake, but that's another story. Each of the Gospels uses the phrase "Jesus of Nazareth" (rather than, say, "Jesus of Bethlehem," or "Jesus Josephson"). It is John's Gospel that tells us that the note above the crucified Christ said, "*Jesus of Nazareth*, King of the Jews." So, yeah, something good can come from Nazareth. *The* something good.

See also: Jesus, John (The Gospel according to).

Nebuchadnezzar

\NEHB-uh-kuhd-NEHZ-uhr\

Status:
Nebuchadnezzar is burning-hot angry.

Profile

Vocation:	King of Babylon, Mighty Warrior, Conqueror of Nations, Destroyer of the Temple, Despoiler of Jerusalem, Enslaver of Israel, etc.
Fun Fact:	My friends call me The Nebunator!
Turn-offs:	Uppity servants who think themselves too good to bow down to my personally commissioned, ninety-foot tall, golden statue; fiery furnaces that don't work
Favorite Book:	*Pizza Pat*; his pizza oven goes to 800 degrees
Favorite Quotation:	"What the . . . ?! Who let that fourth guy into the fiery furnace?!" —Me (I only threw three guys in there.)

King Nebuchadnezzar takes some figuring out—and not just the pronunciation of his name. The Bible depicts him as the enemy of God and of the chosen people (his armies laid siege to Jerusalem, murdered its inhabitants, enslaved the survivors, looted the city, and destroyed the Temple). But the Bible doesn't just hate him for it. On top of being God's enemy, the Bible also depicts Nebuchadnezzar as God's agent. A biblical idea that can be troubling (to modern minds at least) is that God uses folks like the not-so-nice Nebuchadnezzar to discipline and redeem Israel (see Ezra 5:12 or Jer 27:8, for example). But whether you see ol' King Nebuchadnezzar as a good guy or just a Bad Mess O' Potamia, you gotta like the story of The Nebunator's showdown with Shadrach, Meshach, and Abednego. In this story, Nebuchadnezzar not only becomes a believer in the God of the Hebrews, he also gives Sunday school teachers the world over the story of the Fiery Furnace and a vivid lesson on the first commandment: "You shall have no other gods."

Key Verse: "Now I, Nebuchadnezzar, praise and extol and honor the King of heaven, for all his works are truth, and his ways are justice; and he is able to bring low those who walk in pride" (Dan 4:37; see also all of Dan 3 and 4).

See also: Shadrach, Meshach, and Abednego.

Nehemiah \nee-uh-MI-uh\

See EZRA-NEHEMIAH.

New Testament \NOO-TEHS-tih-mihnt\

1. The collected stories, history, prayers, songs, laws, and writings of a bunch of sinners called "God's chosen people," a.k.a. the church;
2. The "younger sibling" of the Old Testament; resource for the next generation(s) of sinful, chosen people.

Follow along now: the opposite of *up* is ... *down*, very good. The opposite of *good* is ... *bad* (we were confident you'd get that one right). The opposite of *strong* is ... wait for it ... wait for it ... *weak*. Excellent! And the opposite of *old* is ... *young*, or maybe *novel*, or maybe *new*. Okay, maybe that last one didn't work so well but you get the point: there is something new about the New Testament.

Like the Old Testament, the New Testament is not a book so much as it is a library, made up of twenty-seven books and letters. (Here's a little numerology to help you remember that: 'new' has 3 letters and 'testament' has 9, 3x9=27. This works for the OT, too: 'old' has 3 letters and 'testament' 9, put those numbers side-by-side and you get 39. Cool!) These NT books and letters tell the story of Jesus' life (the Gospels: Matthew, Mark, Luke, and John) and the story of the early church (Acts). The NT also includes the correspondence of early church leaders (in letters from Paul, John, James, and so forth.) and a record of visions to provide hope for a persecuted people (Revelation). In other words, the New Testament really follows a similar pattern to the Old Testament. This "book" is the story of God's chosen people—the church—and its relationship with God in Christ Jesus.

But there is something really new about the New Testament, rather than merely the "latest edition" or something of a novelty. Also, it's not new because it replaces the old; the NT supplements the OT rather than replaces it. What's truly new in the New Testament is the new covenant (which is basically what "testament" means). Here's the New Covenant: instead of fearing the just punishment that we might deserve and even expect from God, we are forgiven—freely and fully. Instead of taking sacrifices to God, God comes to us. Instead of offering a lamb whose blood we shed as atonement for our sins, the Lamb of God—that's Jesus—sheds his own blood for our atonement. Here's how the Apostle Paul (in 1 Cor 11:25-26) described this truly New Covenant, that is, the New Testament:

"In the same way he took the cup also, after supper, saying, 'This cup is the new covenant in my blood. Do this, as often as you drink it, in remembrance of me.' For as often as you eat this bread and drink the cup, you proclaim the Lord's death until he comes."

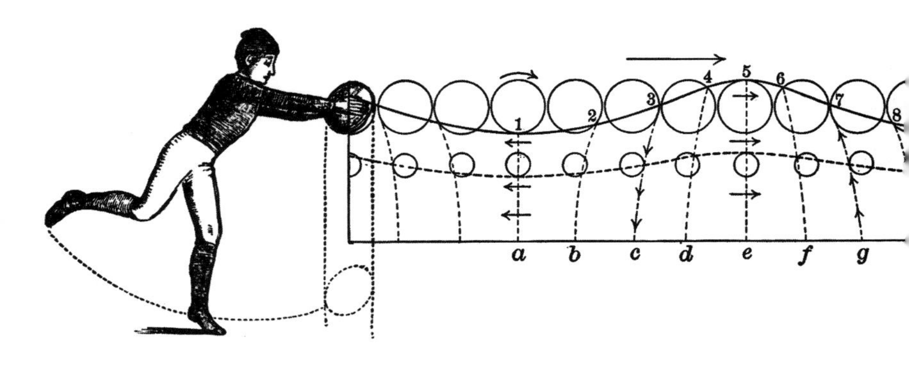

Nicodemus \NIHK-uh-DEE-muhs\

Status:
Nicodemus wishes that he had copyrighted John 3:16 when he had the chance.

Profile

Vocation:	Pharisee—I come from a long line of Pharisees
Favorite Sport:	Football (because they hold up that sign behind the goal posts)
Did You Know?	You know the old spiritual that asks, "Were you there when they laid him in the tomb?" Well, yes, as a matter of fact, I *was* there!
Favorite Quotation:	"You must be born again." I still can't get over this one! You can't go back into your mother's womb, can you!? That crazy-talkin' Jesus!
Favorite Song:	"Night Moves" by Bob Seger

You can thank Nicodemus for John 3:16. You know, the so called "Gospel-in-a-Nutshell"? "For God so loved the world that he gave his only Son, so that everyone who believes in him may not perish but have eternal life." Yeah, *that* John 3:16. According to the Bible,

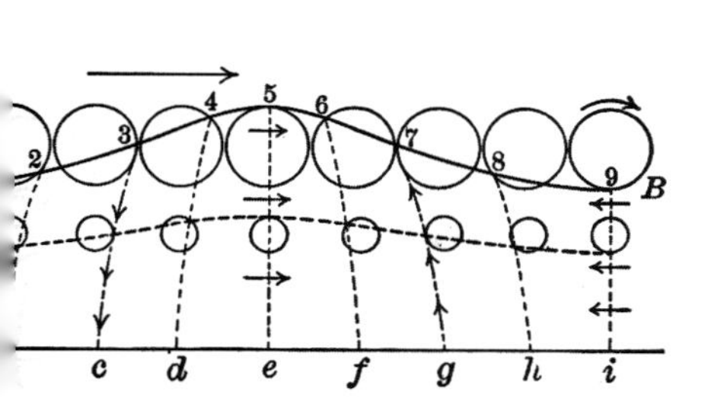

the first and only guy to hear those words was none other than our man, Nicodemus. If Nicodemus hadn't gone to see Jesus that fateful night, there'd be no John 3:16! At the time, Nicodemus had no idea what to make of the man from Nazareth. *Who was Jesus representin'? What were his credentials?* In other words, Nicodemus needed info. What he got instead was crazy talk! Crazy talk about being born anew; crazy talk about being born of water and the Spirit; crazy talk about how the Spirit blows about like the wind, making people born again from above. Nicodemus did manage to get a word in edgewise, namely: "How can these things be?" (Translation: "Saviorsays-what?!") In fact, you get the feeling that Jesus had been holding back, waiting like some football rube for the cameras to show him on the jumbotron so he could flash the original John 3:16 sign. And here comes Nicodemus with his "nobody does signs like you do, JC." Talk about right place/right time.

Key Verse: All together now: "For God so loved the world . . ." (John 3:16).

See also: Creation, Jesus, John (The Gospel according to).

Noah \NOH-uh\

Status:
Noah is dry.

Profile

Vocation:	Ship-builder, Zoo-keeper, Vine-grower
Hometown:	Watertown, PA (not really)
About My Family:	One wife, three sons, their wives, and a boatload of animals
Turn-offs:	Getting caught in the rain (although I might like a piña colada)
Lucky Number:	Forty
Did You Know?	I still feel bad about this, but I just couldn't coax those unicorns to climb aboard the ark.
Song I'm sick and tired of:	"The Rainbow Connection"—why *are* there so many songs about rainbows?!
Most Embarrassing Moment:	The time I had a little too much, er, "fruit of the vine"; ever since then my family just hasn't been the same

Noah was just sitting there, minding his own business, when God showed up and gave him a job to do. We're sure that Noah's first reaction was the same as the reaction of other Bible figures (like Abraham, Moses, Mary, Peter, and Paul) who were just sitting there minding their own business when God showed up with a job to do: "You want me to do *what*?!" God instructed Noah to build an ark and to gather two of every kind of living thing on the earth. (This made the creators of toddler books and the designers of nursery room wallpaper very happy.) So Noah built the ark according to the specs God gave him. (Note to hobbyists: if you are interested in building your own ark, you'll find the instructions in Gen 6:14-16.) The animals were gathered, two by two, boarded the ark, and—as that old camp song puts it so well—"It rained and poured for forty daysie, daysies . . . nearly drove those animals crazy, crazies, children of the Lord."

The story of Noah teaches us a number of things, including: (1) that God can be angry enough to open up a big can of Whoop-H_2O on the creation, and (2) that the same God can be merciful enough to promise never to do that again. But the real lesson lies with Noah himself. At the beginning of the story, we're told that God chose Noah because Noah was the only one righteous in his generation. But after the flood it's a different story. The water had barely receded when we're told that Noah "drank some wine and became drunk" and passed out in his tent, naked. This from the "only one righteous!" (Makes you wonder what everyone else was up to . . . or *down* to, depths wise.) Turns out Noah's a sinner just like all the rest. (Although in Noah's defense, we suppose that after a whole year cooped up in that ark even the best of us might be tempted to crack open a cold one.)

Still, God makes a covenant and offers a promise to Noah: no more, never again—not no way, not no how. Why does God make a promise to Noah? Because in the end God is gracious and merciful to sinners, that's why.

Key Verse: [God said to Noah:] "I establish my covenant with you, that never again shall all flesh be cut off by the waters of a flood, and never again shall there be a flood to destroy the earth" (Gen 9:11; see also Gen 6–9).

See also: Flood, Genesis.

N

Numbers \NUHM-buhrz\

by Anonymous (Old Testament, Pentateuch, thirty-six chapters)

Unless you have an overactive interest in genealogies, censuses, and the lists of names and families, the beginning of Numbers is probably something you should skip. In the annals of uninspiring opening lines of books—"*it was the best of times, it was the worst of times . . . it was the summer of our discontent. . . .*"—Numbers makes a run at the number one spot: "Take a census of all the congregation of the people of Israel, by families, by fathers' houses, according to the number of names, every male, head by head . . ." This reviewer almost put Mr. Anonymous' book down right then and there, had reviewing Numbers not been this reviewer's job.

What then should someone not paid to read and review Numbers do? When confronted with these lists of names that are hard to remember and harder to pronounce, perhaps it is best to follow the abbot's advice and "Skip a bit, brother."

Whether one begins at the beginning of Numbers or slides ahead a few chapters, the industrious reader will be amply rewarded for their perseverance. Numbers is a rich tableau of different types of writing, from its lists of people, to laws and rubrics for worship, to accounts of battles, to stories about Israel's forty years in the wilderness, to the division of the Promised Land between the twelve tribes.

While some might question the choice of literary devices, Mr. Anonymous has cleverly organized Numbers around the census lists. The first list (chapter 1) introduces the first major part of Numbers, chapters 1–25, which continues the familiar pattern of Mr. Anonymous' previous work in Exodus where the Israelites return again and again to their rebellious mistrust of God's promise. The second list (chapter 26) introduces the second half of the book which moves from the older generation of Israelites who have struggled with God to a new generation that—while not free from the problems of its predecessors—is more fully committed to trusting in the promise of a land that will be their own and in their relationship with God.

One final note about the tone and variety of literature in Mr. Anonymous' fourth book. Mr. Anonymous shows a remarkable and, for all the lists and laws that he seems so fond of, surprising gift for storytelling. Numbers has several gems that almost seem hidden in the rest of the work—from the familiar stories of manna and water in the wilderness, to the giants (the *nephilim*) living in the promised land who scare the Israelite scouts silly, to the story of the prophet Balaam and his talking mule. Each of these tales shows the author's gift for storytelling. And these stories alone make it worth both the price of the book and the work of seeking them out.

See also: Genealogy, Pentateuch.

Obadiah \o-buh-DI-uh\ (book)

by Obadiah (Minor Prophets, one chapter)

Clearly, Mr. Obadiah, along with his New Testament buddies 2 John, 3 John, and Jude, didn't read the directions that clearly stated every biblical book must be at least three chapters long. Or perhaps, living and prophesying just after the exile, there just wasn't much paper sitting around. Mr. Obadiah's message is one of hope and restoration for a people who had been defeated and scattered in exile: "The exiles of Jerusalem... shall possess the towns of the Negeb (a fancy ancient word that sort of means "the back 40"). Those who have been saved shall go up to Mount Zion" (vv. 20-21).

See also: Prophets.

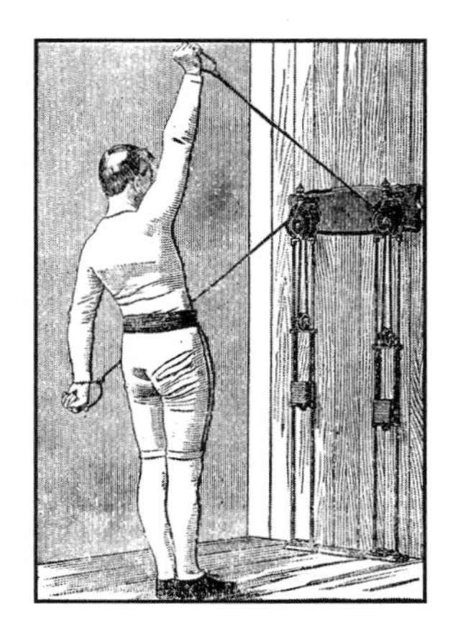

Old Testament \OHLD-TEHS-tih-mihnt\

The collected stories, histories, prayers, songs, laws, and writings of a bunch of sinners called "God's chosen people"; the "elder sibling" of the New Testament; resource for the next generation(s) of sinful, chosen people.

The Old Testament is also called the Older Testament, the Hebrew Bible, the First Testament, the *Tanak*, and That Ponderous Weight In My Backpack. When something has been around as long as this book has (its earliest material dates from over 1000 years BCE), it can pile up quite a list on monikers, titles, names, and the occasional abbreviation—like OT. In the broadest sense, the OT tells the story of God in relationship with and mission through the people of Israel.

The Old Testament is held to be sacred by both Jews and Christians (although precisely what different folks mean by "sacred" remains a point of some disagreement) and is believed to be a source of authority and instruction for daily living. The OT contains thirty-nine books that are often separated into groups: Pentateuch, History, Poetry, Major Prophets, and Minor Prophets.

Some folks say that the OT isn't a Christian book. Hooey. The OT is fully a Christian book and a Jewish book. It is Scripture that these two cousin faiths share. Both Jews and Christians are the spiritual descendants of the *Israelite religion* that makes up the OT.

Christians read the OT as Scripture. Jesus always assumes that his Father is the same as the God of Abraham, Isaac, and Jacob. The Bible is fully God's word for Christians. It provides words for us people to speak to God, points to Jesus as the promised *Messiah*, and on the whole holds for us who read it something uniquely true about who both God is and who we are.

Parable \peh-RUH-buhl\

A story with not only a point, but a skewer.

In the movie *Planes, Trains, and Automobiles*, Steve Martin's character launches (and we mean *launches*) into some good advice: "When you're telling these little stories, here's a good idea: Have a point! It makes it so much more interesting for the listener!"

Because admit it. We have all been there, listening to a story and wondering, "Why is he telling this? There is no point!"

A parable is a story designed not to be entertaining or amusing, or to pass on family history. It is a story with a point. In fact, the biblical parables are often pointed. You might say that they have lance-like point—a sort of "gotcha" moment in which we realize that the point of the story has, in fact, punctured us. (For an example, see NATHAN.) While there are parables in both the Old Testament and the New Testament, most of the biblical parables occur in the Gospel because Jesus often taught using parables.

A key to reading Jesus' parables is to realize that we are the ones who are being skewered by Jesus' parables. He pokes a hole in our illusions about our selves in order to let the hot air out and the Holy Spirit's healing breath in.

See also: Gospels, Jesus.

Passion Narrative, The (a.k.a. Holy Week)

\thuh-PASH-uhn-NEHR-uh-tihv\

The seven 24-hour days that, unlike the days in Genesis 1, really are worth arguing about.

It's not like we shouldn't have seen it coming. In the first three Gospels, Jesus warns his followers that he must go up to Jerusalem to "undergo great suffering, and be rejected by the elders, the chief priests, and the scribes, and be killed, and after three days rise again" (Mark 8:31). The Gospels emphasize that even though from a worldly perspective it may look as if God isn't in control, God was in fact working in, with, and under the events that led to Jesus' crucifixion. For instance, when Peter tried to defend Jesus when soldiers come to arrest him, Jesus told Peter to put away his sword, because Jesus had to "drink the cup" that was assigned to him.

For the Gospels, it is the final week of Jesus' life that is of utmost importance. How much utmost importance? Fully one third (thirty out of eighty-nine) of the chapters in the Gospels are devoted to the events that begin with "Palm Sunday" and Jesus' triumphal entrance into Jerusalem. Six days later, the body of Christ lay lifeless deep inside a borrowed tomb. In between the entry into Jerusalem and his burial just outside the city wall, the Gospels report that Jesus overturned tables in the Temple, argued with the pharisees, taught his disciples, washed their feet, ate a last supper, prayed in the garden, was betrayed by his friend, was arrested, put on trial, mocked, beaten, and crucified. Not the kind of fate you'd expect for a Messiah. That is, starting off on such a high note and ending up "six feet under" isn't exactly "gettin' 'er done" by human standards. But it *got* done. Or, as Jesus said in those final moments on that cross: "It is finished."

See also: Holy Week, Jesus.

Paul (Saul of Tarsus) \pahl\

Status:
Paul is trying to be all things to all people.

Profile

Vocation:	Apostle, Ex-Pharisee, Tent-maker, Numero Uno Sinner
Hometown:	Tarsus
Alias:	Saul (my Hebrew name)
A Place I'd Like to Visit:	I'd love to see Paris in the springtime. I did manage to make it to Rome, though. So, I've got that going for me. Which is nice.
Most Embarrassing Moment:	Pretty much the entire time I persecuted the followers of Jesus was my "most embarrassing moment." I'm still trying to live it down!
Favorite Saying:	"My grace is sufficient for you, for my strength is made perfect in weakness"—this is what the Lord said to me when I was dealing with a particularly pesky "thorn in the flesh."

If Jesus is the main Crazy Talker—and he is, or how else do you explain "Take up your cross and follow me"?—then Paul is the main Crazy Talker *about* the main Crazy Talker. Paul *loved* to talk about Jesus. In fact, you couldn't get him to shut up about Jesus. Paul traveled all over the Mediterranean world talking to people about Jesus. And when he wasn't talking to people about Jesus he was writing to people about Jesus. You see, for Paul, the main thing was to make the main thing the main thing. For Paul, the only thing worth knowing was, as he put it, "Jesus Christ and him crucified." Well, all of that talking and writing about Jesus tended to do two things: (1) introduce others to Jesus and (2) get Paul into a heapin' helpin' lot of trouble. (The book of Acts tells plenty of stories about both 1 and 2.)

Initially, Paul was a hater. That is, he hated Christians. He hated Christians so much that he worked to lock them up in jails and even approved of the occasional execution. So you can imagine that when word got out that Paul had become a Christian, folks had a hard time believing it. Paul's turnaround from hater to lover of Christ is probably one of the better known "Damascus Road" conversions. Come to think of it, it's the *original* Damascus Road conversion. On his way to arresting Christians in Damascus, Paul met the risen Jesus. And he was given a job to do: to tell the good news of Jesus to the "Gentiles"—that is, to folks who didn't have the advantage of having Abraham and Sarah in their family tree.

Perhaps because of his spotty past or perhaps because he didn't pal around with the other Apostles, Paul always seemed to have trouble establishing his Christ-cred. For instance, the Christian congregation in the city of Corinth—a congregation that he started no less—began to wonder if Paul was really *all that.* Making a living as a cred-challenged Apostle didn't come easy—poor Paul even had to moonlight as a maker of tents to supplement his meager income. Making matters worse (in terms of his cred), Paul had this whack idea that, because of Jesus, people were "justified by faith apart from the works of the law" (Rom 3:28). This idea left Paul wide open to his critics: "Hey, Paul, if good works don't matter for salvation, why not just go on a sin-bender? Should I party like it's '99, so that grace may abound?" Paul's response: "No freaking way!" (That's our translation of the Greek phrase, *mei geneto.*) Paul lays out this "faith-not-works" theology pretty aggressively and quite clearly—especially in his letters to the Christians in Rome and in Galatia. Read 'em for yourself!

In the end, after traveling all around the Mediterranean region telling about Jesus and starting churches wherever the good news took hold (and visiting some great tourist sites along the way), Paul got crossways with the Law—with both the Jewish and Roman legal systems, that is. Ironically, his status as a Roman citizen saved his hide for a time. Instead of being executed immediately, he was shipped to Rome and put under house arrest for a number of years. And then they executed him. But the "damage" was done. As a result of Paul's inspired work to plant churches all over the known world, and because of his efforts to join together Jew and Gentile, male and female, slave and free in the Body of Christ, the word was out. And there would be no stopping it.

Key Verse: There are so many key verses for Paul, it's tough to choose just one. But since the writers of this here *Crazy Book* are a bunch of sinners, and since Paul referred to himself as the "Chief of Sinners," we're going with, "God demonstrated his love for us in this, that while we were still sinners, Christ died for us" (Rom 5:8). Perfect time. Perfect line.

See also: Letters (or Epistles).

Pentateuch \PEHNT-uh-took\

From the Greek for "five books" this refers to the first . . . um . . . five books of the Old Testament. Nice name, huh? What marketing expert landed that little gem?

The Pentateuch (also known as the Torah, the books of Moses, and the Law) is the first major section of the Bible. Its volumes include Genesis, Exodus, Leviticus, Numbers and Deuteronomy. The broad sweep of the Pentateuch includes: stories about creation and the earliest days of human life up to and including the great flood (which eggheads like to call the "primeval history," Genesis 1–11); stories about the patriarchs and matriarchs of Israel (the ancestral period from Abraham and Sarah through Joseph, Genesis 12–50); about the sojourn in and exodus from Egypt, (in, drum roll please . . . Exodus 1–15); and about the years the Israelites spent living and wandering in the desert (Exodus 16–Numbers 10). The last book in the Pentateuch, Deuteronomy, is in many ways a summary and retelling of a major portion of the Pentateuch's story, which are the laws given by God to Moses at Mt. Sinai.

Included in these stories are important ideas about how God is in relationship with us people—through a covenant (which is really an agreement, a set of terms that describe and define a relationship)—and about laws for living together both with God and with one's fellow humans. This last bit is where the other name for the Pentateuch comes from: *torah* is translated as "law" but really means "instruction" and instruction really is what the Pentateuch is all about.

The author of the Pentateuch, JDEP—not to be confused with the actor J. Depp (that's two 'p's)—is not, in fact, a single author but an acronym for a collaboration of four authors (or more likely four groups of editors). 'J' stands for the Yahwists (the initial 'J' is a homage to the German spelling of the name), who in the book of Genesis call God by the name "Yahweh"; 'D' is for the Deuteronomists, the same writers' group responsible for *The Jerusalem Times* best-seller Deuteronomy; 'E' stands for the Elohists, who in the Book of Genesis preferred the more generic term "Elohim" for God instead of a personal name; finally 'P' is for the priestly authors who emphasized the fundamentals of right relationship with God. It should be noted that although somewhere in the tradition somebody decided Moses wrote these books, nowhere in these books does it claim that Moses wrote them.

One last thing. In thinking about what the Pentateuch is, and what is in these five books for us, you might find it helpful to remember that the Pentateuch begins with stories. There are rules and instructions, there are the Ten Commandments, and to be perfectly blunt, there are certain parts of Leviticus that might make you think the Torah really is all about the Law. But we are given those instructions and rules and yes laws in the context of stories—stories about our relationships with one another, and even more so about our relationship with our Creator. So the Pentateuch is a story. *The* story. The story of God's ongoing faithfulness to God's chosen people, and God's expectations and hopes and promises for them—for us. For you.

See also: Law, Old Testament.

Pentecost \PEHNT-ih-kahst\

Please refer to APOSTOLIC MISSION.

See also: Acts of the Apostles, Paul (Saul of Tarsus).

Persians \PUHR-zhuhnz\

Purveyors of fine rugs, cats, coffees, empires, and remarkably tolerant religious policies—for a price.

The Persian empire rides onto the scene in the biblical narrative like the mythical seventh cavalry, appearing from over the eastern horizon toward to the end of the Babylonian exile, just as the light was about to go out on God's people. The people had been suffering in exile in Babylon, when God raised up Cyrus of Persia, whom the Bible goes so far as to call, God's "shepherd" (Isa 44:28) and "his anointed" (45:1)—terms otherwise reserved for Israel's own kings.

Cyrus' arrival was good news. He rode into town as the new sheriff of a new empire, a kinder, gentler empire. Cyrus sent God's people home. He commanded them to rebuild Jerusalem and its Temple (see Ezra 5). Unlike the Assyrians or Babylonians, the Persian policy on religion was more tolerant—allowing and even encouraging subject peoples to practice the faiths of their fathers and mothers.

This didn't always mean that life in the Persian Empire was a bowl of cherries. They exacted heavy tribute from their provinces, and life in post-exilic Judea was often a hard-scrabble lot (that is old-fashioned talk meaning "they were always hungry and often starving").

But given a choice between Persia and Babylon, most ancient Judeans would have said that they were happy to pay the Persian price.

See also: Assyrians, Babylonians, Israelites.

Peter \PEET-uhr\

Status:
Peter is fixing to eat at KFR (Kentucky Fried Rooster) now that he is finished eating crow.

Profile

Profession:	Fisherman (But I am networking—Get it? Net-working?—in order to find a new profession.)
What's in a Name?	Simon (the name my mother gave me); Cephas (the Aramaic word for "rock," which is the name Jesus gave me)
Interests:	Rocks, keys, camping on mountain tops, fishing, travel (I would love to visit Jerusalem and Rome someday), water skiing (I am not that good—I often fall—but I have a friend who is so good that it looks like he is practically walking on the water)
Turn-offs:	The courtyard of the high priest's palace, the sound of roosters crowing, storms at sea, and hanging upside down (the first three are because of some things that happened to me, the last is just a weird feeling that I have)
I can relate to:	The 2007 New England Patriots

He climbed so high and fell so far. Right into the arms of forgiveness. And purpose.

He was the first one to recognize that Jesus was the Messiah. He was the chief disciple. Chosen not only to be one of the twelve, but to be a part of Jesus' inner circle. And when Jesus said, "They're coming now to arrest me. When they do, you'll all run away. And that's okay, this is one lonesome valley that I've got to walk by myself," Peter said, "Oh no, even if I have to die, I won't run away."

Jesus shook his head and said, "Before the rooster sings three time, you'll deny that you even knew me."

They arrested Jesus and took him to the high priest's palace, where Peter sort of hung out in the courtyard to see what would happen. A servant girl surprised him, "Didn't I see you with Jesus?"

"Must have been some other fisherman," he said.

She shouted to her friends, "Come here, this dude knows the guy that they are questioning."

"Shhhh!" said Peter, shaking his head. Someone else said, "You're from Galilee, you have to know Jesus."

"Never heard of him," said Peter.

Then the rooster said three words: "Cock-adoodle-doo."

Peter got so close to perfection. And then, in the last two minutes of the last game, he failed. As soon as he heard the rooster, Peter knew he had failed. He knew that he couldn't follow Jesus, that he didn't have the strength, faith, courage, or integrity to be faithful.

And then, a few days later, Peter heard what Mary Magdalene and a couple of other women were told by a messenger from God: "He has been raised... Go, tell his disciples and Peter..."

His disciples and Peter. And Peter? And Peter! When Peter heard those two words, he knew that the love of God, which the grave could not contain, was willing to forgive even him. And more, God still had a place for him on the team that God was sending out to love, save, and bless the whole world.

Key Verse: "I tell you, you are Peter, and on this rock I will build my church, and the gates of Hades will not prevail against it. I will give you the keys of the kingdom of heaven, and whatever you bind on earth will be bound in heaven, and whatever you loose on earth will be loosed in heaven" (Matt 16:18-19; see also Mark 8:27—9:8; 14:26-42; John 20–21).

See also: Mark (The Gospel according to), John (The Gospel according to).

1 and 2 Peter \FUHRST-and-SEH-kihnd-PEET-uhr\

By Simon Peter (New Testament, Letters, eight chapters)

Does that last beatitude in Matthew, chapter five, have special meaning for you? You remember the one: “Blessed are you when people revile you and persecute you and utter all kinds of evil against you falsely on my account” (5:11). If you are getting picked on or worse because of your trust in Jesus, well, then, Peter is for you. 1 Peter was written to Christian groups that had been chased from their homes and were living in exile because of their worship of Jesus. 2 Peter takes aim at false teachers who persecute the church from within and reminds readers of the coming “Day of the Lord.” Mr. Peter wants to encourage Christians in tough times to remain steadfast and to confess their faith with boldness: “Always be ready to make your defense to anyone who demands from you an accounting of the hope that is in you, yet do it with gentleness and reverence” (1 Pet 3:15). Mr. Peter offers both an exhortation to and a resource for this defense of the faith, and makes for some good teaching and preaching.

We should also mention that one of our favorite camp songs—“Lions” by Lost and Found—is based on 1 Peter 5:8: “Like a roaring lion your adversary the devil prowls around, looking for someone to devour.”

See also: Letters (or Epistles).

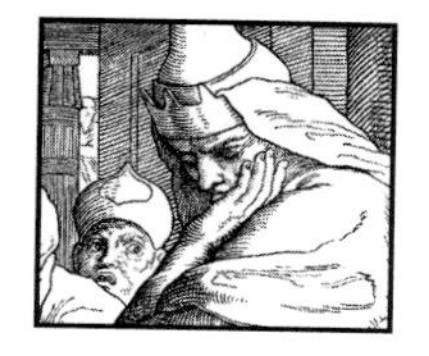

Pharaoh \FEHR-oh\

Status:
Pharaoh is treading water.

Profile

What's in a Name?	"Pharaoh" isn't a name, it's a title!
Pet Peeves:	1. Nine of the plagues—you were expecting ten, but here in the desert a little daytime darkness is really more of a blessing, nice relief from the heat, plus my third wife burns easily. 2. Meddling midwives 3. Flash-floods
Favorite Celebrities:	Yul Brenner, Clint Eastwood
Favorite Band:	"The Pharaohs of Rhythm"—an obscure Scandinavian-American funk-punk-hip-hop-fusion early 90's college band; they rewrote and retitled a Clash song: "Should They Stay Or Should They Go Now?"
Favorite Quotation:	 *

"Pharaoh" is the Egyptian word for "king," and not a name; there are all kinds of different pharaohs mentioned in the Bible, from Pharaoh Shishak (1 Kgs 11:40), to Pharaoh Neco (2 Kgs 23:29), to Pharaoh Hophra (Jer 44:34), to Pharaoh "Braggart who missed his chance" (Jer 46:17).

To most of us, the most famous pharaoh, the most well-known of the pharaohs, the capital 'P' Pharaoh, is from the Exodus story. Pharaoh enslaves the Hebrew people in Egypt. Pharaoh, worried

* Which is hieroglyphic for: "Israel is laid waste; its seed is not"—written by another pharaoh, Merneptah, on a monument.

that he has too many slaves and that they might rise up and drop the smack down on him, orders the Hebrew midwives to kill every boy that is born to the Hebrews. Pharaoh, after losing his showdown with Moses, lets the Hebrews go and then says "Psych!" and tries to run them down in his chariot.

Everybody knows Pharaoh. And every middle school youth group member knows "Pharaoh, Pharaoh." But in a great stroke of irony, this infamous (which is *more* than famous) Pharaoh is never once mentioned by name. The Pharaoh of Exodus is anonymous. He's the original "man with no name," except he's nowhere near as cool as Clint. He is anonymous for a few reasons:

First, villains are creepier when they are anonymous—the Boss (not Springsteen, he's cool), the King, the Pharaoh, the Assistant Principle.

Second, and more importantly, although Pharaoh isn't given a name, Shiphrah and Puah—the two Hebrew midwives who defy Pharaoh's orders because they "feared God"—are. Why do they get names? Because it shows where and how God is at work in the world. God is not at work where we would expect—among the rich and powerful, among Pharaoh. God's presence is hidden. God is at work among the lowest of the low: among enslaved, barren, foreigner women—in ancient Egypt, you couldn't get much lower than that. And THAT is where God is present.

Third, and most importantly, Pharaoh is not named in the story because God *is*. One of the really important things that happens in the Exodus story is that God shares with Moses the Divine Name: "Yahweh" which means something like "I am who I am" (see Exod 3:14-15). God's name is given because in freeing the Hebrew slaves from Egypt we learn that Yahweh is God—which means nobody else is God, and so Pharaoh's name doesn't really matter. In Egyptian religion the pharaoh was thought to be the son of the god Horus. As such he (and sometimes she) was thought to be a god in his own right. So the issue is, who is really God? Whose name really matters?

In fact, Pharaoh himself had to learn whose name mattered. He said, "Who is the Lord, that I should heed him and let Israel go? I do not know the Lord, and I will not let Israel go" (Exod 5:2).

In February of 1967, the great boxer Muhammad Ali faced Ernie Terrell at Madison Square Garden. Before the fight, Terrell had refused to acknowledge Ali's new name (Ali was originally named Cassius Clay), and the champ vowed to punish him for this disrespect. Even though the fight went to a decision, Ali delivered a horrible beating, winning every round decisively. He repeatedly backed away from the staggering Terrell, so that he could continue the beat-down. In between punches, Ali shouted at Terrell, "What's my name?"

In the Exodus story, it is sort of like in between plagues, God shouted to Pharaoh, "What's my name?" It's not good to be the pharaoh.

Key Verse: "For the scripture says to Pharaoh, 'I have raised you up for the very purpose of showing my power in you, so that my name may be proclaimed in all the earth'" (Rom 9:17; see also Exod 1–15).

See also: Egyptians.

Pharisees \FEH-reh-sees\

The spiritual ancestors of Rabbinic Judaism, cousins of Christianity, and the most misunderstood people in the New Testament.

So the Pharisees were a bunch of hypocrites, right? A bunch of self-righteous legalists who thought that they could earn God's grace, right? Not so fast, my friend!

The Pharisees were more like Jesus than any other Jewish group of his day. That is why he and they spend so much time talking to one another. This is not to say they didn't have differences, but Jesus (and Christianity after Jesus) had more in common with the Pharisees than with the Sadducees, Essenes, or Zealots. Like Jesus, the Pharisees acknowledged the entirety of what we call the Old Testament as Scripture. Like Jesus, the Pharisees were a movement of the common people rather than a movement of the elite class. Like Jesus, the Pharisees were a movement of lay people rather than a movement of priests. Like Jesus, the Pharisees believed in the resurrection of the dead and in a dynamic and spiritual interpretation of Scripture.

When the Temple was destroyed in 70 CE and the Sadducees, Zealots, and Essenes faded away (or burned out), it was Pharisaic Judaism that came to the fore. Pharisaic Judaism produced the Talmud and evolved into Rabbinic Judaism. And since Jesus had so much in common with Pharisaism, and since St. Paul described himself "as to the law, a Pharisee," it might also be safe to say that some Pharisees, such as Paul, also became Christians (Phil 3:5).

See also: Jesus, Paul (Saul of Tarsus).

Philemon \fihl-EE-muhn\

By Saul of Tarsus, a.k.a. the Apostle Paul
(New Testament, Letters, one chapter)

What if you had a co-worker in Christ who was also a servant owned by another? And what if you needed that servant for the work of the gospel? What would you do? Why, you'd write a letter muscling the servant's owner (a guy named Philemon, in this case) to give the servant (a guy named Onesimus) his freedom, that's what you'd do. And that's what Paul does in this letter, to great effect. Nice touch: sending Onesimus himself to deliver the letter. Onesimus might have felt a little bit like Uriah the Hittite delivering his own death sentence, but Paul reminds Philemon of the importance of love, forgiveness, and mercy. And this reviewer, for one, is a sucker for love, forgiveness, and mercy.

See also: Letters (or Epistles), Paul (Saul of Tarsus).

Philip (the Apostle) \FIHL-uhp\

Status:
Philip likes leftovers.

Profile

Vocation:	Apostle (and one of the first followers of Jesus)
Hometown:	Bethsaida
Pet Peeve:	Getting confused with Philip the Deacon or with Philip the brother of Herod Antipas
Most Embarrassing Moment:	That time when Jesus wanted to feed the crowd and I told him it couldn't be done. Talk about eating your words! Although they do go surprisingly well with fish and chips.

In terms of speaking parts, Philip doesn't have much. He's got four lines in John's Gospel and that's it. Still, that's four more lines than the disciple called "Simon the Zealot"—who apparently was not zealous enough for a speaking part (or maybe he was too zealous, you now how spiteful directors can be). Philip, on the other hand, maximizes his minimal role. His first line is, "We have found him . . . !" His second line is, "Come and see!" But as with the rest of the disciples, Philip doesn't quite get who Jesus is. For instance, he tries to talk Jesus out of feeding the 5000. And during the Last Supper, Philip says to Jesus: "Show us the Father and we'll be satisfied." Jesus gets up in Philip's face and says, "You've been with me this whole time, and you still don't know me? . . . How can you say 'Show us the Father'?!" You can understand Jesus getting a little miffed at Philip. What's a guy have to do? Walk on water? But Philip figured it out eventually. The resurrection has that kind of effect.

Key Verse: [Jesus said to Philip:] "Whoever has seen me has seen the Father" (John 14:9).

See also: John (The Gospel according to).

Philip (the Deacon) \FIHL-uhp\

Status:
Philip is wondering who he'll run into next.

Profile

Vocation:	Deacon, Evangelist, Bible Study Leader
Home:	I settled in Caesarea (on the coast). The Apostle Paul and some of his buddies once stayed at my house.
Pet Peeve:	Getting confused with Philip the Apostle or with Philip the brother of Herod Antipas
A Place I'd Like to Visit:	Ethiopia. I once met a eunuch from there—worked for the queen. Nicest "guy" you could ever meet.

You know those helpful church people who are always preparing food for potlucks, taking care of the needs of members who are "shut in," and so on? Well, the first Apostles thought they had more important things to do than "wait on tables"—so they appointed others to organize that kind of thing. Philip was one of seven whose job it was to make sure that those in the church who couldn't take care of themselves got taken care of. The word "deacon" means "servant" and Philip was one of the first official deacons of the church. Now we know what you're thinking. You're thinking: *Why those heartless, lazy Apostles! Too busy with prayer and preaching to bother with those in need!* On the other hand, if the leaders have to do everything, they'll burn out. There's a lesson here for modern congregations, it seems to us.

In fact, the New Testament says nothing about how Philip did his job as deacon. It may be that "volunteer coordinator" was not Philip's bag. Instead, the New Testament highlights his role as a preacher of the good news, calling him "Philip the Evangelist." Indeed, Philip is best known for his conversion of the "Ethiopian Eunuch." Philip met him on the road down from Jerusalem. The eunuch was in his chariot reading from the book of Isaiah, a passage that begins, "Like a sheep he was led to the slaughter." The eunuch asked, "What does this mean?" Philip explained that the sheep was Jesus, the crucified and risen one. And faster than you can say, "Candace, Queen of the Ethiopians!"—the eunuch was baptized. (For the whole story, check out the entry on the "Ethiopian Eunuch.") The upshot of Philip's effort: you don't have to be a pastor to teach the Bible or baptize.

Key Verse: "Philip and the eunuch went down into the water and Philip baptized him" (Acts 8:38; see also Acts 6:1-6, 8:26-40).

See also: Acts of the Apostles), Ethiopian Eunuch.

Philippians \fuh-LIHP-ee-uhnz\

By Saul of Tarsus, a.k.a. the Apostle Paul
(New Testament, Letters, four chapters)

Readers of Philippians may get the strong impression that the Christians in the city of Philippi and the Apostle Paul had kind of a crush on each other. At least, based on Paul's flattering prose (Phil 1:3-11) and the fact that the Philippians were always giving Paul cash and prizes (Phil 4:15-18), there's reason to suspect a good amount of mutual admiration. Philippians has some theologically savvy "greatest hits," including, "Work out your salvation in fear and trembling, for it is God who is at work in you, enabling you both to will and to work for his good pleasure" (Phil 2:12b-13), and "the peace of God which surpasses all understanding, will guard your hearts and minds in Christ Jesus." But the greatest of these "greatest hits" is the great hymn giving praise to Christ "who, though he was in the form of God... emptied himself... and being found in human form, he humbled himself and became obedient to the point of death—even death on a cross" (Phil 2:6-8 and there's more great stuff there too, check it out).

One complaint. The Greek word *skubala* is translated "rubbish" or "dung" in English. There is a much better translation. Do a web search for "*skubala*" to learn more about it. (FYI: you'll need to have any parental filters *turned off*—so be warned). Translation challenges

P

aside, the reader will find Philippians to be a faithful word to faithful Christians, full of encouragement and hope in challenging circumstances—some great hits to keep the Christian inspired, uplifted, and rocking. Pretty good for a guy who was writing from prison.

See also: Letters (or Epistles), Paul (Saul of Tarsus).

Philistines \FIHL-uh-steenz, -stinz\

The sort of folks who have been accused of confusing an ocean-going boat for a gravy boat.

At some point, we don't exactly know how or when the term "Philistine" came to mean someone who despises art, culture, manners, beauty, and intellectual achievements. The sort of person who would set down a sweating can of light beer on your teak dining table so that they could wipe the BBQ sauce off their sleeveless shirt.

But in truth, the Philistines were a people with an advanced culture. They came from Crete and arrived in the Promised Land by boat (they were called "the sea people" by the Egyptians) about the same time as the Israelites arrived in the Promised Land by land (and no, the Egyptians did not call the Israelites "the land people"). Whereas the Philistines dwelled on the coastal plain by the Mediterranean in cities such as Ashdod, Ashkelon, and Gaza, the Israelites dwelled in the highlands. For much of Israel's history—especially during the period of the Judges and the early monarchy, but right down to the time of the Kingdom of Judah—the Philistines and Israelites struggled with one another. The Philistine name still survives in the name of the promised land—Palestine.

See also: Goliath, Israelites.

Poetry \POH-ih-tree\

Words ordered in lines.
Parallels, strophes, and rhythms.
Lilies in autumn.

It may surprise you to learn that there is a lot of poetry in the Bible. When we think "Bible," most of us think stories, history, and laws. But in fact several of the major collections of material in the Old Testament are best described as poetry. Psalms, Proverbs, Ecclesiastes, most of the prophetic books, Lamentations, even Job, and that naughty little Song of Solomon's—all poetry. But not, probably, the kind of poetry that you're used to. Not the kind of poetry you studied in tenth-grade English, or that you read to your significant other when your heart's all atwitter, or listen to on the radio. And certainly not like the bad Haiku in the definition above.

Poetry in the Old Testament is different. When it comes to the poetry of the Bible there are lots and lots and lots of little details that you could think about, way too much to deal with in a dictionary. So here are the bare bones basics: it isn't about rhyming, it's about two basic things: couplets and parallelism. Here's an example of Old Testament poetry that will show you what we mean:

> As a deer longs for flowing streams, 'A'
> so my soul longs for you, O God. 'B'

This is the first verse of Psalm 42. This verse is made up of two parts (labeled 'A' and 'B'), these are called couplets and many verses of poetry in the Old Testament are made up of these couplets (some have more, but this is by far the norm). Notice that between the two couplets there are some ideas that "parallel" or balance each other: deer = my soul; flowing streams = you, O God. These ideas are held together and make a fuller (more full?) image or reflection of what the poet is trying to say.

The prophets, the wise, the pray-ers, and the occasional king all did their thing poetically. So it's a fair bet that if you like the Bible, then you like poetry, too. Who knew?

See also: Old Testament.

Pontius Pilate \PAHN-shuhs-PI-liht\

Status:
Pilate is suffering under the "suffered under" line in the creed.

Profile

Vocation:	Roman Governor of Judea
Home:	Jerusalem (until Caesar moves me out of this god forsaken backwater and gives me a plusher assignment—I hear Pompeii is nice)
Fifteen Minutes of Fame:	Fifteen minutes? More like Fifteen Centuries! I'm smack in the middle of that Apostles' Creed—my name gets uttered by millions of people every single week!
Pet Peeves:	People who don't wash their hands. "Cleanliness is next to godliness," I always say. People who spell my name "Pilot" (a crucifiable offense if you ask me).
Favorite Movie:	*Monty Python's Life of Brian*. My wife doesn't think the movie portrays me very accurately but, man, it kills me every time. "Wewease Bawabbas!" Pretty funny stuff.

How would you like to be forever remembered by the words, "Crucified under Pontius Pilate"? You can almost feel for Pilate. He was just minding his own business, oppressing the Jewish people with his Roman Empire authority, when along comes this prisoner, Jesus of Nazareth. With Jesus standing before him, Pilate found himself in a quandary. On the one hand, it seemed clear that Jesus had done nothing that deserved the death penalty. On the other hand, the religious leaders and the angry crowd wanted Jesus dead. What's a local despot to do? "I know," thought Pilate, "I'll see if I can't get Jesus to defend himself." But that didn't work. "Maybe if I get him into a philosophical discussion about 'What is Truth'?" But that didn't work. "Maybe if I give the rabble a choice between Jesus and some real criminal?" But that didn't work. "Maybe if I have him flogged within an inch of his life?" But that didn't work. "I've got it!" said Pilate, "I'll wash my hands of the entire matter—that ought

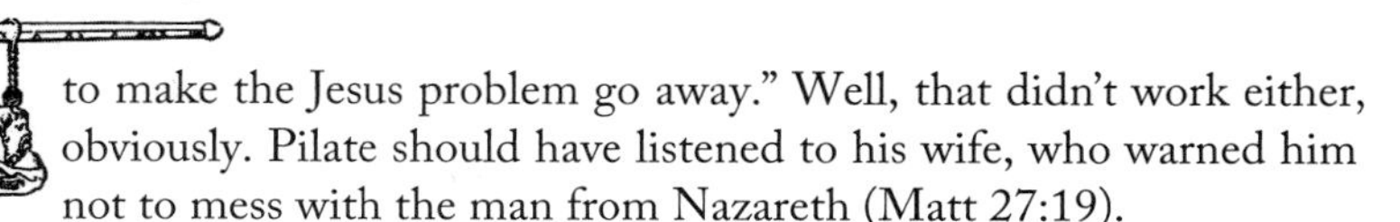

to make the Jesus problem go away." Well, that didn't work either, obviously. Pilate should have listened to his wife, who warned him not to mess with the man from Nazareth (Matt 27:19).

Key Verse: [Jesus said to Pilate:] "You have no power over me, except that which has been given to you from above" (John 19:11a; see also John 19, Mark 15, Luke 23, and Matt 27).

See also: Barabbas, Holy Week, Jesus, Passion Narrative.

Prophetic Message \ prah-FEH-tik\

The handwriting on the wall, the names pinned on kids, the harness worn around the neck, or the divine homework that was eaten—anything the prophets did to get across God's message.

Here is a little advice. If a prophet ever rings your doorbell and says, "I've got a message for you . . . from God," think twice before signing for the delivery. The prophets, who were God's message deliverers, would do just about anything to get a point across. Daniel saw handwriting on the wall; Isaiah and Hosea gave their kids funky names; Jeremiah wore a harness around his neck; Ezekiel ate a scroll. And so on. If it would help to get God's point across, a prophet would pretty much do it.

Speaking very broadly, the prophet's messages came in two flavors: good news (called messages of salvation) and bad news (called messages of judgment). The good news messages often start off, "Fear not!" The bad news messages often begin, "Woe unto you!"

But one person's good news is another person's bad news. For example, God might say, "Fear not! For I am going to save you from the person trying to smite you . . . by smiting that person." Or, God might say: "Woe unto you! For I going to smite you because of the evil you are doing to your neighbor . . . because I love your neighbor." So, even God's bad news shows God's good side—depending on which side of God you are on.

See also: Ezekiel, Jeremiah, Prophets (Major and Minor).

Prophets, Major \MĀ-juhr-PRAH-fihts\

As tuba players are to lesser band members, so these prophets are to other musicians whose choice of instruments may not be less important but only smaller. And like tuba players, the major prophets made the other, "minor," prophets (the percussion section?) nervous. So the band geeks in the percussion section (that is, the "minor prophets") might be heard to say something like, "That Isaiah, he sure is a major prophet, isn't he? What an über-dork."

Prophets, Minor \MI-nuhr-PRAH-fihts\

Those prophets who knew that a few well-chosen words are worth more than the heaping-up of words you get from those tuba players, er, "major" prophets.

When it comes to the prophets, the first thing you need to know is that the categories "major" (which refers to Isaiah, Jeremiah, Ezekiel, and Daniel) and "minor" (which refers to Hosea, Joel, Amos... and the rest of the other twelve) have nothing to do either with the quality or importance of the books. "Major" and "Minor" simply describe the relative size of the books. Isaiah, Jeremiah, Ezekiel, and Daniel are the big boys, and we mean that literally. All the rest are short by comparison. Major means bigger and Minor means smaller. For the most part, that is all there is to it.

In fact, there is a lot that the Major and Minor Prophets have in common. All of the prophets deliver a message from God, often introduced by the phrase, "Thus says the Lord." All of the prophets believed that Israel (and oftentimes Israel's neighbors, too) had failed to keep faith with God in some way, and their words called Israel (and yes sometimes even Israel's neighbors) to repent or suffer the consequences of its sin. The prophets also have much to say about justice, about how the poor, the widows, the orphans, and the strangers that are in Israel's midst were being treated. In other words, the prophets all had something to say about right relationships: right relationship with God and right relationship with one's neighbors (especially those less fortunate).

Whether large or small, big or little, Major or Minor, the prophets present a message from God that is still very important. And that message is ultimately one of hope and promise. Through the prophets God still is calling us back into a right and good relationship with him.

See also: Old Testament.

Proverb \PRAH-vuhrb\

A short saying that, once you hear it, you know it's true; valuable for those who don't know it.

A proverb is a short saying that teaches a practical truth based on common experience. Every coach or music teacher knows dozens of proverbs, such as, "Can't is a four-letter word. We don't use four-letter words here." Or, "Focus on what you can control." These aren't in the Bible. But this one is: "Like a dog that returns to its vomit is a fool who reverts to his folly" (Prov 26:11). So, take our advice. Check out the Bible. It has a whole book of these things.

See also: Proverbs (book).

Proverbs \PRAH-vuhrbz\ (book)

by Various-and-Assorted (Old Testament, Poetry, thirty-one chapters)

Benjamin Franklin, the more or less great American whose wit gave us such classics as "A penny saved is a penny earned" and "Anyone who trades liberty for security deserves neither liberty nor security," ain't got nothing on Proverbs. A sampling of Proverb's fare shows it equally acerbic and likewise apropos: "Like vinegar to the teeth, and smoke to the eyes, so are the lazy to their employers" (Prov 10:26); "Like a gold ring in a pig's snout is a beautiful woman [or man] without good sense." (11:22); "It is better to live in a corner of the housetop than in a house shared with a contentious spouse" (21:9).

Of all the types or genres of literature in the Bible, none is more recognizable or more readily appropriated as the proverb. Proverbs are a part of everyday language in virtually every culture. This is part of what makes Mr. Various-and-Assorted's anthology so appealing. For the record, some believe that these sayings can be attributed to King Solomon, but the book includes sayings attributed to other authors. And genuine authorship of these sayings is difficult to ascertain—not that Solomon didn't surely quip off with a proverb now and then—as we said, such things are part of everyday life.

The biblical proverbs address a wide range of subjects, from wise and righteous living to fear of the Lord, to common courtesy (don't laugh too much, talk too much, drink too much, or, well, anything too much). The collection begins as an address to "my child," which may refer to the "son of Solomon," that is the prince, or to young men in general, or perhaps both. Whatever the case, the book provides sagacious advice for any young person. Another distinctive feature of Proverbs is the personification of wisdom as a woman. Woman wisdom in Proverbs is employed by Mr. Various-and-Assorted as a counterbalance to the "loose" or wicked woman who will distract a young man and lead him astray. This is, according to the book, to be avoided. One ought to dedicate oneself to a right relationship with God and woman wisdom can nurture that relationship, and no one better.

A broad outline of Mr. Various-and-Assorted's book is as follows: 1:1—9:18 "the proverbs of Solomon, son of David"; 10:1—22:16 "the proverbs of Solomon"; 22:17—24:22 "words of the wise"; 24:23-34 "these are also words of the wise"; 25:1—29:27 "... other proverbs of Solomon ..."; 30:1-33 "Sayings of Agur"; 31:1-31 "Sayings of King Lemuel."

See also: Poetry, Old Testament.

Psalm \sawlm\

A biblical poem that is often sung ping-pong style during worship.

The first thing to know about the psalms is that they are poetry. But unlike the poetry you learned once upon a time, the lines of these poems don't end with a rhyme (even in the Hebrew language in which they were originally composed). So what makes them poetry if they don't rhyme? The fact that each line of a Hebrew poem parallels the one that comes before or after it. For example:

Line A Then our mouth was filled with laughter,
Line B and our tongue with shouts of joy. (Ps 126:2a)

In order to get the hang of reading the psalms, it is key to get comfortable with this parallel rhythm.

The second thing to know about the psalms is that there are a few flavors. Most of these types of psalms do exactly what they say:

hymns of praise
songs of thanksgiving
laments (also known as prayers for help)
songs of trust
royal psalms (which talk about God's gracious deeds through the ancient human king)
wisdom psalms (which teach about God's ways)
liturgies (which were used in communal worship)

Each of these types of psalm is meant for a different mood or time of life. There are poems for when you are lonely or angry with God or feeling good about God. There are 150 of these things. Go ahead and try some out.

See also: Poetry, Psalms (book).

Psalms

\sawlmz\ (or, as they say on the East Coast, \sahmz\) (book)

by Various-and-Assorted
(Old Testament, Poetry, one-hundred-fifty chapters)

The book of Psalms is a collection of various types of poetry authored by an assortment of bards, scribes, and poets for any number of occasions and uses. The Psalter (another name for this collection) includes (take a deep breath): poems of praise, prayer, complaint, thanksgiving, travel, reflections on wisdom and divine instruction, history, and theology, as well as for specific events like religious festivals or important moments in the life of the king. These various psalms are attributed to the quill of David, Asaph, the Sons of Korah, Solomon, nobody at all, and even Moses.

Like most anthologies of poetry, there is little coherence to the book as a whole. In fact the book of Psalms is divided into five books or smaller collection of psalms (1–41, 42–72, 73–89, 90–106, and 108–150). Some psalms seem to have been placed next to each other because of shared themes, and there is some subtle movement throughout the book as a whole, moving from a more somber tone at the beginning of the collection to one of praise and thanksgiving at the end.

Mr. Various-and-Assorted has here assembled an admirable collection of spiritual poetry that will be a welcome source of comfort, insight, prayer, and praise for every believer in most any time of their life. Indeed, as another reviewer of this work once remarked, "The Psalter . . . might very well be called a little Bible. In the Psalter everything that is contained in the entire Bible is comprehended so beautifully and so briefly that it constitutes an excellent 'Enchiridion,' or handbook" (Martin Luther). To take it a step further, Psalms by itself is worth the price of the Bible.

See also: Poetry, Old Testament.

P

Queen of Sheba

\KWEEN-uhv-SHEE-buh\

Status:
QoS is in awe of that Solomon fellow—wow!

Profile

Vocation:	Queen (duh!)
Home:	Sheba (c'mon!)
Turn-ons:	Wealth, wisdom, power—and guys who have them.
Favorite Song:	"Material Girl" by Madonna
Favorite Quotation:	"Give me an Escalade, a two-way, bling bling on E-Bay"—Dr. Evil in *Austin Powers in Goldmember*

The Queen of Sheba is famous for one thing and one thing only: Buh-ling. When Solomon was king of Israel, the Queen of Sheba came to Jerusalem to check Solomon out. She wanted to see for herself if Solomon's wisdom (and wealth) matched all the hype. Perhaps to butter Solomon up a bit, the Queen brought with her camel-loads of precious spices, gold, and jewels. Not to mention lumber, lots of lumber. (Solomon used the lumber to make terraces for the royal palace.) Solomon, who wasn't exactly known for his restraint when it came to women, gave the queen a royal welcome. When Solomon answered all her questions (even the trick ones like, "Does a falling tree make a sound when there's no one to hear it?" and "Can God make a square circle?" Answers: *Duh*! and *Don't be stupid*.), she was so overwhelmed with his awesomeness that she bestowed on him the title "QuizMaster 950 BCE" and lavished upon him her many camel-loads of riches.

Key Verse: "I did not believe the reports until I came and my own eyes had seen it. Not even half had been told me; your wisdom and prosperity far surpass the report that I had heard" (1 Kgs 10:7; see also 1 Kgs 10:1-13).

See also: Solomon.

Rachel \RĀ-chuhl\

Status:

Rachel and her sister are definitely *not* bff (best friends forever).

Profile

Vocation:	Co-wife
Home:	Somewhere in the desert
Pet Peeve:	Bigamy and its sticky, unanticipated results: like my sister's kids not knowing whether to call me "mom" or "aunt" or some ridiculous combination of the two
Least Favorite Song:	"Torn between Two Lovers" by Mary MacGregor

If Rachel lived today, she'd be on Oprah telling stories about how she survived her messed up family. First off—cue intro lick to "Dueling Banjos"—Rachel married her cousin, Jacob (of Abraham, Isaac, and Jacob fame). The wedding itself was lovely, with Rachel looking radiant in white chiffon. The wedding night, on the other hand, presented complications—the main complication being Rachel's older sister, Leah. Turns out Rachel's dad, Laban, didn't think it right that the younger sister should marry first. You can imagine the conversation. Laban: "Rachel, great wedding. Say, I was wondering if you'd let your sister take your place tonight?" Rachel: "What!?" Laban: "Yeah, I think Jacob has had enough to drink where he won't be able to tell the difference." Rachel: "What?!" Laban: "So your sister Leah will spend the night with Jacob, if that's okay with you." Rachel: "What??!" Laban: "But don't worry. If Jacob works for me for seven more years, you can be his wife, too." Rachel: "What?!!"

If you think two sisters sharing a bathroom is tough, imagine sharing a husband. That's a whole 'nother thing. Making matters worse was the fact that Rachel was having a tough time getting pregnant, while Leah was having baby after baby. Like her great aunt, Sarah, Rachel even tried the old "I'll-Let-My-Husband-Sleep-With-My-Personal-Assistant" trick in an attempt to produce offspring. (A trick which worked, by the way. Her maid, Bilhah, had two children—Dan and Naphtali.) But in the end, the Lord had mercy upon Rachel and "opened up her womb" (as the Bible so delicately puts it). Rachel bore two children, Joseph and Benjamin, which resulted in the musical *Joseph and the Amazing Technicolor Dreamcoat*, which resulted in Donny Osmond's career comeback.

Key Verse: "With mighty wrestlings I have wrestled with my sister, and have prevailed" (Gen 30:8; see also Gen 29, 30).

See also: Jacob.

R

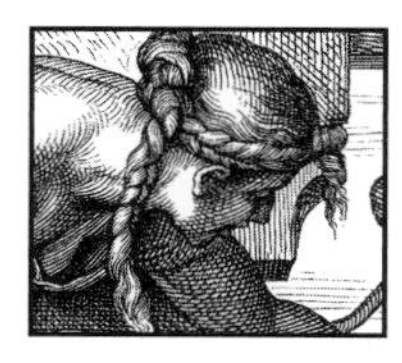

Rahab \RĀ-hab\

Status:
Rahab is sweeping up.

Profile

Vocation:	Formerly a member of "The World's Oldest Profession," and, no, I don't mean "farmer"
Home:	Jericho (before the walls came a-tumblin' down)
Little-known Facts:	I'm King David's great, great grandmother, *and* I'm one of only four women named in Matthew's family tree of the Messiah.
Favorite Movie:	*Pretty Woman*

March 1. Dear Diary: Last night, some new customers stopped by the shop. At least, I thought they were new customers. Turns out, they're advance spies, scoping out the city on behalf of their general, someone called Joshua. Today, the local cops stopped by, looking for the spies. Apparently, they're something called Hebrews. I wonder if this is the same bunch whose God opened up a can of whoop-Asherah on the mighty Egyptians. Well, if these Hebrews are as invincible as everyone says they are, I didn't want to get on their bad side, did I? So I told the cops, 'Those guys you're looking for?—they went that-a-way!' But actually they were hiding up on my roof.

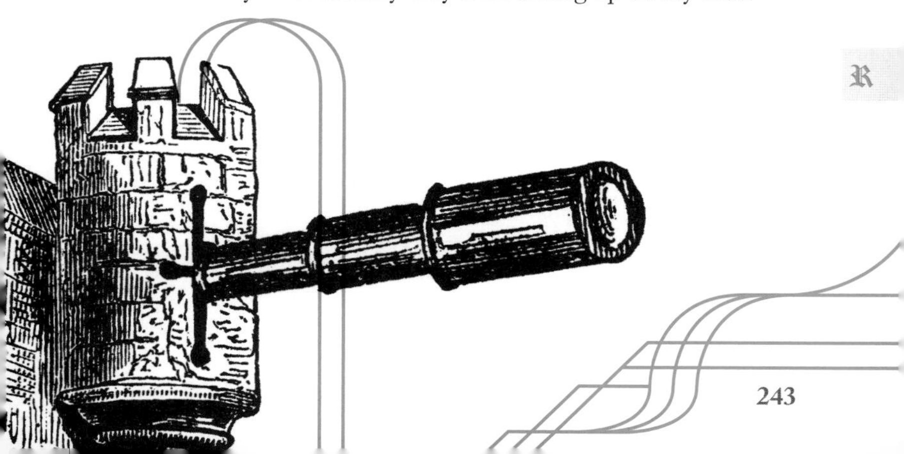

R

March 2. Dear Diary: Call me naughty, but today I helped the two spies escape. Since the entrance to the city was all sealed up, I had to do some quick thinking. Lucky for me, my place is built right into the city wall. I took one of my best ropes (the scarlet one) and the two guys used it to climb out of my window. But I made this deal with them: In exchange for my help, they had to promise to spare me and my family when they invaded Jericho. They agreed.

March 29. Dear Diary: Well, long story short: after much fanfare, the Hebrew army flattened the city, the spies came to get me, and now I'm living with the Hebrews. Everyone's really nice to me. And then there's this guy named Salmon who seems to be interested in me (in a good, wholesome, "no money down" sort of way). It's funny how things turn out.

Key Verse: Rahab said: "We have heard how the LORD dried up the waters of the Red Sea . . . the LORD, your God, is God in heaven above and on earth below" (Josh 2:10a, 11b; see also Josh 2 and 6:22-25).

See also: Jericho, Joshua (book).

Rebekah \ruh-BEHK-uh\

Status:
Rebekah is playing favorites (and we don't mean favorite songs).

Profile

R

Vocation:	Cunning Matriarch
Hometown:	Aram of the Two Rivers (or "Up North")
About My Family:	I married my dad's cousin, and my youngest son married my brother's daughters. Talk about "family systems issues" . . .

Rebekah wasn't looking for love when she went to the local watering hole that fateful day. Little did she know that the stranger with all the camels loaded with cash and prizes was on a mission to find a wife for Abraham's son, Isaac. By the end of the day, Rebekah had wedding plans, not to mention fistfuls of silver and gold and a fantastic new wardrobe. Still, marriage to a complete stranger requires a leap of faith. Rebekah took the leap. When asked by her family, "Will you go with this guy?" Rebekah said, "I'll go!"

It's easier to like the young Rebekah—bright-eyed, free spirit that she was—than it is to like the older Rebekah, who "played favorites" with her children in a big way, and who deceived her husband in outrageous fashion. The rules of the day said that the firstborn son, Esau, should get Dad's blessing—and all the cash and prizes that went with it. But Rebekah wanted her second-born, mama's-boy Jacob, to get the blessing. So she came up with a plan to trick her husband, Isaac, into blessing Jacob rather than Esau. You might say that it's one thing to slip an extra cookie in one kid's bag lunch, or to slide a few extra denarii to him/her on the side, but Rebekah went to what you might call an extreme inheritance makeover. Is it any surprise that Rebekah never won any Mother-of-the-Year awards? Then again, she is the mother of the father of the Twelve Tribes of Israel. So she's got that going for her. Which is nice.

Key Verse: "May [your descendents] increase to thousands upon thousands" (Gen 24:60a; see also Gen 24 and 27).

See also: Ancestral Period, Esau, Isaac, Jacob.

Resurrection of Jesus, The

\thuh-REHZ-uh-REHK-shuhn-uhv-JEE-zuhs\

Although the resurrection happened at a particular point in time, its effects are beyond time. You quantum physicists out there know that we humans can measure the space-time continuum in four dimensions (with one dimension being time itself), but to account for the complexities of the universe we observe, some theorists have imagined anywhere from six to twenty-two (!) additional dimensions. In some of these models, time is not only relative, it's an afterthought. Fortunately, you don't have to be a rocket scientist to appreciate the fact that the resurrection of Jesus Christ is a one-time, once-and-for-all-time, now-and-forevermore-time event, in the light of which "there is a new creation: everything old has passed away; see, everything has become new" (2 Cor 5:17)!

In the weeks that followed the crucifixion, the followers of Jesus experienced a bit of the rupture of the time space-continuum when the Risen Christ appeared and disappeared to them, hiding himself and revealing himself to them, eating and drinking with them, comforting them, and reassuring them. Because God had raised Jesus from the dead, these followers came to learn that all of time—past, present, and future—had been transformed from dark to light, from death to life.

Still, those resurrection appearances were perhaps a bit risky. As everyone who remembers the *Back to the Future* trilogy well knows, you don't want to interrupt the space-time continuum too much. On the other hand, since human existence on the space-time continuum was headed for hell in a hand-basket anyway, maybe the divine idea was similar to the thinking of *Back to the Future*'s Doc Brown. When Marty McFly asked him about the risks of messing with the space-time continuum, the good doctor replied: "What the hell." For sinners stuck in the space-time continuum, the resurrection of Jesus means death and hell no longer have the last word. Thanks be to God. Amen.

See also: Creation, Gospel, Jesus.

Revelation to John, The

\thuh-REHV-uh-LĀ-shuhn-too-JAHN\

By John of Patmos*

(New Testament, Apocalyptic Literature, twenty-two chapters)

Long appreciated by heavy metal aficionados because of sinister elements like "The Beast" and "666," Revelation can be appreciated by Christians as well. (That's not to say that heavy metal aficionados can't also be Christians. They can. More cowbell!) Mr. O'Patmos begins with three chapters that proclaim words of comfort and warning to Christian congregations in various contexts. Revelation ends with a vision of a New Jerusalem where Christ, the Lamb of God, the Alpha and the Omega, reigns for eternity. In this New Jerusalem, every tear will be wiped away and there will be "no more death or mourning or crying or pain" (Rev 21:4). As for the material in between the beginning and ending of Revelation, it can be summed up in the following manner: "What the . . . ?!"

If you struggle reading Revelation, you are not alone. Even early church leaders commented that Revelation was "covered thickly and densely by a veil of obscurity," that there is a "concealed and more wonderful meaning in every part," and that "it is beyond my comprehension."* Consider the following passage: "I took the little scroll from the angel's hand and ate it. It tasted as sweet as honey in my mouth. But when I had eaten it, my stomach turned sour" (Rev 10:10). How should this be interpreted? Don't eat little scrolls? Chase that with some Maalox®? That God's word sometimes seems sweet—especially when we're reciting God's judgment to someone *else*—but that living with that judgment can be harder than you'd expect? It's a little hard to tell.

On the other hand, there is no shortage of folks who will be more than happy to tell you the meaning behind each and every implausible event and fantastic image recorded in Revelation. Whether it's the arrival of four, color-coordinated horses (white, black, red, and

---

*Reported in Eusebius, *Church History*, VII:vvx.

an understated yet effective shade of pale green) or the seven-headed woman with ten horns whose cup is filled with the "abominations and impurities of her fornications" (Rev 17:4), history is chock full of (false) prophets explaining the true, hidden meaning of every detail. Often these prophets will include in their explanations a timeline of end-of-times events. It is an obvious point—but one worth repeating—that not one, single prediction of the world's end has yet to come to pass. *Countdown to Armageddon* is not only a terrible 1998 "documentary," it's an even worse method of biblical interpretation.

But let's not let a bunch of crackpots spoil Revelation for the rest of us. The fact is that countless Christian communities and individuals have been able to read their own trials and tribulations, persecutions and sufferings, through the lens of Mr. O'Patmos's fantastical visions. In this sense, Revelation is not so much a book for predicting the future as it is a book for giving comfort and hope in the present. If Revelation does make one thing absolutely clear, it is this: no matter how bad it gets, Christ has already emerged victorious over sin, death, and the power of the devil. And because you have been joined to his crucified and risen body, the day is coming when you will emerge victorious as well.

* Some early Christian leaders (like Irenaeus) held that John of Patmos and John the Apostle were the same person, while others (like John Chrysostom) held that the two figures were not the same.

See also: Apocalyptic Literature.

Romans \ROH-mihnz\

By Saul of Tarsus, a.k.a. the Apostle Paul
(New Testament, Letters, sixteen chapters)

In Romans, Paul offers a reasoned argument in support of his proclamation of the good news about Jesus Christ. This is Paul's most profound and lucid argument to date. Originally a letter to Christians living in Rome, Paul makes his case for a Jesus who redeems humanity not by rewarding people for obeying the rules but—get this—through establishing a relationship based on trust alone. Paul invites his readers to consider this seemingly preposterous proposal from the standpoints of reason, the Hebrew Scriptures, the history of Israel, and his own personal experience. Paul is particularly effective in countering the question that if we are saved apart from legal standards, then why not sin as much as you want?

In chapters one through eight Paul carefully builds his argument—an argument which crescendos to the promise that nothing "will be able to separate us from the love of God that is in Christ Jesus our Lord" (Rom 8:39b). "Really?" the reader may ask, "Nothing? What if I reject this love?" But Paul anticipates this question and spends chapters nine through eleven demonstrating how even such rejection is part of the divine plan. In the end, however, even Paul recognizes that reason has its limits. Paul says it best: "Oh, the depth of the riches of the wisdom and knowledge of God! How unsearchable his judgments, and his paths beyond tracing out!" (Rom 11:33). In chapters twelve through fifteen, Paul outlines a vision for the Christian life, before concluding in chapter sixteen by showing off a bit by listing all the people he knows.

Except for the rather plain title (what would have been wrong with something like, *Friends, Romans, Countrymen: Since Faith Comes Through Hearing, Lend Me Your Ears?*), Paul's Romans has it all.

See also: Letters (or Epistles), Paul (Saul of Tarsus).

Rome \rohm\

A place where one might do things in a manner in which one does not normally do things, but in a manner consistent with local custom. Like Vegas.

Rome is now called the Holy City. But back in the biblical day, it was the unholy City. At least in the New Testament, it was considered so vile and violent that the book of Revelation refers to it as "Babylon," which was another rather unwholesome city.

The Roman empire dominated the then known civilized world, which included both the promised land (Judea) and most of the places where the early church spread. The Roman emperor was considered a god (see Caesar). And while the *Pax Romana* (peace of Rome) provided the benefit of an often stable political world, the *pax* was established through rather un-peace-full methods. Such as crucifying potential troublemakers and Messiahs.

When in Rome, do as the Romans. So since the Romans conquered, the church eventually conquered Rome by means of a mostly peaceful winning-of-the-day. Rome became the center of the Christian Church. Unfortunately, in Rome, the church later often learned to do as the Romans did, and so the (institutional) church fell prey to the temptation to make others its prey. But that really should be another book, don't you think?

See also: Caesar.

Ruth \rooth\ (book)

by Anonymous (Old Testament, History, four chapters)

In the book of Ruth, Mr. Anonymous picks up where Judges left off. It is often hard for a person to properly understand just what kind of story one is reading in Ruth. For the purposes of this review, let it suffice to say that the work is something of a prequel; something of a bridge story; something of a foreshadowing of a testament to come.

Ruth begins, "In the days when the judges ruled, there was a famine in the land, and a certain man of Bethlehem in Judah went to live in the country of Moab, he and his wife and two sons." Not the most ominous of beginnings, perhaps, but the fallout is remarkable.

Ruth's story begins with one of those deeply ironic statements of which the biblical authors are so fond and of which most readers are ignorant because they do not know the first thing about the Hebrew language. Famine comes to Bethlehem—*beth-lehem* in Hebrew means "house of bread." The author is telling his readers that when famine can touch even the very house of bread, times are difficult indeed.

Of the family that leaves Judah for greener pastures, only the mother Naomi who calls herself Mara (which in Hebrew means "bitter") returns, accompanied only by her son's foreign-born widow, Ruth. Ruth finds new love with Boaz, and through her faithfulness to her mother-in-law, brings life and hope back to Naomi and ultimately to Israel as well, as her great-grandson will be David.

While brief by almost any editorial standard, Mr. Anonymous sets out to accomplish at least two things in this courageous and ambitious little book. First, the story introduces a foreign woman in a favorable light—a widow from Moab, historically one of Israel's greatest enemies, is ultimately the character who is most faithful and hopeful, and who in turn provides faith and hope for her family and her adoptive nation. This is a bold and daring plot line around which to build a story. Second, Ruth sets the stage for the stories of Israel's great king (and ultimately for its messiah), bridging the gap historically between the eras of judges and kings. Ruth is one of those books that one will, perhaps, leave unread and never realize what one has missed. But upon reading this powerful little story, the reader's eyes will be opened in new ways to the wondrous and mysterious ways in which God works good for God's people.

See also: Naomi, Ruth.

Ruth \rooth\

Status:
Ruth is glad to be done threshing on the threshing floor.

Profile

Hometown:	Moab originally, now Bethlehem
About My Family:	I'm the daughter-in-law of Naomi, the wife of Boaz, and the great grandmother of David the king.
Did you know . . .	. . . that I am one of only four women mentioned in the family tree of Jesus the Messiah (Matt 1:5)?

Ruth's story is about traditional things like marriage, home, and family. Except in Ruth's case, she did not come by these traditional things in the traditional way. We meet Ruth in the aftermath of a tragedy. Both Ruth and her sister, Orpah, had become widowed. To make matters worse, their dead husbands' mother, Naomi, was also a widow. Widows and orphans had it tough in those days—they still do—and so Naomi decided to head back to her hometown, Bethlehem. Not wanting the baggage of two widowed daughters-in-law, Naomi told Ruth and Orpah to go home and live with their own mothers. Orpah goes. But Ruth tells Naomi, in short, "I'm sticking with you whether you like it or not" (for Ruth's actual words, see the key verse below).

Here's what Ruth does. Ruth ditches her own homeland (Moab), her own people (Moabites), and even her own god (Chemosh), in favor of a new life in Naomi's homeland (Judah), with Naomi's people (Israelites), and with Naomi's God (Yahweh). And for such ditching, the Holy Scripture is eternally grateful—a gratefulness shown by awarding Ruth with her own book of the Bible.

Ruth, chapter one, tells how the foreign-born, husbandless Ruth, arrived in Bethlehem with her husbandless mother-in-law, Naomi. In a culture that didn't leave widows much recourse, what do two widows do? They get busy. The clever way in which the two women conspire to get Ruth hooked-up with the dashing sugar daddy, Boaz, is a story we'll let you check out on your own. But the upshot is that Ruth's marriage to Boaz produces a son, Obed. Who becomes the father of Jesse. Who becomes the father of David. And the rest, as they say, is (salvation) history. (David is the necessary forefather of Jesus—do we have to spell it out for you?) Ruth proves, once again, that even the "outsider"—sometimes *especially* the outsider—has a special place in God's plan to redeem the world.

Key Verse: "Where you go, I will go; where you lodge, I will lodge; your people shall be my people, and your God my God" (Ruth 1:16b; see also the book of Ruth).

See also: **Boaz, Naomi, Ruth (book).**

Sadducees

A group of Jews whose fate it was to be too closely connected with the Second Temple—rather sad, you see?

The Sadducees—a Jewish group prominent from about two centuries BCE until roughly the year 70 CE—thought they had it pretty good. They were a priestly group, which meant that with Rome in control of the land, they had a lot of power. They held most of the key leadership posts at the Temple, which gave them further power. And they were largely aristocratic, which added even more to their power. All in all, when compared to the lowly Pharisees, they thought they had it pretty good.

Like the Samaritans, the Sadducees only acknowledged the first five books of the Bible. They didn't believe in the resurrection of the dead or a spiritual interpretation of the Bible or the Psalms (for which we hold them in particular derision—we like the Psalms).

So what happened? When one too many Jewish rebellions convinced the Romans that it was time to destroy the Temple in 70 CE, the base of the Sadducaic power and influence evaporated. You gotta dance with the one who brung you, and when the one who brung you is destroyed stone by stone, brick by brick, you've got nobody left to dance with. That is what happened to the Sadducees, who disappeared from history following the Temple's destruction.

See also: Pharisees, Temple.

Salome \SAH-luh-mā\

Status:
Salome is winded.

Profile

Vocation:	Dancer, Head-on-a-Platter Server
Favorite Play:	*Salome* by Oscar Wilde
Favorite Opera:	*Salome* by Richard Strauss
Favorite Movie:	*Bring Me the Head of Alfredo Garcia* by Sam Peckinpah

Thanks to Salome, we know what it means to have your head served on a platter. Thanks to this young—and by all counts, effective—exotic dancer, John the Baptist got his noggin turned into an entrée. You'll find the gory details in Matthew 14. Seriously, read the twisted tale for yourself. It's not the kind of story they cover in Sunday school. You've got a young girl, Salome, with an uncle who's having an affair with her mom who wants John the Baptist dead. But it's Salome who does all the dirty work: it's Salome who does the dance that gets her uncle to promise her anything—anything!—she wants; it's Salome who makes the request for John's head on a plate; it's Salome who delivers the dastardly dish to her mother.

Funny thing is, this Salome isn't mentioned by name in Matthew's account of John the Baptist's demise. We learn her name from the first-century Jewish historian, Josephus (who conveniently includes additional sordid details of the affair between Herod and Herodius). Still, there is a Salome named elsewhere in the Gospels. In Mark's Gospel, a certain Salome is among the women who witness the crucifixion and the empty tomb. There's no reason whatsoever to think that it's the same Salome who bumped off John the Baptist. But wouldn't it be cool if it was?

Key Verse: "The head was brought on a platter and given to the girl, who brought it to her mother" (Matt 14:11).

See also: Herod Antipas, John the Baptist.

Samaria \suh-MEHR-ee-uh\

A place filled with people who do good deeds on the side of roads.

Samaria was just a hill. But a king of Israel (the Northern Kingdom) bought the hill and built himself a new capital city there. Kind of like King David before him, who had moved Israel's capital to Jerusalem. Or kind of like the American founders after him, who created a new capital city in Washington, D.C., the strategy was to unify a disparate people by creating a new central city. And it worked.

Samaria eventually was destroyed by the Assyrians when they laid waste to the Northern Kingdom. But its name lived on as the name of the region and as the name of a religious people known as the Samaritans.

See also: Monarchy.

Samaritans

The second cousins twice removed from both Jews and Christians.

Jesus was always bumping into people who are called "Samaritans" in the New Testament (also mentioned once in the OT in 2 Kings 17:29). In order to figure out who the Samaritans were, it is helpful to remember that around the year 922 BCE, the nation of Israel split into two kingdoms:

The southern kingdom was called Judah. The capital was Jerusalem. Its people were called Judeans. And much, much, much later, the spiritual descendants of Judah were called Jews.

The northern kingdom was called Israel. A capital was eventually built at Samaria. Much, much, much later, the spiritual descendents of the northern kingdom were called Samaritans.

Like Jews, Samaritans worshiped the Lord and were strict in their obedience to God's law. But they didn't acknowledge the Temple in Jerusalem. They had their own temple, at Mt. Gerizim (destroyed about 150 years before Jesus). The Samaritan Bible includes only Genesis through Deuteronomy (slightly altered).

See also: Monarchy.

1 and 2 Samuel

\FUHRST-and-SEH-kihnd-SAM-yoo-uhl\

by Anonymous (Old Testament, History, fifty-five chapters)

The books of Samuel are really two volumes that make up a single work. One can only assume that reasons of marketability and profit margins moved the publisher to divide Samuel into two separate books. What's more "Samuel" may be a misleading name for the book, and for two reasons—first because it has implied to some that Samuel was the author, and second because it may intimate that Samuel is the main character of the whole work. There is nothing in the book to suggest that Samuel authored this work, and indeed Samuel's death is reported in the twenty-fifth chapter of the first volume, making his continued narration of the subsequent thirty chapters suspect, to say the least. The astute reader will also note that mention of Samuel's death less than halfway through the book bearing his name gives lie to the idea that Samuel is the primary protagonist.

What Samuel is, and perhaps herein we find the *why* of the titling of these volumes, is a "beginner." The opening story of 1–2 Samuel is Samuel's story—he is a gift from God to an otherwise barren mother (a story which should by now be familiar to readers). The mother, Hannah, in turn re-gifts her son to the Lord as a Nazirite. What follows is "Samuel the early years," as he grows and serves the Lord at the ancient sanctuary at Shiloh, where Samuel is called to be a prophet of the Lord. It is Samuel's calling and work as a prophet that is the beginning of these volumes. Samuel is also a beginner in that he serves as Yahweh's kingmaker. It is Samuel who calls and anoints Israel's first king, Saul, and Israel's second king, David. Samuel is God's agent of beginnings and change throughout his life's story. The book is aptly named for Samuel, despite any confusion; Mr. Anonymous has chosen well.

1–2 Samuel tell the story of Samuel, Saul, and David. The volumes may be roughly divided as follows:

1 Samuel 1–7 are the call of Samuel; 1 Samuel 8–15 tell of Saul's rise to kingship; 1 Samuel 16–31 recount Saul's decline and David's stellar rise; 2 Samuel 1–10 are about David as king of Judah and Israel; 2 Samuel 11–12 relate the sordid tale of David's dalliance with Bathsheba; and 2 Samuel 13–24 covers the rebellion of David's son Absalom and David's continuing struggles against foreign powers.

In 1–2 Samuel, Mr. Anonymous traces the early history of the Israelite monarchy, inscribing that history with brutally honest portrayals of its flawed characters—its flawed kings—and in terms of what God is doing, first through Samuel and then through a variety of agents.1–2 Samuel is historical story-telling at its best—with truth about all and for all.

See also: David, Nathan, Saul.

Sarah \SEHR-uh\

Status:

Sarah is—what else?—laughing.

Profile

Vocation:	The Mother of all Matriarchs
Hometown:	Ur (just to the west of Um)
What's in a Name?	The name means "princess" but believe me, I'm no Snow White.
My Friends Tell Me . . .	. . . that for a new mom, I don't look a day over 90!
Favorite Song:	"Sara Smile" by Hall and Oates—what else?
Least Favorite Song:	"Havin' My Baby" by Paul Anka
Favorite Comic:	Hagar the Horrible
Favorite Quotation:	"As for your wife, Sarah . . . I will bless her and moreover I will give you a son by her. I will bless her, and she shall give rise to nations; kings of peoples shall come from her"—God, to my husband Abraham. Incidentally, just before God said this, he told my husband that all of our descendents would have to be circumcised. Ouch!

It couldn't have been easy being married to Abraham. Like there was that time that Abraham let Pharaoh make Sarah a part of his harem (Gen 12:10-20). But that was peanuts compared to the on-going issue about having children. See, Sarah's husband kept getting these visits from the Lord, who kept promising that Abraham would have more descendents than there are stars in the sky. One itty-bitty problem: Sarah was "barren" as the Bible bluntly states (Gen 11:30). And so as one childless decade passed into the next, you can imagine that the pressure from Abraham got pretty bad at times. One time, Sarah offered Abraham her handmaiden, Hagar, as a "surrogate." (If anything, Sarah probably thought that

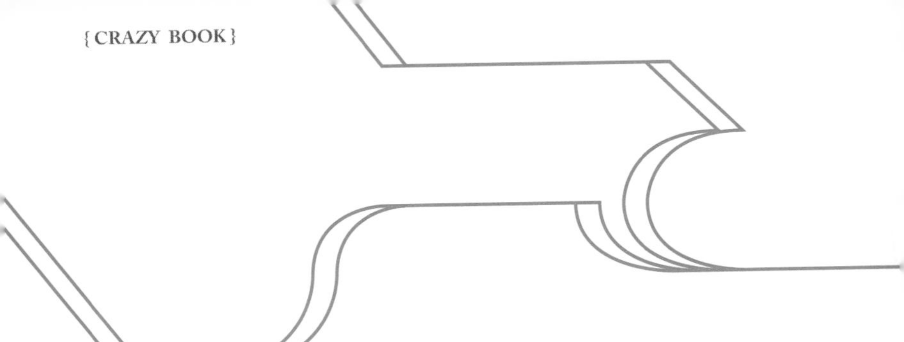

this would be a good way to find out if her "barrenness" wasn't in fact her husband's fault.) But when Hagar got pregnant, it only translated into more pressure on Sarah—not to mention jealousy and a handmaid with an I'm-better-than-you attitude.

When Sarah was pushing ninety years old, the Lord finally came through with some specifics: "Next year at this time, there will be the pitter-patter of little feet." Of course Sarah laughed! A cynical, jaded, bitter, and unbelieving laugh. The Lord, who can smell unbelief a mile away, asked Sarah: "Did you laugh?" Sarah: "I didn't laugh." The Lord: "Oh yes, you laughed. But it is I who is I AM who will laugh last and loudest and longest. But my laughter will not be at you, it will be for you, and because I laugh, you will too." Nine months later, at the birth of her son, Sarah's sarcastic snort was transformed into joyous laughter. Sarah named her son "Isaac" which means "he will laugh." It's safe to say that even though the Lord had the last laugh, Sarah didn't mind one bit.

Key Verse: "God has brought laughter for me; everyone who hears will laugh with me" (Gen 21:6; see also Gen 17 and 21).

See also: Abraham, Ancestral Period, Hagar, Isaac.

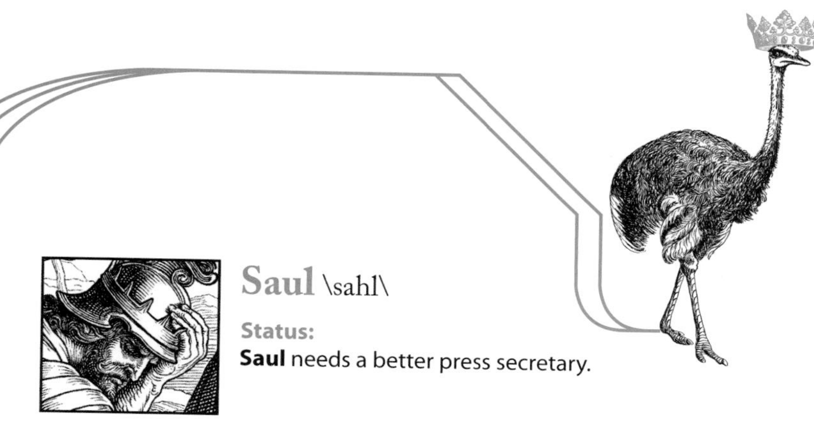

Saul \sahl\

Status:
Saul needs a better press secretary.

Profile

Vocation:	Donkey-Chaser and Israel's First King
Hometown:	The Land of Benjamin (not far from Jerusalem)
What's in a Name?	My name means "asked for" because I was the king the people asked for.
Pet Peeve:	Young snots who think they can be king
Fun Fact:	The King James Version calls me "a choice young man."
Favorite Quotation:	"When you gotta go, you gotta go"—anonymous
Favorite Shake-spearean Tragedy:	*King Lear*

It's important to realize that Saul was God's reply to the Israelites' request for a king. God took the request as an insult, but went ahead and granted the request anyway (1 Sam 8). It should come as no surprise then that Saul was out chasing donkeys when he stumbled into the role of king (1 Sam 9–10). Saul was a tall drink of water and stood out—a quality that seems to have been his only qualification for the monarchy. Yet when it came time for the coronation, Saul hunched down and hid behind some boxes. "He's over here!" some in the crowd called out. "Long live the king!" cried the rest. And with that, Israel's first king was off and running—or loping, or slouching, or whatever.

Despite some early successes—massive smack-downs on the Philistines and the Amalekites, for instance—Saul's gig as king did not end well. Saul got on God's bad side (read 1 Samuel 15 to learn the disturbing reason for this), and from that day the Lord began to back David as Israel's next king. As a result, Saul tried to eliminate David. But a plot to kill David was foiled because Saul's own son, Jonathan, tipped David off. And Saul's daughter (and David's wife) didn't help either. Saul's inability to finish off his rival for the throne reached its low point when Saul had David cornered near the Dead Sea. When Saul ducked into a cave to "relieve himself," David was hiding deeper in the same cave (1 Sam 24:3). Think about it: David was within reach and literally caught Saul with his pants down! Oh, the humiliation! It's enough to make a guy wanna fall on his sword. Which Saul eventually did. There's no happy, uplifting ending here. The Bard's words apply: "All's cheerless, dark, and deadly" (*King Lear*, Act V, Scene III). For Saul that was most certainly true. Sorry to bum you out.

Key Verse: "You have rejected the word of the LORD and the LORD has rejected you from being king over Israel"
(1 Sam 15:26; see also Sam 8, 9, 15, 24, 31).

See also: David, 1 and 2 Samuel, Monarchy.

Second Temple Period

\SEH-kihnd-TEHM-puhl-PEER-ee-ihd\

The time in between when everything memorable happened.

The few people who know the biblical story can probably tell you that story from the time of Abraham right down to the destruction of Solomon's Temple (a.k.a. The First Temple) and the Exile in Babylon. Then they will skip ahead about 600 years to the birth of Jesus.

That's right. They skip ahead about 600 years. As if nothing happened.

Well, a lot happened. First, the Temple was rebuilt. The walls were rebuilt. But the kingdom was not re-established. Well, at least not in a permanent way. The idea that not much happened during this time betrays a rather Christian focus—as if nothing happened that matters until God kept the promise that the Messiah (Christ) would come.

The Second Temple Period marks the time from roughly 520 BCE when the temple was rebuilt down to 70 CE, when the Second Temple was destroyed by the Romans. (Trivia: on the Temple mount there now stands the Muslim mosque known as the Dome of the Rock, the third holiest place in Islam). During this period, God's people endured the reigns of the Persians, the Greeks, the Romans, and a few other tyrannical powers. They even achieved some autonomy during the Maccabeean Revolt (about 160 BCE). During this period, the priests played a really important role in leading the people. For this reason, some misguided Christians later saw this as "downtime" for God's people, assuming that the priests led the people into a strict, non-gracious form of law-observing. For the record, this Christian view is anti-Jewish and quite misguided.

Among the biblical books that cover this period are the last chapters of Isaiah, Ezra, Nehemiah, Haggai, Zechariah, and Malachi. The disputed books of 1–4 Maccabees and 1–2 Esdras also shed light on this period.

One of the most important developments for God's people that happened during this time is that the evolution from "Israelite religion" to either "Jewish religion" or "Christian religion" was in process. The Old Testament is really a book of Israelite religion, which developed into both Judaism and Christianity. The destruction of the Temple marked the final catalytic moment in this evolution. As part of this development, the Jewish Talmud started developing, the Old Testament books were finalized, and the faith of God's people changed from "holy place and holy nation" to "holy book and holy people."

See also: Persians, Temple.

Settlement (Period of) \SEHT-uhl-mihnt\

Having nothing to do with divorce or the gradual yearly lowering of the backend of one's spouse (hopefully not measurable in cubits), this is the more genteel, polite, and PC word for the conquest of the Promised Land by Joshua and the boys.

One day Joshua was eatin' up some food, when down from the sky came a hoverin' dude—the commander of the army of the Lord, that is, angel, that is, seraphim. The Lord's Angel said, "Josh, it's time for you to go." So Joshua and the Israelites surrounded Jericho—gateway to the Promised Land, first city to fall, domino number one.

Following the Exodus from Egypt and the long wilderness years, the now-Joshua-led people of Israel were poised on the brink of the Promised Land. Nowadays there are several theories about just how Israel came to possess the land. Some say it was outright conquest (exactly as some parts of the Bible suggest it was). Some say it was less an invasion and more of a "peasant" uprising—local people throwing off the yoke of foreign oppressors (exactly like the story of Rahab throwing in with the Israelites against her king would suggest). Some say it was more of a gradual migration—nomadic people settling down over time or folks leaving the Canaanite cities to join the tribes of Israel (exactly as other parts of the Bible suggest it was). Some even say that it was a combination of all three.

Whatever.

The details of the Settlement, or conquest, or Move-In Day are much less important than what is at stake in this time period.

On the day that Joshua was met outside the camp by the commander of the army of the Lord, something very important happened. (You can find this in Joshua 5:13—6:7). The angel of the Lord said to Joshua, "Remove the sandals from your feet, for the place where you stand is holy." Sound familiar? It's pretty much the same thing God said to Moses from the burning bush (Exod 3:5). This may not seem like a huge big deal, but it is. Joshua is chosen to follow Moses, and that's important. But it is important that God is *with* Joshua, just as God was with Moses. The crazy story of trumpet blowing and yelling that brings down the walls of Jericho is really about nothing else than God winning the victory. God gives Jericho to Joshua (and the Israelites). And after that, all the rest of those domino shaped cities, and kings, and nations start to fall—because God is with Joshua (and the Israelites).

In the end this is what the Settlement is all about—God is settling up with Israel. All of the promises that were made to Israel's ancestors, about land for the people and for each of the tribes, about God making something out of this ragtag collection of people and tribes, about God being with them and being their God and making them God's people, in the Settlement these promises are made good.

See also: Joshua (book), Joshua.

Shadrach, Meshach, and Abednego

\SHAD-rak-MEE-shak-and-uh-BEHD-nih-goh\

Status:

S.M.A. are chillin'.

Profile

Vocation:	Government Officials
Hometown:	Babylon
What's in a Name?	Our Hebrew names are Hananiah, Mishael, and Azariah. But those names don't quite roll off the tongue like "Shadrach, Meshach, and Abednego."
Turn-offs:	Ninety-foot tall statues, fiery furnaces
Favorite Songs:	"Light My Fire" by the Doors; "Fire" by the Pointer Sisters; "Burning For You" by Blue Öyster Cult; "Shadrach, Meshach, Abednego" by the Beastie Boys
Least Favorite Song:	"The Bunny Song" (see below)

Quick. What's the first commandment? Right. "I am the Lord your God; you shall have no other gods." Most of us fail wretchedly when it comes to keeping this first commandment. Martin Luther (in his *Large Catechism*) once defined a god as that "from which we expect all good and to which we take refuge in all distress." With such a definition in mind, then it's clear that we bow down to just about any god that presents itself, be it possessions, power, politics, wealth, work, fame, family, food, science, celebrities, or a certain bottle of fifteen-year-old scotch we've got stashed away and that would probably be the first thing we would save in a fire.

Speaking of fire, consider Shadrach, Meshach, and Abednego. These guys are famous for the time they kept the first commandment in spectacular fashion. "Rack, Shack, and Benny" (as they are called in the "Veggie Tales" version of the story) were Israelites living in captivity in Babylon. The three young men refused to bow down to a ninety-foot statue of a Babylonian god. A statue the Babylonian king (Nebuchadnezzar) had been made for just such a purpose. Annoyed, Nebuchadnezzar had the three tossed into a giant furnace. But the Lord was present with them, and Shadrach, Meshach, and Abednego escaped the flames without so much as a singed hair. The king was impressed; the ninety-foot statue, on the other hand, didn't have much to say. (Note: In the "Veggie Tales" version, the statue is a ninety-foot chocolate bunny—yummy!—and to worship it, one must sing the dreaded "Bunny Song." All together now: "The bunny, the bunny; oh, I love the bunny . . . ")

Key Verse: "If our God whom we serve is able to deliver us from the furnace of blazing fire and out of your hand, O king, let him deliver us. But if not, be it known to you, O king, that we will not serve your gods and we will not worship the golden statue that you have set up" (Dan 3:17-18; see also Dan 3).

See also: Babylon, Daniel (book), Nebuchadnezzar.

Shiloh \SHI-loh\

The place where God dwelled in a tent before 'movin' on up' to the big city.

Shiloh was, once upon a time, the semi-permanent encampment site of the Tent of Meeting (or Tabernacle), the portable sanctuary where the Ark of the Covenant was kept. Shiloh was a holy place, where priests such as Eleazar and Eli ministered before the Lord (Josh 21; 1 Sam 1). Shiloh is also where the great prophet and judge, Samuel, got his start. Shiloh lost its pride of place as a sanctuary when the Philistines attacked and captured the Ark (1 Sam 4). The Ark was recovered and then King David went suburban yuppie on the bit and moved it to the new capital city of Jerusalem.

Key Verse: "[God] abandoned his dwelling at Shiloh, the tent where he dwelt among mortals... but he chose the tribe of Judah, Mount Zion, which he loves" (Psalm 78:60, 68).

See also: Israelites, Philistines.

Shiphrah and Puah

\SHIHP-ruh\ \POO-uh\

Status:
Shiphrah and Puah are changing diapers.

Profile

Vocation:	We are midwives and political activists—think of us as nannies who vote and disobey civilly.
Pet Peeves:	Pharaohs who think they're all that
Great Loves:	Wriggling, giggling, bouncing babies; defying pharaohs who think they're all that
Favorite Sports Bit:	Dick Vitale's "Diaper Dandies"
Favorite Quotation:	"We will not all sleep, but we will all be changed." 1 Cor 15:51

The book of Exodus begins with the pharaoh (that's the king of Egypt) deciding that the Hebrew people, who were his slaves, were becoming too numerous and therefore a danger to national security. Too late for racial profiling at the harbor or to build a giant wall at Egypt's borders, the pharaoh decided to have all male children put to death. Now apparently the pharaoh wasn't all that bright, not the "toothiest croc in the Nile" as it were, and he instructed two of the Hebrew midwives to kill every boy that was born. Hebrew midwives were told to kill Hebrew baby boys—people experienced, trained and committed to the joys of child-birth told to commit post-term abortions. Well naturally they didn't. Instead, they defied the king of Egypt and let the boys live. Gutsy.

This fact alone is enough to warrant a place of honor in any dictionary of biblical terms (stuffy or not-so-stuffy) for the names of these two brave women—Shiphrah and Puah. But the very fact that we know their names offers an insight into what the book of Exodus is all about. In the Jewish tradition, Exodus is called "These are the names," which may not seem like much of a title but that's OK because it's really just the first couple words of the book (which is where books got their names back in the biblical day). What's really crazy and cool is that we never, ever, never ever never learn the name of the Egyptian pharaoh. Never. But right here, right out of the gate, we learn that these are the names of the kind of people God loves, the kind of people God would later send Moses to deliver, the kind of people God chooses to get the job done. These are the names—not the names of the pharaohs or the powerful people, but of two Hebrew midwives. These are the names: Shiphrah and Puah. You go, girls.

Key Verse: "But the midwives feared God; they did not do as the king of Egypt commanded them, but they let the boys live" (Exod 1:17; cf. Exod 1).

See also: Egyptians, Exodus, Pharaoh.

Simeon \sɪʜᴍ-ee-uhn\

Status:
Simeon can't believe his eyes.

Profile

Vocation:	Righteous and Devout Man
Hometown:	Jerusalem
Pet Peeves:	Getting confused with Simeon, the second son of Jacob and Leah—wrong Testament
Favorite Song:	The *Nunc Dimittis*, of course

At Christmas time, most people only read up through the part (in Luke 2) where the shepherds head for Bethlehem to worship the baby Jesus. This may be due to the fact that the next section begins with the words, "After eight days, it came time to circumcise the child." (Is there anything less Christmas-y than circumcision?) Anyway, if you *do* keep reading, you meet the AARP representation for the Christmas story. First up is Simeon, a man "righteous and devout," followed by Anna, an elderly prophetess (with her own entry in *Crazy Book*).

Simeon's "bucket list" had only one item: to see God's Messiah with his own eyes. This makes Simeon a better person than you, since your bucket list contains mundane stuff like "Learn French" or "Build a tree fort" or "Visit Yellowstone." Anyway, when Jesus was presented at the Temple (to be *circumcised*), Simeon got his wish. Simeon's response, consequently, has been etched into Christian worship ever since. Simeon's thanksgiving prayer—known by the shorthand "*Nunc dimittis servum tuum*" (Latin for "Now let your servant be dismissed")—has, for centuries, been repeated in worship services worldwide. Not bad for an old guy whose name sounds awfully monkey-ish.

Key Verse: "Lord, now let your servant depart in peace, according to your word; for my eyes have seen your salvation, which you have prepared in the presence of all peoples, a light for revelation to the Gentiles and for glory to your people Israel" (Luke 2:29-32).

See also: **Anna, Jesus, Temple.**

Solomon \SAHL-uh-mihn\

Status:
Solomon is looking forward to his son, Rehoboam, ruling over Israel one day.

Profile

Vocation:	King of Israel, Builder of the Temple, Satyr
Hometown:	Jerusalem
What's in a Name?	"Solomon" is related to *shalom*—"peace"
About My Family:	David and Bathsheba are my parents—yes, *that* David and Bathsheba
Interests:	Female spirituality
Did You Know?	I've been credited with writing three books of the Bible: Proverbs, Ecclesiastes, and Song of Songs. Honestly, given my other interests, I'm not sure how I found the time to write all of that. Well, maybe Song of Songs.
Favorite Player:	Wilt Chamberlain
Favorite Quotation:	"It's good to be the king"—Mel Brooks (as King Louis XVI in *History of the World, Part I*)

Let's get the really disturbing part out of the way here at the start. We're speaking of course about that verse (1 Kgs 11:3) that notes that King Solomon had seven-hundred wives and three-hundred concubines. ("Concubine" is an old-timey way to refer to "friend with benefits," except from the point-of-view of the concubine, there usually wasn't much in the way of either friendship or benefit.) So here's the question: If Solomon "loved many foreign women" (including, we're told, the daughter of Pharaoh and many "Moabite, Ammonite, Edomite, Sidonian, and Hittite women"), then when did he have time to rule over Israel?

But let's not let King Solomon's hyper-indulged libido define the man. There's the Temple, too. He built that. There's the time he asked God to give him wisdom. So God gave him wisdom. So he had that going for him. Which was nice. There's that story about the two prostitutes fighting over a baby—they wanted Solomon to decide who was the real mother. ("Cut the baby in half," for example) There's the time that Solomon hosted the Queen of Sheba, with whom he shared his "royal bounty"—as the Scripture puts it (we're not making this up). Okay, okay. Let's be honest. All those women were a problem. But not for the reason you might think. Turns out, the Lord's only complaint about Solomon's colossal promiscuity was the fact that some of the women introduced Solomon to their foreign gods and goddesses, "such as Astarte the goddess of the Sidonians, and Milcom the abomination of the Ammonites." So actually all those wives and pillow-pals make a nice metaphor for Solomon's theology—all gods welcome. And for God, that sort of arrangement just doesn't work.

The moral of the story? Polygamy is one thing; polytheism is quite another.

Key Verse: "So Solomon did what was evil in the sight of the LORD, and did not completely follow the LORD, as his father David had done" (1 Kgs 11:6; see 1 Kgs 1–11).

See also: David, Monarchy, Temple.

Song of Solomon (a.k.a. Song of Songs)

\SAHNG-uhv-SAH-luh-mihn\

by Mrs. Solomon (Old Testament, Poetry, eight chapters)

When one thinks of biblical literature, one is unlikely to also be thinking of erotic literature but, at least in part, that is what one finds in the Song of Solomon—erotic biblical literature. In graphic terms, Song of Solomon describes the relationship between a man and a woman. What is striking is that it is the woman who takes center stage, not just in the vivid description of her beauty, but through her voice, the ways in which her sexuality is not just described but celebrated, and in the predominance of language about mothers. It is for this reason that many have speculated that it was not a Solomon who wrote the "song of songs," but a Mrs. Solomon.

As if the tone and vocabulary were not shocking enough, there is literally no explicit mention of God in the Song of Solomon; none. What then does the reader make of Mrs. Solomon's vivid and intensely sexual poetry, and why is this book billed as biblical at all? Well, if you don't mind getting all allegorical about it, the Song of Solomon is best taken as profound metaphor for God's love of the people of God—whether the love of the Lord for Israel or of Christ for the church; perhaps both. This is very much a love song, sung by one lover to another.

And your mother probably wouldn't approve of your reading it.

See also: Poetry.

Stephen \STEE-vihn\

Status:
Stephen is cool under pressure.

Profile

Vocation:	Deacon, Martyr (although that was more of a 'temp' situation)
Hometown:	Jerusalem
What's in a Name?	*Stephanos* is a Greek word meaning "crown" or "laurel wreath."
Not-So-Fun Fact:	When I was murdered, the soon-to-be Apostle Paul watched in approval. (You owe me one, Paul.)
Did You Know?	I was chosen (along with six others) to be one of the first church deacons—"deacon" comes from a Greek word that means "servant."
Favorite Quotation:	"No one is to stone anyone until I blow this whistle—do you understand?!"—John Cleese (as Elder Praline) in *Monty Python's Life of Brian*

Stephen is best known for being stoned. No, not that kind of stoned. Although, we're sure that those who stoned Stephen thought he was smoking something.

Stephen was an early follower of "The Way" and—more significantly—the first Christian martyr. The word *martyr* is from a Greek word for "witness" or "testifier." For Christians, "martyr" refers specifically to those who are put to death for bearing witness or testimony to Christ. In other words, martyrs are those who are so captured by the Holy Spirit that when it comes to choosing between denying Christ and dying for Christ, it's no choice at all: *off with my head!*

Stephen got himself into trouble when he preached about Jesus to the *Sanhedrin*—a kind of religious Supreme Court. Stephen's sermon is a Torah-based, learned, and well-developed "history of salvation," not to mention the longest sermon recorded in the book of Acts. Alas, Stephen's sermon was not well received—and not because his illustrations were lame or because he failed to use the time-honored three-point sermon. When Stephen ended his sermon by telling the court members that they had murdered the Messiah, it was the last straw. They ground their teeth, covered their ears, and yelled at Stephen to shut up. Then they dragged him out of the city and began to stone him. As he died, Stephen spoke in Christ-like fashion: "Lord Jesus, receive my spirit" and "Lord, do not hold this sin against them." With these words, "Stephanos" received the martyr's crown.

Now there's a servant and a witness we can look up to.

Key Verse: "Stephen, full of grace and power, did great wonders and signs among the people" (Acts 6:8; see also Acts 7–8).

See also: Acts of the Apostles, Paul (Saul of Tarsus).

Story \sTOH-ree\

A verbal means of communication that has a beginning and an end. In between, things happen (often to people).

The Bible is a big story that is filled with many little stories. Like a good loaf of bread (flour, water, yeast, salt, oil), a story is made up of simple ingredients (plot, characters, setting, time) that can be combined in infinitely complex and wonderful ways.

When it comes to digesting stories people too often ask the unfulfilling question: Did this happen exactly like this? This isn't a bad question; it is just leaves you empty if it is the only question you ask. Would you ever eat a great piece of bread and then ask, "Did it happen?" Better to ask questions such as: What was good about it? What worked about it?

The point of reading the biblical stories is to ask what they mean about who God is, what God is up to in our world, what God wants for and from us, and what we need from God. Ask the big questions. Then pass the bread.

See also: Gospels, Parable.

Syria (Aram) \SEER-ee-uh\ \AR-uhm\

A place of well-lined-up breakfast foods in bowls.

The name may sound like a breakfast food or well-ordered progression of numbers, but in fact, it is a place—populated by many Syrians (also called Arameans). Syria was to the north of Israel, and often the two nations fought—even though they each had their own room.

See also: Syrians (Arameans).

Syrians (Arameans)
\SEER-ee-uhnz\ \ar-uh-MĀ-uhnz\

A people one might meet on the road, but probably would confuse for someone else.

The Syrians, or Arameans as they are often called, were a people whose nation (conveniently known either as Syria or Aram) was located directly north-northeast of Israel. The Syrians, who worshipped the storm-god Hadad among other deities, were often in conflict with Israel (see the story in 1 Kings 22 and many other stories throughout 2 Kings). At one point, they were allied with the Northern Kingdom of Israel against the Southern Kingdom of Judah (see the story in 2 Kings 15:29—16:20 and Isaiah 7). But they were often also allied with Israel against the bigger, badder empires—such as the Assyrians (with whom the Syrians hate being confused on account of how mean and nasty the Assyrians were).

The capital of Syrian was Damascus, famous for the technology that allowed it to make better steel, and also famous for a road that led to it. Upon which the Lord later appeared to a troublesome young Pharisee named Saul.

See also: Monarchy, Syria (Aram).

Tamar \TĀ-mahr\

Status:
Tamar is trying to clear her name.

Profile

Fun Fact: When I can't remember something, I tie a red piece of string on my hand, which reminds me . . .

Favorite Song: "Respect" by Aretha Franklin

Tamar's first husband, Er Judahson, died before the two of them had children. As the good ol' Bible says, he was "wicked in the sight of the Lord." So what was a girl to do?

<<<Warning to Readers (sound foghorn):
We are not making this up.>>>

Back in Old Testament times, when a man left his wife childless, the husband's brother was legally required to sleep with the woman so that she could have a child to take care of her and to inherit her husband's name and property. The child would be considered the son of the dead man, not the son of the living man. This was called Levirate marriage.

So Tamar's father-in-law, Judah, ordered his second son, Onan, to provide a child for Tamar in this way. When he didn't do this, he died.

So Tamar said, "Judah, how about your third son?" But Judah got to thinking that Tamar was cursed, and he only had one more son. So he made excuses, put Tamar off, avoided her, and didn't return her calls or e-mails.

So what was a girl to do?

One day, and not on Halloween, Tamar dressed up like a prostitute.

<<<Warning to Readers (sound foghorn):
We are not making this up.>>>

Judah's wife had died, and when Judah saw who he thought was a prostitute, he did with Tamar what men will do with prostitutes (but don't take this as permission—he isn't a role model in this case). "I don't have any cash," he said, "Will you take a check?"

"Just leave me your driver's license, I'll wait here while you hit the ATM," she told him. But when he got back, the woman he thought was a prostitute was gone.

A few months later, the town know-it-alls said to Judah, "Your daughter-in-law Tamar is pregnant!" "Well," he said, "We'll just have to kill her on account of her sins. Don't want to do it, but I feel I owe it to her."

Flashing Judah's driver's license, Tamar said, "What were you doing the last time you saw this, Judah?"

Judah repented. He realized that his refusal to provide a son for Tamar had driven Tamar to provide for herself. And he realized that she was righteous.

God must have realized this, too, since God made sure that Tamar's DNA found its way into the family tree of Jesus.

Key Verse: "Then Judah acknowledged [his possessions] and said, 'She is more in the right than I . . .'" (Gen 38:26; see also Gen 38).

Temple, The \thuh-TEHM-puhl\

God's house; fixer-upper that could be torn down and rebuilt in three days (if you have a good carpenter); a house with many dwelling places with one reserved just for you. Not a place for doing business.

When you're talking about the Temple, you need to be as clear as possible with what you're talking about. First things first: in Hebrew the word for temple is *bet*, which also means palace and—more importantly—house. It makes some sense if you think about it: a regular old house-house is your house, the palace is the king's house, and the temple is God's house. So when you read "temple," think "house," too. Second, there is a problem with speaking of "The Temple." When people say "The Temple," they usually use the definite article—this is *The* Temple, not a temple. And then there's the fact that you can just hear the capital 'T' when people talk about it. Both of which are misleading because "The" Temple in the Bible can actually be one of three temples.

The first Temple is often called Solomon's temple, 'cause Solomon built it, during the tenth century BCE. You can read a very (*very*) detailed description of it in 1 Kings 6–8. Solomon built this Temple as a place for the Ark of the Covenant to be kept. This first Temple was destroyed in 587 BCE when the Babylonians conquered Jerusalem, took everything of value from the Temple, and burned it to the ground. (Ouch!)

The second temple is often called the Second Temple, 'cause it was built . . . um . . . second. This Temple was built during the period after the Babylonian Exile with the permission of the Persian Empire (in roughly 520 BCE). This second Temple was an important rallying point for the restored people of Israel.

The third temple is really a refurbishing and expansion of the second temple and is often called Herod's Temple, 'cause—you guessed it—Herod refurbished and added on to it. Herod started work on this version of the Temple is 37 BCE and it was not yet finished when he died. Herod's Temple was destroyed in 70 CE by the Romans who put down a rebellion and put an end to the Temple pretty much once and for all.

The New Testament doesn't say too terribly much about the Temple. What it does say gets back to the basics of having the right kind of relationship with God. The Temple becomes a symbol for Jesus' death and resurrection, and an image of heaven. In this heavenly image, God's house (temple = house, remember?) is a big ol' house with lots of room and lots of rooms. And there's a room with your name on it.

See also: 1 and 2 Kings, Second Temple Period, Solomon.

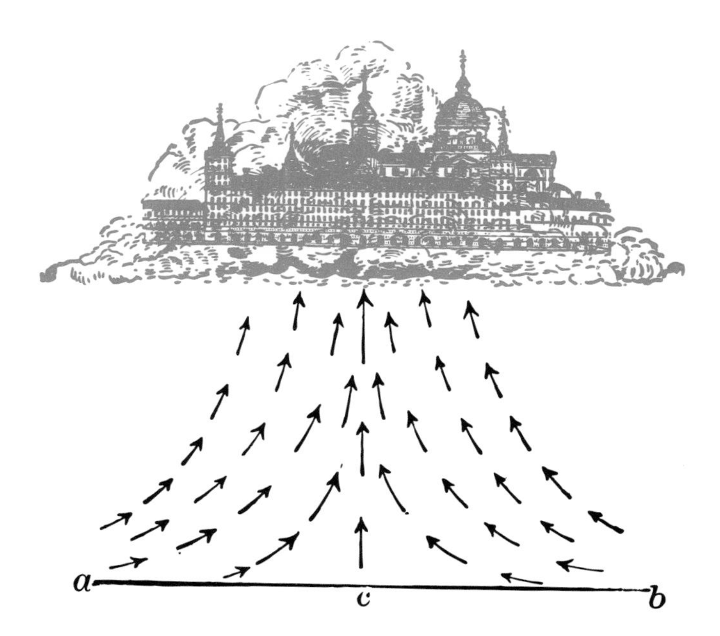

1 and 2 Thessalonians

\FUHRST-and-SEH-kihnd-theh-suh-LOH-nee-uhns\

By Saul of Tarsus, a.k.a. Paul (New Testament, Letters, eight chapters)

In this first letter to the Thessalonians, we find Paul doing what he does best: encouraging a congregation. In the case of the Christians in Thessalonica, Paul is encouraging them to have a little patience! "You turned from idols to serve a living and true God," Paul reminds the congregation, "and to *wait* for his Son from heaven" (1 Thes 1:10). In fact, Paul spends about half of the letter reminding them of the ways in which they "received the word of God . . . not as a human word but as what it really is, God's word." It would appear that the Thessalonians were losing heart because (1) they were being persecuted for their faith and (2) some of them had died. To the second concern, Paul offers the Thessalonians a rapturous vision of Christ's return at the end of time (1 Thes 4:13-18). Some readers will be tempted to pair this passage with verses from books like Daniel and Revelation to come up with something called a pre-tribulation Rapture, but why do such a thing when the plain meaning of the text will do so much better than any fanciful, imaginary mambajahambo?

As for Paul's second letter to the Thessalonians, it's (a) shorter than the first letter (b) thematically similar to the first letter, and (c) hard to always recognize Paul's usual verbiage and style. Still, it provides a nice epilogue to the first letter.

See also: Letters (or Epistles), Paul (Saul of Tarsus).

Thomas \TAH-muhs\

Status:
Thomas is wondering why there aren't many churches named after him.

Profile

Vocation:	Apostle (in spite of myself)
Pet Peeve:	Being called "Doubting Thomas" all of these centuries
Did You Know . . .	. . . that if I hadn't asked Jesus, "How can we know the way?" He might never have said "I am the Way, the Truth, and the Life"? (See for yourself in John 14:5-6.)
Favorite Song:	"Faith" by George Michael
Favorite Toy:	Brightly colored model trains

Thomas's reputation as "Doubting Thomas" is undeserved. Everybody thinks that Thomas doubted that Jesus had risen from the dead. But to doubt means to be uncertain or unsure about the truth of something. Thomas, on the other hand, *was certain and sure* that Jesus was dead. Thomas was no doubter. He was an unbeliever. Here's what Thomas said when his fellow Jesus-followers tried to convince him that they'd seen their Lord alive: "Unless I see the mark of the nails in his hands, and put my finger in the mark of the nails and my hand in his side, I will not believe" (John 20:25). Do you hear any doubting in those words? No. You hear unbelief straight-up.

When Jesus does finally show up he invites Thomas to dig around in his wounds (eww). And the best way to translate what Jesus says next is: "Do not *not* believe, but believe!" (Thereby proving our point about Thomas being an unbeliever rather than a doubter.) Then Jesus says, "Have you believed because you have seen me? Blessed are those who have not seen and yet have come to believe." Jesus is talking about you here—you haven't seen or had the benefit of the icky finger-poking, and yet the promise of Christ's resurrection is for you. You can believe it.

Key Verse: "Jesus said to Thomas, 'Put your finger here and see my hands. Reach out your hand and put it in my side. Do not ~~doubt~~ not believe but believe.' Thomas answered him, 'My Lord and my God!'" (John 20:27-28).

See also: John (The Gospel according to), Resurrection of Jesus.

1 and 2 Timothy

\FUHRST-and-SEH-kihnd-TIHM-uh-thee\ (books)

By Paul (New Testament, Letters, ten chapters)

These letters addressed to Timothy have the pastoral tone you'd expect from a seasoned veteran writing to a young protégé. That said, the discriminating reader will frankly find it difficult to recognize in 1–2 Timothy the same Apostle Paul who gave us Romans or Corinthians or Galatians or Philippians. It may be impolitic to raise this notion, but could it be that Paul's advancing age is beginning to show—"I have fought the good fight, I have finished the race" (1 Tim 4:6-8)—and he's letting his assistants help with the letter writing? It may be further impolitic, but maybe one of these assistants has a problem with women. How else to explain 1 Tim 2:8-15? Fortunately, we can discern in Timothy the apostolic sensibility that we've come to appreciate: a desire to encourage struggling believers, warnings against false teachers, strong exhortations to godly behavior, reliance on the Hebrew Scriptures (see 2 Tim 3:16), and high praise for Jesus Christ. There's also much excellent guidance for church leaders (bishops, deacons, and elders) and some ahead-of-its-time information about the health benefits of a glass of wine. Let Paul's words to Timothy be his words to you as well, O leader in your local church: "Set the believers an example in speech and conduct, in love, in faith, in purity. Do not neglect the gift that is in you . . . Put these things into practice, devote yourself to them, so that all may see your progress" (1 Tim 4:12, 14-15).

See also: Letters (or Epistles), Paul (Saul of Tarsus), Timothy.

Timothy \TIHM-uh-thee\

Status:
Timothy is off on another church-related errand.

Profile

Vocation:	The Apostle Paul's Little Helper
Hometown:	Lystra (in Lycaonia)
About My Family:	Mom = Eunice; Grandma = Lois
Pet Peeve:	Apostles who don't practice what they preach. Didn't Paul say, "if you let yourselves be circumcised, Christ will be of no benefit to you" (Gal 5:2)? Wish he'd thought of that back when I first started hanging out with him!

Here's what Yoda would have said to Timothy: "The force is strong in this one. But much you have to learn, my young Padawan. Young you are. Not let others despise you for your youth you must. For believers, an example in speech, conduct, love, faith, and purity you must set." But Yoda wasn't Timothy's Jedi-master, the Apostle Paul was.

Timothy's initiation as the Apostle's protégé and coworker was a little harsh. In order to appease certain Jewish believers in Timothy's neighborhood, Paul had Timothy circumcised. (Here, the writers of *Crazy Book* would like to express regret that, once again, the subject of circumcision has come up. Hey, we wouldn't keep bringing it up if the New Testament didn't keep bringing it up.) But after the rough start, Timothy settled into his role: traveling around Asia Minor and Greece, visiting and strengthening the churches in the various cities, sometimes with Paul, sometimes on his own.

You can learn something about how much Timothy meant to the Apostle Paul from the Paul's own correspondence. Timothy was with Paul when Paul sent letters to the congregations in Rome, Corinth, Philippi, and Thessalonica. Paul saw Timothy as a "co-worker for God in proclaiming the gospel of Christ" and as a young man who "strengthened and encouraged" believers for the sake of faith (1 Thes 3:2). In the words of Grace (Principal Rooney's secretary in *Ferris Bueller's Day Off*), Timothy was "a righteous dude."

Key Verse: "Timothy's worth you know, how like a son with a father he has served with me in the work of the gospel" (Phil 2:22; see also Phil 2:19-23; Acts 16:1-5; 1 Cor 4:17, 16:10,11; 1 Tim 4:12-16).

See also: **Paul (Saul of Tarsus), 1 and 2 Timothy (books).**

Titus \TI-tuhs\

By Paul (New Testament, Letters, three chapters)

If brevity is the soul of wit, then Paul must be soul-brother number one. In Titus, Paul gives us one chapter aimed at church leaders and how they should respond to false teachers, another chapter telling different groups of people how to behave, and a third chapter that contains a verse that really preaches: "God saved us, not because of any works of righteousness that we had done, but according to his mercy through the water of rebirth and renewal by the Holy Spirit" (Titus 3:5). As in his letters to Timothy, in Titus Paul is offering instruction and encouragement to his protégé and fellow worker in spreading the gospel. Paul's words are fitting (except for gratuitous and regrettable cheap-shot at the Cretan people) for us who read him now, as much as they surely were for Titus. You are saved in Christ Jesus. His mercy is yours, and the gift that you have to share with your fellow man and woman. Paul desires that we insist on these things, for this is the heart of the good news, and the heart that you too can wear on your sleeve as a witness to your neighbor.

See also: **Letters (or Epistles), Paul (Saul of Tarsus).**

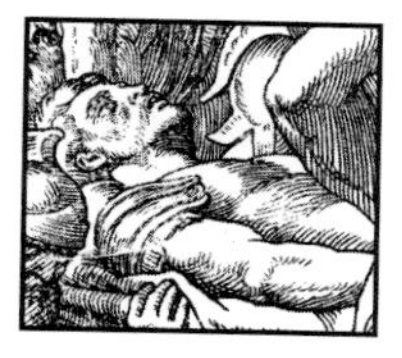

Uriah the Hittite

\yoor-I-uh-thuh-HIH-tit\

Status:
Uriah is waiting for orders.

Profile

Profession:	A Soldier in King David's Army
Hometown:	Hittite-ville
What's in a Name?	My name—which means "The Lord is my light"—is also the name of a Charles Dicken's character, which became the name of a classic rock band.
About My Family:	Happily married to my loving, faithful, and beautiful wife
Interests:	Serving my king with loyalty, sacrifice, and honor
Will Somebody Please Tell Me . . .	. . . what the word *cuckold* means? I keep hearing it but haven't figured it out yet.

See also: Bathsheba, David.

Versions \vuhr-zhuhnz\

A buffet of alphabet soup, served up to satisfy the universal hunger for God's word, necessitated by the fact that Christ sent us to make disciples of all those nations that don't speak Hebrew or Greek.

A "version" is simply a translation of the Bible from Hebrew and Greek into a different language. So that people can have a Bible in their own language that they don't read, bring with them to church, or study.

Versions fall into two broad categories—ancient and modern. The first ancient versions were translations of the Hebrew Old Testament into such languages as Greek (abbreviated, LXX), Latin (VUL), Syriac (SYR), and so on. But that doesn't mean that there was only one translation into each language. For example, an early church leader named Origen made a version of the Old Testament called the *Hexapla*, in which there were six columns. The various columns contained:

1. A Hebrew text of the Old Testament
2. The Hebrew words transliterated into Greek letters
3. A Greek translation of the OT by a fellow named Aquila
4. A Greek translation of the OT by a fellow named Symmachus
5. Origen's own Greek translation of the OT
6. A Greek translation of the OT by a fellow name Theodotion.

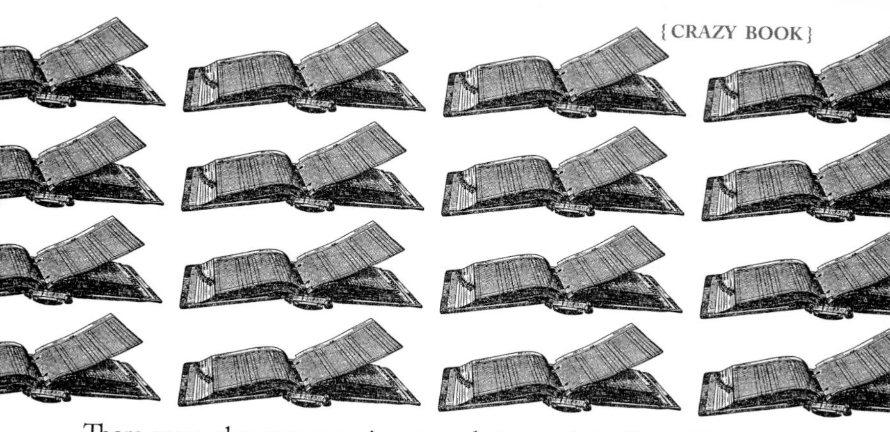

There were also many ancient translations of the New Testament into various languages, such as Coptic, and the like.

Modern versions of the Bible are translations into languages that people speak and read today. In English, there are too many to name. Modern versions come in two basic flavors—translations and paraphrases. A translation strives to be very faithful to nearly each and every word of the ancient text. A paraphrase tries to say what the Bible means, but in a way that is more folksy and easily understood. Among the more popular translations are the New International Version (NIV), the New Revised Standard Version (NRSV), the King James Version (KJV, which was translated way back in the year 1611), the New American Standard Bible (NASB). Among the more popular paraphrases as the Living Bible (TLB) and the Message (by Eugene Peterson).

Why so many versions? Well, language changes over time. So you can't translate the Bible just once. In addition, different translations have different guiding principles. The NRSV, for example, never refers to humanity as "man" but rather as "humankind." Or again, the Good News Bible (or Today's English Version, TEV) was written for about a sixth-grade reading level.

So which translation is right for you? Why stop at just one?

See also: Essenes, New Testament, Old Testament.

Vespasian \vehs-PĀ-zhuhn\

Status:
Vespasian is looking for some Pepto Bismol®.

Profile

Profession:	Roman Emperor
Interests:	World domination, history (of a sort)
Pet Peeves:	Pesky Christians and their numerically headed riddles
Favorite TV Show:	*Dynasty*
Lucky Number:	666

Vespasian was a military general and then Roman emperor during a key time for early Christians. Vespasian was assigned the job of crushing the "Jewish rebellion" that broke out in Galilee and Jerusalem in 66 CE. When Vespasian became emperor, the job of conquering Jerusalem and destroying the Temple fell to his son, Titus. (This is *not* the Titus of the New Testament's Letter to Titus.) It was during Vespasian's reign (69–79 CE) that Christians as well as Jews began to flee Judea in large numbers. It was also during this period that the Gospels of Matthew, Mark, and Luke took shape.

Vespasian was a bit of a history buff—especially when history made him look better than his predecessors. Therefore, he supported the work of some key early historians, including Josephus, Tacitus, and Pliny the Elder. Why are we telling you this? Because it's these historians who give us "outsider" information about early Christianity. Take, for instance, Tacitus, who wrote: "Christus, from whom the name 'Christians' had its origin, suffered the extreme penalty during the reign of Tiberius at the hands of one of our procurators, Pontius Pilatus, and a most mischievous superstition, thus checked for the moment, again broke out not only in Judaea, the first source of the evil, but even in Rome . . ."

Vespasian does not appear by name in the New Testament. Still, it could very well be that he rears his ugly head (among six other heads) in the book of Revelation. Most of the imagery in the book of Revelation is code language for the political troubles and persecutions that Christians were facing in the closing decades of the first century. So if it's true that the seven-headed beast in Revelation 17 originally represents seven Roman emperors, then Vespasian—"the one who is living"—is head number six.

Vespasian died of intestinal complications resulting in diarrhea. According to one ancient historian, he last words were, "Woe! I think I'm becoming a god."

Key Verse: "This calls for a mind that has wisdom: the seven heads are . . . seven kings, of whom five have fallen, one is living, and the other has not yet come; and when he comes, he must remain only a little while" (Rev 17:9-10).

See also: Caesar, Rome.

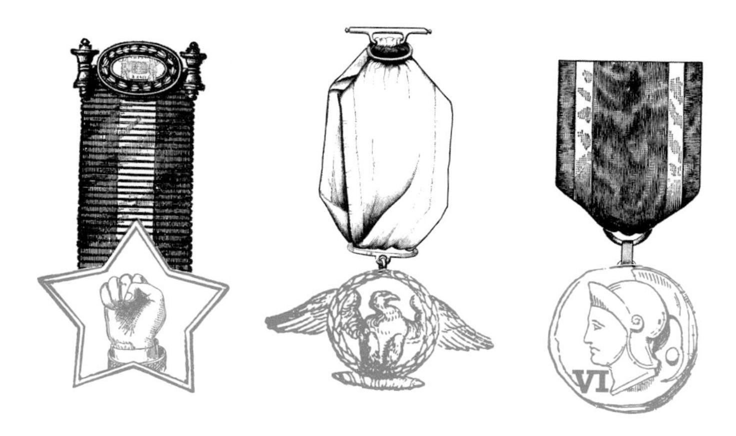

Wise Men, The \thuh-WIZ-mehn\

Status:
The Wise Men are shocked—shocked!—and appalled that Herod tried to con them.

Profile

Vocation:	Magi, Astrologers
Hometown:	Somewhere East of Judea
What's in a Name?	That our names are Melchior, Gaspar, and Balthasar, is just one of dozens of non-biblical legends about who we are and where we're from.
Pet Peeves:	Nativity scenes that put us in Bethlehem at the same time as those rowdy shepherds
Did You Know . . . ?	In the twelfth century, Marco Polo visited our tombs in Persia, reporting that our bodies—including hearts and hair—were in tact? And if you believe that then we've got some land in, uh, Persia that we'd like to sell you.
Least Favorite Song:	"We Three Kings of Orient Are." Look, this one's more than 150 years old. Can we get an update for grammar's sake?!
Favorite Quotation:	"Well, if you're dropping by again, do pop in. And thanks a lot for the gold, and frankincense, but don't worry too much about the myrrh next time"—Mandy (played by Terry Jones) in *Monty Python's Life of Brian*

We begin by invoking Monty Python's Mother Mandy once more: "What are you doing creeping around a cow shed at two o'clock in the morning? That doesn't sound very wise to me!" "Wise men" is the lame, King James translation of the Greek word *magoi*. Matthew's Gospel—the only one to report that "magi from the east came to Jerusalem"—probably has in mind a priestly caste of Zoroastrian astrologers. But who gives a rip what Matthew had in mind? Even if those magi weren't "kings" or "wise men" originally, they are now—your church's Christmas pageant will have it no other way. You can't have a bunch of Zodiac-believin', What's-Your-Sign?-askin' occultists marching up to the altar on December 24th, can you? Hence, "Wise Men." Furthermore, Matthew never gives the number of magi. There could have been seven or seventeen magi, for all we know, with the treasure chests being carried by pack animals!

So, yeah, we've made the story of the magi a bit more palatable and stage-able over the centuries, not only for our younger audiences, but also for our more romantic ones. Matthew's original story is a tale of political intrigue, deceit, and escape—a tale that ends with the Holy Family ducking for cover in Egypt (in a kind of reverse Exodus) and the wicked King Herod slaughtering the innocents back in Judea. Still, our nativity scenes get at least one thing right: that wayward star led those "pagan" magi to an epiphany regarding the Light of the World.

Key Verse: "On entering the house, they saw the child with Mary his mother; and they knelt down and paid him homage. Then, opening their treasure chests, they offered him gifts of gold, frankincense, and myrrh" (Matt 2:11; see also Matt 2).

See also: Herod the Great, Matthew (The Gospel according to), Persians.

Xerxes \zuhrk-zeez\

Status:
Xerxes is quite fond of alphabet games.

Profile

Vocation:	Emperor
Aliases:	Ahasueres (in various English versions of the book of Esther, my name appears one way or the other)
Marital Status:	Married
Favorite Quoation:	"I'm the king of the world!"—Muhammad Ali
Pet Peeves:	Wives who forget that I am the king of the world

Ol' Xerxes had a bit of a temper on him. One day, Xerxes decided he wanted to show off his hot wife, Queen Vashti, to all of the people who had come to fawn over him. But she refused. Who knows why? Maybe she was just sick of getting jerked around like a yo-yo whenever X-man wanted to display her like she was a department store mannequin.

Her punishment for refusing the king? She was banned from his presence forever. And like us, you're probably thinking, "Isn't that what she wanted in the first place?" Precisely.

But there is a bigger story here. And that is the story of Esther. Because the X-ster decided that he still needed a queen to display. So he went on a search for a new queen. You can read more about it in the story on Esther.

Key Verse: "On the seventh day, when the king was merry with wine, he commanded . . . the seven eunuchs who attended him, to bring Queen Vashti before the king, wearing the royal crown, in order to show the peoples and the officials her beauty; for she was fair to behold. But Queen Vashti refused to come . . . " (Esth 1:10-12; see also the book of Esther).

See also: **Esther (book), Esther.**

Yahweh \YAH-weh, -wā\

Status:
Yahweh is.

Profile

Nicknames (titles):	The Great I AM (which is pretty much what *Yahweh* means), El Shaddai (God Almighty), El Elyon (Most High God), Adonai (Lord), God of Hosts, Rock, Refuge, Savior, Friend—and there's more where those came from.
Pet Peeves:	People who call me "Jehovah"; sinners who keep on sinning the same sinful sins that they're always sinning.
Great Loves:	People who call me "Lord"; sinners who keep on sinning the same sinful sins that they're always sinning.
Favorite TV Episode:	"The Prime Mover," *Twilight Zone* season 2 episode #21 starring Dane Clark and Buddy Ebsen
Favorite Quotation:	"Not everyone who says to me, 'Lord, Lord,' will enter the kingdom of heaven . . . " (Matt 7:21) "Then everyone who calls on the name of the LORD shall be saved . . . " (Joel 2:32)

See *Crazy Talk: A Not-So-Stuffy Dictionary of Theological Terms*, p. 183.

Key Verse: "God said to Moses, 'I AM WHO I AM.' He said further, 'Thus you shall say to the Israelites, 'I AM has sent me to you'" (Exod 3:14).

See also: Jesus.

Zacchaeus \zak-EE-uhs\

Status:
Zacchaeus is out on a limb.

Profile

Vocation:	President of the JTCA—Jericho Tax Collectors Association
Interests:	Money
Turn-offs:	Not having any money; short jokes; jokes about money that end with "and you can't be any shorter than that"
Favorite Song:	Toss-up between "Money" by Pink Floyd, "Money for Nothing" by Dire Straits, and "Money (That's What I Want)" by The Flying Lizards; on the other hand, "Money, Money, Money" by Abba just does not rock.
Favorite Quotation:	"Money is better than poverty, if only for financial reasons"—Woody Allen in *Without Feathers*

All together now: "Zacchaeus was a wee little man, a wee little man was he. . . ." How would you like to be immortalized in a Sunday school lyric like that? Zacchaeus is the height-challenged, tree-climbing tax-collector introduced in Luke 19. Because Zacchaeus was (a) short, (b) not able to see Jesus for the crowd, and (c) able to get a leg up into a Sycamore, Jesus thought to himself: "Hmmm, maybe

I should invite myself over to this guy's house for dinner." Now why would Jesus think something like that? Why go dine with a tax collector, a guy who is selling out his own people to the Romans? Why? Because Jesus came for exactly this kind of person—a sinner. To paraphrase another, similar story, Jesus came not to heal those who are well, but those who are ~~short~~ . . . sorry, sick.

Key Verse: Jesus said to Zacchaeus, "Today salvation has come to this house . . . For the son of Man came to seek out and to save the lost" (Luke 19:9-10).

See also: Jesus, Luke (The Gospel according to)

Zealots \ZEHL-uhts\

Persons opposed to the idea of rendering unto both God and Caesar. As vegans are to vegetarians, zealots were to Jews.

At first, to be called a "zealot" just meant that a person was intensely devoted to God and to keeping God's law. Later, a group of Jews who lived about the same time as Jesus said, "Hey, since Caesar considers himself a god, and since the Roman empire controls the promised land, if we are truly devoted to the True God, we have to be opposed to Caesar's occupation."

For the record: this policy didn't work out so well.

See also: Caesar, Rome.

Zechariah \ZEHK-uh-RI-uh\ (book)

by Zechariah Ben-Berechiah, with an afterward by Anonymous
(Minor Prophets, fourteen chapters)

Zechariah Ben-Berechiah has authored a book (or at least half of a book) that is sure to confound (or at least confuse) many (or at least some). Similar to his fellow post-exilic prophet Haggai, Mr. Ben Berechiah's began to prophesy in the year 520 BCE. But while Haggai's writings are practical, down-to-earth, and no-nonsense (he said, "Let's finish this temple so that we can enjoy the blessings that come from proper worship"), Zechariah's pen tends toward the dreamy, visionary, utopian... the impractical. Check this out: "I see a flying scroll; its length is twenty cubits, and its width ten cubits" (Zech 5:2). Or this: "I see a lampstand all of gold, with a bowl on the top of it [Haggai interrupted him, "That's just your skinny brother, who just got a bad haircut!"]; there are seven lamps on it, with seven lips on each of the lamps that are on the top of it. And by it there are two olive trees, one of right of the bowl and the other on its left" (4:2-3).

Although not our preferred cup of tea (no, that's not a vision), it is still true that temperamental, artistic types have their value. Zechariah's vision promises a future of peace, hope, and of God working through everyday humans beings (such as the Davidic descendant Zerubbabel and the high priest Joshua). And those are visionary promises that we all need.

The second half of the book, which may have been added by a later and anonymous hand, also offers visions of peace, holiness, victory of God's people, and hope. Even though these chapters were written during one of the most disillusioned times in the history of God's people—when the return from exile brought the people back to a land that was sorely disappointing and where they were beset by famine and difficulties—the prophet who wrote these chapters promises God's ultimate triumph. And who hasn't had a few days when *that* message wouldn't have been welcome!

See also: Haggai, Prophets, Old Testament.

Zechariah (husband of Elizabeth)

\ZEHK-uh-RI-uh\

Status:
Zechariah is dumbfounded.

Profile

Profession:	Priest
Hometown:	Jerusalem
Pet Peeves:	Angels with an attitude; mimes
Favorite Celebrity:	George Burns
Favorite Movie:	*On Golden Pond*

April 16. Dear Journal. Yeah, I know I'm way too old to be keeping a journal. But I've been forced into it. Here's what happened. Today, I had the honor of going into the Temple sanctuary and making the offering. So I'm in there and—you won't believe this—the angel Gabriel appears! Scares the bejeebers out of me! Well, Gabe tells me that Elizabeth (my wife) is going to be pregnant and that we should name the kid "John." I say, "You're kidding, right? We've never had any kids and, given our age, that ship has sailed." So Gabe goes, "Unbeliever! Just for that, I'm going to make it so you can't talk." Just because I thought he was kidding. I was speechless. Still am.

August 31. Dear Journal. Well, Elizabeth is twenty weeks along and showing. Her friends are teasing her about having to take prenatal vitamins with her Geritol. On the other hand, the fact that her husband (that's me) hasn't been able to utter a word in over four months makes her the envy of all.

January 14. Dear Journal. This will be my last entry. John was born today. And I think I'm getting my voice back. In fact, I feel a prophecy coming on. [You'll find Zechariah's prophecy in Luke 1:68-79—ed.]

Key Verse: "Blessed be the Lord God of Israel, for he has looked favorably on his people and redeemed them. He has raised up a mighty savior for us in the house of his servant David . . ." (Luke 1:68, 69).

See also: Elizabeth, John the Baptist.

Zephaniah \ZEHF-uh-NI-uh\

by Zephaniah Cushison (Old Testament, Prophets, three chapters)

Mr. Cushison has written a book that makes up for the vice of being largely derivative (at times Mr. Cushison sounds remarkably like Misters Obadiah, Joel, Amos, Micah and others), by possessing the virtue of being relatively short.

In chapter one, Israel is criticized and warned for its failure to commit exclusively to Yahweh. In chapter two, the warnings are extended to Israel's neighbors. In addition, some of Israel's less friendly neighbors are cautioned not to take too much comfort in their victories over Israel, for God will restore Israel in due time. The third chapter marks a sudden and dramatic shift in tone and also the most striking element of Mr. Cushison's book: a musical duet featuring God and the people. In the final paragraphs, Mr. Cushison describes a musical number, with God and Israel singing to each other. God will not punish Israel forever; rather, God will restore Israel. First, Israel is called to "sing aloud" over its forgiveness and pending restoration, and then God will exult over the forgiven and restored Israel with "loud singing." It all makes for a triumphant conclusion for God, for Israel, and for Mr. Cushison's book. Zephaniah is not only a good, quick read, it's also a godsend for anyone thinking about creating a biblical resource that covers the books of the Bible from A to Z.

See also: Prophets.

Zion, Mount \zɪ-uhn\

A mountain that's a little more like a molehill but which God nevertheless makes mountainous by choosing to live and meet God's chosen people there.

While it's no Mount Everest (or Olympia, for that matter), Zion towers over the biblical story like . . . well . . . a mountain. The importance of Zion as the dwelling of God cannot be overstated. God lives on Zion (Ps 46:4). God is worshipped on Zion (65:1). God calls all the nations to pay homage to God on Zion (Mic 4:2). And God blesses the world from Zion (Ps 46:4).

Zion as the mountain of God lies at the center of Jerusalem, and so "Zion" is employed as a synecdoche (which is a fancy word meaning "a part of something can represent the whole" that we had to look up and so we thought we'd save you the time) for Jerusalem; in other words, Zion can be synonymous with Jerusalem (see 2 Sam 5:7).

See also: Jerusalem, Psalms (book).